SHAMANS

Shamans

Siberian Spirituality and the Western Imagination

Ronald Hutton

Hambledon and London
London and New York

Hambledon and London

102 Gloucester Avenue
London NW1 8HX (UK)

838 Broadway
New York
NY 10003–4812 (USA)

First Published 2001

ISBN 1 85285 324 7

A description of this book is available from
the British Library and the Library of Congress

Typeset by Carnegie Publishing, Carnegie House
Chatsworth Road
Lancaster, LA1 4SL

Printed on acid-free paper and bound
in Great Britain by Cambridge University Press

Contents

Introduction   vii

PART ONE: WHY WE THINK WE KNOW ABOUT SHAMANS

1   The Creation of Siberia   3
2   The Creation of Siberians   9
3   The Transformation of Siberians   15
4   The Records of Shamanism   29

PART TWO: WHAT WE THINK WE KNOW ABOUT SHAMANS

5   What Shamans Did   47
6   Shamanic Cosmologics   59
7   Shamanic Apprenticeship and Equipment   69
8   Shamanic Performance   85
9   Knots and Loose Ends   99

PART THREE: SIBERIA IN THE SHAMANIC WORLD

10   The Discovery of a Shamanic World   113
11   The Discovery of a Shamanic Past   129
12   The Discovery of a Shamanic Future   151

Notes   163
Bibliography   193
Index   205

To Valera Racowski and Natasha Konstantinova

Introduction

Since the 1970s, the word 'shamanism' has become one of the most heavily worked among scholars of anthropology and religious studies, as well as having a major presence in counter-cultural groups in the western world. It has flourished especially among American academics, but is by now almost as commonly used by those of other nations.[1] Virtually all who use it are aware that it derives originally from Siberia, even while it has long been applied to phenomena in many other parts of the globe. The word 'shaman' was apparently first printed in the memoirs of the exiled Russian churchman Avvakum, in 1672, and seems to have reached Western and Central European scholarship twenty years later in the work of Nicholas Witsen. By the late eighteenth century it was current among authors from Russia westward to Britain to denote a phenomenon which was encountered in Siberia and impressed western writers as both dramatic and alien: an individual who claimed to contact spirits through an often spectacular public performance, and to use this power to help or blight other human beings.[2]

'Shamanism', by contrast, is recognised among experts to be a scholarly construct, used to group together beliefs and activities across the world which have some apparent relationship with those observed in Siberia. It is also generally admitted that no commonly agreed definition has ever been ascribed to the term, and that the recent boom in studies associated with it has only worsened the confusion and diversity in its use.[3] There seem to be four different definitions circulating at the present time. In one, shamanism is the practice of anybody who contacts a spirit world while in an altered state of consciousness. A second limits it to specialist practitioners who use such contacts at the behest of others. A third attempts to distinguish shamans from other such specialists, such as 'mediums', 'witch doctors', 'spiritual healers' or 'prophets', by some particular technique. This is the definition most commonly accepted among modern scholars, but there is no agreement upon what that technique should be. To some the definitive characteristic is that shamans exert control over the spirits with whom they work, while to others it is the ability to undertake a personal journey into an alternative reality and to accomplish tasks there. The fourth definition stands on its own, being the use of the expression 'shamanism' to characterize the native religions of Siberia and neighbouring parts of Asia. This is the only one to lack logic in itself, because shamanism (by any of the first three usages) represents only one component of those religions, and rarely the dominant one. Its employment to describe them is a matter of practical convenience, in that no apparent alternative exists to act as an umbrella term for the complexes of tribal beliefs concerned. In a European context they would be called paganism, and while western academics have an understandable reluctance to apply this word to cultures far removed from the one which produced it, they are being almost as Eurocentric by highlighting shamanism as the defining characteristic of North Asian religious systems. They are simply drawing attention to the aspect of those systems which appears most striking to them.

Amid all this confusion two things at least are clear. One is that shamanism, in any of the above four senses, has been one of the phenomena against which modern western civilisation has defined itself. As such, it takes its place within a set of complex adversarial relationships: between the developed world and indigenous peoples; between science and magic; between established and charismatic religion; and between institutional and 'alternative' medicine. As modernity has come under sustained critical examination during the late twentieth century, and those relationships have been re-evaluated, the profile of shamanism has been raised in turn. The other patent truth is that, whereas most of the new data for a reconsideration of shamanism has come from the Americas or South Asia, Siberia is still commonly regarded as its classic homeland. To some authors Siberian shamans have provided a norm against which those of other regions can be judged, while to others they have represented the most elaborate and highly-developed example of the phenomenon. It may be helpful, therefore, to attempt here a concise general survey of what is known of the shamanism of Siberia, and of the conclusions which may be drawn from it.

Such a survey depends heavily upon the preoccupations of the author, an academic specializing in the history of Western Europe. An orientalist concerned primarily with Siberia itself would have very different emphases. There is no doubt that the best method of providing a better understanding of the functioning of shamans within native Siberian society would be to concentrate upon one of the peoples of the region, or even on one community within them. Such a study would combine a comprehensive survey of all relevant published and archival material with spoken history collected in interviews with living individuals. The present work, by contrast, depends almost wholly upon published sources, although these include a large quantity of primary material and much of that represents the classic data upon which former general conclusions concerning Siberian shamanism have been based. It seeks to re-examine that material with a more critical eye than it has received hitherto, to propose a new synthesis of it, and to go on to examine ways in which the shamans of Siberia have been viewed by western scholars and some of the limitations and difficulties of their traditional synthetic approaches to the subject. Although the subject-matter is largely Siberian, it is in essence intended as a contribution to the history of European and American culture.

PART ONE

WHY WE THINK
WE KNOW ABOUT SHAMANS

1

The Creation of Siberia

It is as well to start from the apparently solid basis of the land itself. The word 'Siberia' is used here in its most common sense, to signify those areas of North Asia which are directly or indirectly under the rule of the present Russian state. Some would employ the expression 'Greater Siberia' for this purpose, confining Siberia 'proper' to the Arctic regions and the huge band of coniferous forest to their south. The problem with this more scrupulous approach is that the word itself is a political rather than a geographical construct. The Khanate of Sibir just happened to be the first state conquered by the Russians as they pushed across the Ural Mountains in the late sixteenth century, and they projected its name onto the whole vast land mass beyond, as far as their power could advance. If 'shamanism' and 'Siberia' are both mental constructions, moreover, then so are 'Europe' and 'Asia'. Europeans, having invented the concept of continents, chose to ignore its rules on their own doorstep by arbitrarily dividing what is physically one land mass. This anomaly was a legacy of the roots of European identity in Greek and Roman civilization, which found it convenient to designate the three main shores of the Mediterranean Sea as Europe, Asia and Africa. Only further north did the distinction between the first two become meaningless, and having become one of the European family of states, the Russian monarchy found itself the custodian of the boundary with Asia. For centuries it was deemed to lie along the River Don. Not until 1736 did a Swede, Philip von Strahlenberg, who had enlivened thirteen years as a prisoner of war of the Russians by exploring their empire, propose that the Urals represented a more appropriate dividing line.[1] Only since then have Siberia and North Asia shared common boundaries.

Those boundaries consist of clear natural frontiers to north and east, in the Arctic and Pacific Oceans. To the west, the Urals do indeed form a dividing line, but there are mountain ranges just as high within Siberia itself, and at the south west is a large gap, where the Siberian steppes run on into those of European Russia and Turkestan. The southern boundary presents worse problems. For the western third of its length it runs along a genuinely impressive barrier, the Altai and Sayan Mountains. The central portion, however, is a political line drawn during the eighteenth century across the Mongolian plains, and the eastern section is defined by the Amur and Ussuri rivers, which are frozen for half of each year. Their historic role has been to unite their region, and only a period of Chinese weakness in the mid nineteenth century allowed the Russians to press forward to them and turn them into a division between states. The reason why this southern frontier has become etched into the imagination of the modern world is that it is the only land boundary on the planet across which two of its Great Powers, Russia and China, come face to face, and is accordingly one of the most heavily defended of all time.

The area enclosed within these bounds is too vast to have a single geographical identity. It is as large as Europe and the USA put together, stretching across a third of the Northern Hemisphere. In the eighteenth century, Russians travelling overland from the imperial capital to Kamchatka, that peninsula which hangs like a long beard from the protruding head of north-east Asia, took an average of two years to complete the journey. It actually took only half that time to sail there around the world, crossing the length of the Atlantic and Pacific and rounding Cape Horn. The heavily-laden Bering expedition of the 1730s, ordered to explore the seas beyond Kamchatka, needed eight years to reach it and commence the task.[2] Anybody making the same journey today has to cross seven time zones.

In general the western third of the region consists of marshy plains, the centre of uplands, and the eastern third of mountains and plateaux. All are threaded by the valleys and flood plains of some of the world's largest rivers. The Arctic zone of the far north is snow-covered for eight or nine months each year and bursts during the brief summer into a profusion of flowers, lichens and berries. The ground remains frozen more than a foot or two down, and the thawing topsoil forms an endless bog with no trees except willow scrub in the more southerly areas. Europeans give this terrain, worldwide, the name of tundra, which they learned from the Saami or Lapp people in Europe's own far north. Below it on the map begins the world's largest forest, stretching over most of the southern two-thirds of Siberia. In the west it consists mostly of pine, with fir, spruce and cedar taking over closer to the centre and larch predominating in the central and eastern regions. The Russians call it *taiga*, a word which is itself a mistake, being used by the Turkic-speaking peoples of the south west to mean mountains, and confused by the invaders with the trees which grew upon them. In the 1960s it still covered almost 2000 million acres.[3] To the south west are the pasturelands, flat or rolling, which Russians call steppe, while the Amur and Ussuri districts have deciduous forest, with tropical animals such as leopards and tigers.

The variety of the terrain is more than equalled by the capacity of human beings to differ in their perceptions of it.[4] Siberia is certainly inclined to alternating extremes and changing moods. The Kolyma basin in the north east contains the coldest inhabited places in the Northern Hemisphere, where winter temperatures can fall to less than –70 degrees centigrade. Across most of the other regions they are usually far below freezing, and remain so for at least six months in each year. It is equally true, however, that summer temperatures on the Kolyma can top 30 degrees centigrade, and the other parts of Siberia, away from the coasts, get as hot or hotter. At the southern city of Khabarovsk, on the Amur, the air in May can warm by about 20 degrees in a few hours, so that the ice on the river shatters with a sound like cannon fire. None the less, seasonal and climatic variations alone cannot account for the differences in emotional responses to the Siberian terrain. To some, the tundra is a dreary and monotonous waste even in summer, the land surface being viewed from the air (which is how most modern travellers see it) as having a uniform bluish tinge. To others, it is a feast of colour as the flowers and lichens flourish in many different hues. It is even more common to lay emphasis on the beauty of the summertime *taiga*, its floor carpeted with flowers of every shade from white to purple, and dark green mosses and ferns, all overhung by the softer greens of larch and cedar, or the dark fragrant fronds of pine among which slender trunks of silver birch shine out at intervals. Others see only a dreary tangle of branches and undergrowth embedded in a trackless swamp within which even local residents can easily become hopelessly and fatally lost. Such accounts lay particular emphasis upon the swarms of flying, biting insects which appear as soon as the topsoil unfreezes. The only certain way to protect your face from them is to bend over a smoking fire – and then they bite the back of your neck.

Reactions to the long months of winter are similarly diverse. Foreigners routinely emphasise the sheer scale of the cold; tales circulate about how in the Kolyma region it is possible to get frostbitten while crossing a street from one house to another. Such accounts stress the numbing and dulling effect of extreme cold, so that the air feels almost solid to a person walking through it. Siberians themselves, whether Russians or natives, are much more inclined to praise the dry quality of the winter climate and the rarity of heavy snowfalls. These combine with the firmness of the frozen ground and the absence of insects to make overland travel much easier and more pleasant than in summer. The winter, too, has beauties for those able to perceive them. Even the sunless zone above the Arctic Circle is redeemed by the glories of the sky. In clear weather it has that magnificent polished aquamarine hue found in the western heaven of more southerly climes just after sunset. Rarer and even more stupendous is the aurora borealis, rippling, flickering or melting in all the rainbow's colours. Below a certain degree of frost, a person's breath freezes into crystals, which tinkle to the ground with a sound which locals call 'the whispering of the stars'.

Objectively, therefore, this is a hard land, or series of lands. Of all the inhabitable areas of the globe, Siberia remains the most thinly populated. Many of its indigenous peoples had to live in small, scattered populations, often seasonally or continually wandering about vast territories. Subjectively, it is also a region of considerable evocative power, capable of inspiring fear, love, awe, loathing and admiration by turns.

2

The Creation of Shamans

The natives of Siberia are themselves identified, and to some extent have actually been fashioned, by western perceptions. In a manner common in colonial societies, the Russians tended to assign names to indigenous peoples which they did not apply to themselves but which were used of them by (often hostile) neighbours whom the invaders encountered first. Another common Russian habit was to categorise peoples according to the languages which they spoke. Both approaches regularly made nonsense of the way in which natives viewed themselves and their world.[1] Until the twentieth century Russians employed a crude shorthand for the linguistic groupings which they had encountered earliest; thus they referred to the Turkic-speaking peoples of south-western Siberia as 'Tatars', to most of the forest-dwellers of the west as 'Ostyaks', to the tundra-roaming nomads of the north west as 'Samoyeds', and to the reindeer-herders of central and eastern Siberia as 'Tunguses'. These terms recur in the older ethnographic works but have now been largely abandoned except in language studies. When Russian adventurers entered the Kolyma river basin of the north east, they encountered a series of clans who spoke a language unrelated to any other and divided into two very different dialects. The groups concerned had no concept of themselves as one people, and often had long-standing enmities with each other, but the newcomers lumped them all together under the single name of Yukaghirs, which was used of them by the Tungusic-speaking clans to their south. Another unique language was spoken by a set of tribes dwelling in the *taiga* of central Siberia, who likewise had no sense of collective loyalty. At a loss to find a common word for them among neighbouring peoples, Russians dubbed them 'Kets' after the name of one river along which they lived.

In this manner, a probable total of around 120 linguistic communities (let alone social or political groupings) which existed in the year 1600 were transformed by the Soviet period into thirty-five 'nationalities'. The process was more successful in some cases than others. After the October Revolution the Bolshevik regime declared that henceforth the five Turkic-speaking clans or tribes of the steppes around Minusinsk, in the south, should comprise the Khakass nation. The name was invented for the occasion, and the groups concerned had no previous common identity, but by the late twentieth century a collective pride, and genuine sense of nationhood, had indeed grown up among them. Further south still, in the Altai Mountains, the same process put together seven more tribes into the Oirot nation, a name taken from a political confederacy which had existed in that region two hundred years before. Here it was less successful, for one of them, the Teleuts, had never identified with that confederacy, and so could not accept its status as part of the new nationality.

When the Russian and Chinese empires drew that notional frontier across the plains of Mongolia, a number of Mongol tribes were left on the Russian side. The name adopted to distinguish them was Buryats, and, despite the fact that previously they had no common political, social or religious identity, they came to use it of themselves. They have long represented the most numerous and powerful of the native nationalities. Second place to them in both respects is taken by a set of cattle-rearing tribes speaking a Turkic language who had migrated from the southern steppes to the Lena valley of eastern central Siberia before the Russians arrived in the area. The latter called them Yakuts, and duly named the Lena region Yakutia, with its capital at Yakutsk. 'Yakut', however, was the name used of them by their enemies, the Tungusic-speaking clans, and they called themselves Sakha. Almost four centuries of foreign rule could not reconcile them to the imposed name, and in the 1990s they were finally allowed to style their territory the Sakha Republic. Just as in the case of the Buryats, however, this sense of collective self is itself a product of Russian rule.

The most sinister aspect of the process of labelling concerns the claim, made by some twentieth-century authors, that not a single native people disappeared as a result of the Russian impact on Siberia. This is asserted in contrast with the extinction of so many indigenous peoples in the Americas and Australasia, and used to argue for the uniquely benign nature of Russian imperialism in comparison with those of other European colonial empires.[2] The problem here is that since Russians controlled the definition of a people, they were superbly well placed to paper over the cracks which appeared amongst their subject races. For example, about half of the clans which they called Yukaghir disappeared completely after being brought under their rule. According to the Russian way of reckoning, this meant that the 'Yukaghirs' were reduced in numbers but still in existence; but the clans concerned had known no other loyalty and identity than that inspired by their own separate units. In March 1996 the newly-formed Association of the Peoples of the North carried out a brisk exercise in redefinition and formally charged the Russian state with having been responsible for the extermination of six distinct native groups.[3]

When all these problems have been taken into account, the following rough impression can be gained of the ethnic map of Siberia at the time of the Russian conquest of each respective part. In the Urals and the forests of the west lived the Khants and Mansi, two related groupings of clans who hunted, fished and farmed in varying combinations. North of them, on the tundra of north-west Siberia, were reindeer hunters and herders speaking languages which the Russians called Samoyed. From west to east, they comprised three cultural groups which became known as Nenets, Enets and Nganasans. In the south-east part of west Siberia were two groups of forest tribes, with lifestyles similar to those of the Khants and Mansi. One used Samoyed tongues and its members were called Selkups; the others were the enigmatic Kets. The woods and steppe of the south west were home to various Turkic-speaking peoples, dependent on farming or pastoral economies, whom the Russians called Tatars.

Much of the *taiga* and tundra of central and eastern Siberia was roamed by reindeer-herding tribes and clans who spoke the languages which Russians termed Tungus. They were divided into two groups, the Evenks to the west and the Evens to the east, by the

great wedge of the Sakha who had pushed into the Lena basin.
North east of the Sakha and north of the Evens, around the Kolyma,
were the Yukaghir clans, and the Kamchatka peninsula was occupied
by the salmon-fishing and plant-gathering Itelmen people. North
of Kamchatka and east of the Kolyma was the broad peninsula
thrusting out into the Bering Sea which forms the extremity of Asia.
Its easternmost headlands and offshore islands were populated
by communities speaking languages from the family known to
Europeans as Eskimo: the Yupik and Unangan. The remaining coasts
of the peninsula, and the interior, were home to natives who fished
and hunted sea mammals on the former and herded reindeer in the
latter. The two economic groups had quite distinct identities, but
each was divided by language, and the Russians preferred to distinguish them by this means, lumping together the coastal and inland
communities of the western linguistic area as 'Koryaks', and those
to the east as 'Chukchi'. Both of them, and the Itelmens, had more
cultural traits in common with native Americans than with other
Siberian peoples.

    In ethnicity, as in other respects, the southern frontier zone was
the most problematic. In the Altai Mountains at the western end
of this sector were the Turkic-speaking groups formed into the Oirot
nation under Soviet rule, and on the steppes to their north, those
who became the Khakass one. Next to the Khakassi was a metal-
working set of clans whom the Russians called 'Blacksmith Tatars'.
The Soviet regime formed them into a single administrative group,
and arbitrarily named it after one clan among them, the Shors.
Another Turkic language group, the Soyots, occupied the territory
of Tuva in the Sayan Mountains to the east. East of Tuva in the
same mountains was another, the Tofa. In the woods and steppe-
lands east of the Sayans was the large mass of Buryat tribes, divided
into a western and an eastern group by the long inland sea of Lake
Baikal. In the south east of Siberia, along the Amur and Ussuri
valleys, in the wooded hills between, and on the coast and offshore
islands, was a cluster of small peoples. Most – the Nanais, Udeghes,
Ulchi, Nedigals, Oroks and Orochi – spoke languages of the
Tungusic family, but two, the Ainus of the southern part of Sakhalin
island and the Nivkhs of northern Sakhalin and the mouth of the

Amur, formed two more of Siberia's distinct linguistic groups. Archaeology suggests that the Nivkhs may have been the original inhabitants of the whole region.

This panorama covers a range of cultural systems as vast as the swathe of the globe concerned. At the time that Russians moved into their territory, the Khants had a way of life equivalent to early medieval Europeans. They were ruled by chiefs or princes who operated out of fortresses with wooden and earth ramparts, prized silver ornaments and drinking vessels, and led war-bands armed with long bows, spears and mail coats. At the far end of Siberia the Chukchi recognised no authority or collective responsibility higher than family networks. Their dwellings were tents and their weapons bone-tipped arrows and spears, with armour made of bone-plated seal hide. They were therefore essentially a Stone Age people, but not necessarily a more 'primitive' one than the Khants, for they were perfectly adapted to their environment and (as will be seen) could be a formidable military force.

Complex as this ethnic map is, it embodies three further difficulties which have implications for a study of shamanism. The first is that cultural traits did not necessarily correspond to genetic patterns. Most of the natives of the south-western steppe and southern mountains had taken over a language and a way of life (based on livestock rearing) from the Turks of Central Asia. Ethnically, however, the majority of them were related to the Samoyedic or Ket-speaking peoples further north. The second problem is that in some regions there was no neat match between language and territory either. The lands occupied mostly by the Nivkhs also contained Ulchi, Nedigals, Nanais, Oroks and Ainus, and occasional Sakhan, Evenki and Korean immigrants. Almost every Nivkh settlement was ethnically and linguistically mixed, and several clans who spoke the Nivkh language by the mid nineteenth century were recently descended from Nedigals, Ainus, Ulchi, Nanais or Oroks.

The third complication is that the distribution of peoples described above was the one encountered by the Russian state and then frozen by it. Left to themselves, the natives of Siberia were capable of a great deal of mobility, competition and dramatic territorial alteration. The Sakha and Buryats were themselves conquerors. They had advanced northward expropriating Tungusic, Samoyedic or Ket-speaking groups or turning them into vassals. Perhaps propelled by them, Tungusic-speaking tribes had also gone on the move, driving out or assimilating Ket and Samoyedic peoples all over central, northern and eastern Siberia. They had proved to be the most adaptable of all Siberians, taking over technologies, beliefs and customs from their victims and flourishing in forest, tundra and maritime economies alike. In the south east their language-group was found all over the Amur and Ussuri region, as seen, and south of the Amur some Tungusic clans learned horse-riding and cattle-rearing from the Mongols. The most successful of all founded the Manchu state, and in 1643 its ruler seized control of China and established the Qing dynasty which was to lead the Chinese empire until 1911. The Samoyedic tribes were quite capable of fighting amongst themselves with as much determination; at the time of the Russian conquest, the Enets, Nenets and Selkups all preserved stories of how the Enets had been evicted from their former homeland by the other two peoples, in a series of long wars.[4]

In a few cases, this process survived the arrival of the Russians. From 1649 onward the latter made sporadic attempts to subdue the Chukchi, and in 1742 the Tsarina Elizabeth and her Senate declared that this people should be utterly destroyed as a punishment for continued resistance. The order proved to be impossible to enforce, as the target was too mobile, too scattered and too ferocious, and operated in a vast and trackless terrain which afforded no economic reward to Europeans. In 1764 the Russians called off the attack. Having repelled them, the Chukchi went in for some empire-building of their own, annihilating or absorbing many Yukaghir, Yupik and Even communities. They also launched seaborne raids against Alaskan natives, to bring back plunder and slaves. The result was a great increase in their population and territory before they formally accepted the Tsar's overlordship in 1837, on the condition that Russian settlement was forbidden in their land.[5]

3

The Transformation of Siberians

The immediate preface to any survey of Siberian shamanism must consist of a consideration of the nature of Russian rule. The conquest of most of Siberia, including almost the whole of the northern two-thirds, was effected in the space of just one lifetime, between 1580 and 1650. It was begun by private enterprise and continued by government-sponsored expeditions, initiated and led by military adventurers. The lure which drew them was fur, 'soft gold', which the animals of Siberia furnished in vast quantity. It was the only product in which Russia itself could outsell all competitors in Europe and the Middle East, and which provided the Tsars with the flow of commerce, and foreign currency, needed to build their state into a first-class power. The annexation of Siberia confirmed Russian supremacy in the fur trade, and met the challenge presented by western European exploitation of the forests of North America. Its conquest involved the successive repetition of the same pattern: the forcible subjugation of a new group of natives, who would then be put to work to hunt the animals and hand over their pelts. The natives concerned would usually rebel against this treatment, sometimes repeatedly, and the Russian demands were such that the most desirable fur-bearing species would be brought close to extinction within two decades. The first problem was met with military repression, and the second by reducing the quotas required and moving on to conquer fresh territory.[1]

As colonial economies went, this one had some advantages for the indigenous peoples; they were, after all, essential to its functioning and therefore the imperial power had a vested interest in their survival. Furthermore, as long as the tribute of furs was paid, they were at first left to run themselves more or less according to their traditional political, social and religious ways. As those who converted to Christianity were excused from paying tribute, the colonial authorities had the stongest practical motive for discouraging a missionary effort. As a result, most Siberian peoples not only survived but, aided by the end of inter-tribal warfare and a general increase in economic prosperity, grew in numbers. The Sakha swelled from 26,500 in 1700 to 226,000 in 1900, while the Buryats increased ten fold, to 289,000, over the same period; by its end, the two peoples together made up two-thirds of the native population of Siberia. The majority of the others, however, had also registered some expansion.

As in the case of other European colonial empires, the conquest would have been impossible without the military support of the natives themselves, who entered Russian service both to obtain employment and to share some of the booty taken in the first waves of expansion, and to pay off old scores against traditional local enemies. This is particularly obvious in the case of the clans whom the Russians grouped together under the foreign nickname of Yukaghirs. One of them, the Khoromo, allied with the newcomers to overcome another, their traditional enemies the Yandin. As the Russians pushed into the north east of the Yukaghir region they found themselves besieged in a fort by the Khodin clan, only to be saved by the immemorial rivals of the latter, the Chuwan. The Chuwan subsequently supported the Russians in attacking another of their traditional enemies, the Chukchi. When the Cossack chief Afanassy Shestakoff moved against the Koryaks in 1730, he took with him a host of native irregulars speaking Yukaghir and Tungusic languages. These allies soon became appalled by his cruelty, and in particular his habit of wiping out Koryak villages by blocking the doors of all the houses and then burning the inhabitants in them alive. They abandoned him, leaving Shestakoff reduced to his tiny force of Russian soldiers, who were soon overpowered and killed with him by a Chukchi war band. The Siberians were thus not merely vital to the Russian imperial project; they could at times exert a restraining influence over the manner in which it was carried out.

None of this is sufficient to tint Russian colonialism with rose. A minority of native groups declined sharply as a result of it and (as seen) some disappeared. More generally, the system depended on exploiting the labour of the natives for profits which were almost completely appropriated by their foreign masters. The tribute of furs was often exacted with considerable brutality, including the murder, torture, plunder, imprisonment and enslavement of those who fell behind in it, and Russian officials normally levied further payments to make private fortunes. From 1697 onward the central government repeatedly forbade the ill-treatment of aboriginal peoples, and was almost as consistently ignored. The principal British historian of Siberia, James Forsyth, has summed up the first three centuries of Russian rule as 'a hierarchy of power in which there were practically no effective laws and no ethical imperatives'.[2] The worst development of all, as far as the indigenous populations were concerned, was that they were turned into minorities in their own lands. By 1700 there were already about as many Europeans settled in Siberia as there were natives. By 1900 the latter were reduced to about 10 per cent of its inhabitants, and during the twentieth century that figure halved again. Furthermore, the initial disposition to tolerate local customs and beliefs ended dramatically in 1706, with the publication of an imperial decree requiring the conversion of all natives to Christianity, with death the penalty for any who refused.

The results must be put into perspective by emphasising that Christianity was only one of three missionary faiths operating in Siberia at this period. One of the others was Islam. The first step in the Russian conquest, the attack on the khanate of Sibir, was inspired partly by the militantly Moslem identity which that state had adopted shortly before. Thereafter the same religion continued to make less spectacular inroads among the Turkic-speaking peoples of the south west, the most notable being the conversion of those of the Baraba steppe in the 1740s.[3] The other faith was Buddhism, which reached the eastern Buryats in the 1710s and became dominant among them. By the 1820s a fifth of their male population were monks. Over the same period many of the Soyots of Tuva, and the Nanais, Oroches and Evenks of the Amur region, were also converted. Between 1904 and 1921 a new revelatory religion based on Buddhism, and essentially anti-Russian, swept through the Altaian peoples.[4] At first sight, Buddhism should have made a better fit with native beliefs than Christianity or Islam, because it could incorporate traditional deities and rituals, but the reality was different. Monks viewed shamans and other tribal spiritual functionaries as rivals with opposed moral codes, and took ruthless action against them. In the eastern Buryat lands, according to one historian, 'the poor shamanists were everywhere hunted down. No forests, no mountain could hide them from the vengeance of the lamas'.[5] In Tuva the monks erected their shrines on traditional sacred sites, razing the latter to make way for them.[6] In the Altai believers in the charismatic Buddhism which appeared during the 1900s abolished traditional sacrifices, beat shamans, burned their equipment and trampled their fields.[7]

In this competition for allegiance, Orthodox Christianity had the advantage of being supported by the imperial state, with the limitation that the decrees of the latter were effective only where churchmen and administrators were numerous and zealous enough to enforce them. Such a place was Kamchatka in the 1740s, where the Itelmens were literally thrashed into accepting baptism. A similar campaign was mounted in the period between 1710 and 1760 among the Nenets, the Khants and Mansi, and the Turkic-speaking groups of the south-western steppes, officials being sent out to burn shrines and impose the new faith. The death penalty was rarely, if ever, exacted unless religious resistance was coupled with armed rebellion, but the process of evangelism could still be brutal. In 1762, for example, four Khants were convicted at Tobolsk of sacrificing a horse for good luck on a hunting and fishing expedition. All were given a public flogging, and the ringleader was sentenced to three years' imprisonment in a monastery on a 'strict fast'. It seems that by the mid eighteenth century most Siberian natives made a profession of Christianity, sometimes sincere, wherever they lived or moved in the vicinity of Russian settlers or colonial authorities. This consideration did not apply, of course, to the majority of the territory under nominal Russian rule.[8]

The missionary effort flagged in the second half of the century, as Catherine the Great adopted the general trend among European rulers towards religious toleration. This policy was reversed in turn by nineteenth-century Tsars, who tried to build a new Russian nationalism around their monarchy, based in part on confessional orthodoxy. New efforts were now made to convert the native peoples, with tax incentives and programmes of preaching and pastoral work added to coercion. By the 1850s the Sakha were all said to have been baptized, in a campaign led by Ioann Veniaminov who became archbishop of eastern Siberia. In 1824 a new mission was sent to the Nenets, which provoked a revolt that was only fully suppressed after three decades. Another was sent to the Altai and Sayan Mountains in 1830, to preach to the Turkic-speaking inhabitants. In 1876 it subjected three thousand people to compulsory baptism in a single event. The outward achievement among some groups was impressive; a traveller among the Tofa of the Sayans in 1871 noted that all of them attended church, wore copper crosses around their necks, genuflected on entering a cabin, crossed themselves before and after meals, and owned icons. The Nanais and Oroches of the Amur and the Oroks of Sakhalin were also exposed to vigilant evangelism in the later nineteenth century. By 1900 most Siberian natives were nominally Christian.[9]

The reality, as far as it can be recovered at all, was clearly complex. In the face of the first onslaught upon their traditional religion, many of the Khants, Mansi and Nenets had retired deeper into the taiga and tundra, taking the images of their deities with them, to create new shrines out of reach of government agents. Travellers in remote areas during the late nineteenth century reported the continued existence of these. Those dedicated to the most important deities were most carefully hidden, and protected by springtraps.[10] It was also obvious that the sort of Christianity practised by the natives was often decidedly unorthodox and blended with the older customs and beliefs. Observers in Kamchatka in the 1740s and 1780s alike commented that the enforced Christianization of the Itelmens had produced a set of strange hybrid sects.[11] During the nineteenth century some Buryats responded to missionary pressure by altering their calendar of *tailgans*, horse sacrifices to the land-spirits and ancestors, to coincide with the feasts of the church. Some of these sacrifices were offered to St Nicholas.[12] Wealthy Buryat landowners at the opening of the twentieth century still sometimes practised the old religion without even this overlay, offering the sacrifices to a wide range of spirits and deities, and setting up images of the latter to protect their property. They discouraged the presence of strangers at such rituals; photographs of one *tailgan* taken by an American traveller in 1900 show the men going about the sacrifice attired in Russian caps and coats, indistinguishable save by their activity from any other smartly-dressed people in the empire at that period.[13]

Similar descriptions of syncretism, and of confusion, are found among other groups. A Christian Evenk from east of Lake Baikal, interviewed in 1912 or 1913, did not understand the concept of Hell, and thought that an angel was the 'Master of Men', a saint the 'Master of Bears', and St Nicholas the 'Master of Shamans'. He had little interest in Christ.[14] A traveller among the outwardly pious Tofa, in the same years, noted that they confused God with St Nicholas, could not explain who the figures were in icons, and hung images of pre-Christian deities next to those of Christ and the saints.[15] The Khants were likewise observed sometimes to be offering blood sacrifices to St Nicholas along with traditional gods.[16]

Such data have often been used, since the eighteenth century, as evidence for the essential failure of Christianity among Siberian natives, and for the almost universal survival of the old religions, at least in secret. They can, however, be read in a different way, for the pattern suggested here, of the combination of pre-Christian with Christian elements, of the primacy of patron saints rather than the Trinity in personal devotion and their conflation with earlier deities, and of a general lack of understanding and interest concerning the more sophisticated points of theology, are typical of 'folk' Christianities all over the world. They can be perceived as much as signs of the success of the conversion experience, and its assimilation into local cosmology, as of its failure. The prominence of St Nicholas was certainly derived from his importance to ordinary Russian settlers in Siberia, many of whom believed that the Trinity consisted of the saint, Jesus, and the Virgin.[17]

It is instructive to reverse the picture, and observe how much impact Russian imperialism had made upon native religion even in areas where the church and the secular authorities had no direct

power. Such an area was that occupied by the Koryaks at the end
of the nineteenth century. They were by that time the Siberian
people least known to Europeans. Although they had accepted
formal Russian rule in 1757, this only involved the payment of a
light tribute, and no officials or missionaries were imposed upon
them. The Russians settled among them amounted to no more than
6 per cent of the population of their territory and were mostly
merchants, although American traders and whalers were also familiar figures in their coastal settlements. When an anthropologist,
Waldemar Jochelson, visited them in 1900–01, he found that 45 per
cent of them were baptized Christians. Even this minority made
only a nominal profession of the new faith, such as one man who
appeared devout while visiting Russians but still sacrificed dogs to
the old spirits and deities; the difference was that, out of respect for
his new allegiance, he offered puppies instead of grown animals.
On the other hand, Jochelson also reported that traditional religion
itself was in deep decline. Its cosmology, rites and functionaries
were disintegrating into a mass of fables and folk magic, and re-
treating from the public to the private sphere. The solvent forces
of Christianity, and the contempt expressed by foreigners for native
beliefs, were wearing them away even among these most remote of
all Siberians.

This situation was not very different from that at the far end of
the region, among peoples who had been some of the very first to
be conquered by the Russians and to have submitted to enforced
conversion to the Orthodox Church. Such were the Mansi, living
up against the Ural Mountains, who were systematically studied by
a Finnish scholar, Artturi Kannisto, between 1901 and 1906. He was
able to observe in detail what earlier travellers had noted in general;
that the natives were all baptized Christians but that many still
carried on older rites at shrines hidden in forests and bogs. The
deities venerated at these places were, however, a supreme sky god
and his son, 'the Man-Who-Looks-On-The-World', who was associated with the colour white and to whom only white animals were
offered. This was a mirror image of Christianity, adapted to traditional places and observances, with the principal difference that the
third member of the Trinity was not the Holy Ghost but a female

spirit in the form of a bear, daughter of the sky-god and patron of this most revered of local animals. Furthermore even this syncretic system of belief was in deep decline, and largely confined to elderly people. Kannisto, describing a sacrifice, commented that 'I am almost in tears, as I see such darkness. Yet, I believe those old men to be happier than the youngsters that have forsaken the religion of their fathers, but know nothing more of the new one than their elders'.[18] Whether Christian or not, natives at the end of the nineteenth century were operating in a world of composite religions, in which elements of the old mixed often indistinguishably with the new. European knowledge of the pre-Christian beliefs and practices was doomed to be a matter of conjectural reconstruction, rather than of observation.

The figures called shamans, though rooted in those beliefs and practices, were not necessarily incompatible with Christianity. After all, European Christians had regularly provided theoretical justifications for the practice of ritual magic, which likewise involved personal dealings with spirits to achieve specific ends. They had, admittedly, as regularly been condemned by established churches, but they remained both persistent and sincere. The real problem in Siberia was that which drew Buddhist hostility upon shamans: that they represented alternative foci of power and loyalty, and to some extent different moral values, to the priests of the incoming faith. Their treatment by the imperial authorities was therefore bound up with the latters' policies towards native religion. In the seventeenth century they were generally tolerated, if with disapproval. Some Russians asked their help to locate lost or stolen goods. In 1679 the military governor of Yakutia asked one to use his arcane skills to prevent the governor's own transfer. In 1696, however, shamans were forbidden to practise in Yakutsk and Russians ordered not to attend their rites. Official hostility strengthened in the following century, with the drive against native religion, and whereas Catherine the Great disapproved of missionaries, she had an even greater detestation of shamanism. To her, it represented the most vivid example of the barbarism and ignorance with which her empire was identified by other Europeans, and she wrote against it in person.[19]

The burning of shrines and deity-images was therefore accompanied by the destruction of the equipment of shamans, and public humiliation of them. It is not surprising that, from the 1720s onward, Europeans interested in their performances regularly commented on how secretive, and how reluctant to appear before strangers, they had become.[20] The same sense of an underground, but still persistent, tradition is sustained in accounts from the nineteenth century and the first decades of the twentieth. Clearly the degree to which shamanism survived, and the openness with which it was practised, varied considerably according to district and region. A Pole living among the Sakha in the 1880s noted that shamans in the remoter parts of this people's territory still wore the long hair associated with their vocation in Sakhan culture, but those dwelling around Yakutsk had cut it short to evade detection. One of these, an old man called Tiuspiut, had been punished many times by the authorities and had suffered the burning of his ritual dress and drum.[21] When travelling among the Koryaks in 1900–01, Waldemar Jochelson could only identify two shamans, neither of them well respected and one very reluctant to perform before a foreigner. Among the Yukaghir in 1895–96 and 1901–02, he could find none still active, although he persuaded a retired one to display his former skills on condition that the local parish priest did not find out.[22] In the same years, by contrast, shamans among the Turkic-speaking groups who were to become the Khakass nation still performed in public and in full costume.[23] Another scholar visiting Selkup communities in 1911–13 reported that every large family had its own one, and that from almost every hut in the evening he could hear 'the dull roar of the magic drums and the strange chanting of the shamans'.[24]

Had the Tsarist regime survived, the most likely history of native Siberian spirituality during the rest of the twentieth century would have been one of a continued gradual decline and adaptation of traditional ways. The Soviet government, however, set out to make a clean break with former colonial policies. Initially this promised many benefits for Siberian natives, as the new regime proclaimed the equality of all peoples and the free development of ethnic minorities, with rights of self-determination. It went on to abolish the fur tribute, cancel all debts owed by natives, prohibit the sale of alcohol to them, establish university departments to study their cultures, and admit them to local government. In 1924 it established a Council of Assistance to the Peoples of the North, which till its dissolution in 1935 worked hard to provide the indigenous inhabitants of north and central Siberia with better education, medical care, vocational training, and equipment for hunting and fishing. This was a programme of modernization as well as of philanthropy, and the same regime abolished customs which it viewed as barriers to that process, such as bride purchase and blood feuds. On the whole, however, Soviet rule in Siberia until the end of the 1920s was characterized by a genuinely benevolent paternalism, dedicated to the improvement of material wellbeing rather than the disruption of traditional ways of life.[25]

One of the customs abolished by decree was shamanism, but there seems to have been little immediate enforcement of this ruling. On the contrary, in some areas shamans appear to have enjoyed a new freedom of operation and authority during the 1920s because of the Soviet disempowerment and persecution of their old enemies, the Orthodox Church and Buddhist monasteries. This pattern was reported among Selkups, Evens, and Buryats.[26] It was reversed, along with the whole of official policy towards native cultures, on the advent of Stalinism. What ensued was partly a local imposition of the processes of social and economic reconstruction introduced throughout the USSR, and partly a specific process of Russianization of ethnic minorities. Between 1929 and 1938 collectivization of farming, herding, hunting and fishing was enforced across most of Siberia, often at the price of considerable social trauma and physical destruction. Chiefs and the wealthier natives were eliminated and elders deposed, and a further attack mounted upon traditional religions. The few groups which escaped consisted of those Nenets, Nganasans, Evenks, Evens and Chukchi who were able for the last time to exploit the size and wildness of their terrain by withdrawing out of Russian reach. Even these, however, were finally brought into the Soviet economic and political system in the 1950s and 1960s, and a further degree of collectivization was imposed on the other peoples which often involved a drastic reduction in the number of their settlements. Russian immigration was further encouraged, especially in the far north east where it had hitherto been least effective. The Koryaks, who had made up 94 per cent of the inhabitants of their territory in 1900, were reduced to 7 per cent of them by 1980. Over the same period the economic exploitation of Siberia increased at an even greater pace. Ever since the eighteenth century, mining, fishing and logging had joined fur-hunting as extractive processes, and the massive increase of all in the twentieth century, joined by oil wells, gas pipelines, and the official assault on traditional culture, brought the Russian impact on native ways of life at last to 'annihilatory proportions'. By the 1970s only a few bands of Evenks and Evens still roamed with their herds in something like the old manner.[27]

Shamans were naturally prime targets of this transformative process, being designated as agents of backwardness, superstition, fraud and social inequality, and as enemies of the Communist Party. Persecution, of course, often turned the last charge into a self-fulfilling prophecy. If the stories are to be believed, Evenk shamans joined the wealthier clansmen in opposing Soviet propaganda, and encouraging their people to avoid the new hospitals, burn schools and slaughter collectivized reindeer herds. One of the new school-masters sent among the Chukchi in 1932 later recounted how the local shaman had told him that the school, and the smell of Russians, frightened away the sea mammals on the hunting of which the community depended. The first attempt to organize a fishing collective among the Kets, in 1928, was allegedly thwarted by one who warned that the fishing grounds had been contaminated by evil spirits. Nenet shamans were supposed to predict the same fate for those who consulted Russian doctors.[28]

Repression was accordingly often savage. There are tales of shamans thrown out of helicopters by Soviet agents challenging them to display their powers of spirit-flight. One KGB officer under Stalin is said to have adopted the tactic of visiting small settlements pre-tending to be ill and asking for the local shaman. When the latter appeared, the Russian would take him aside, shoot him, and take his drum as a trophy. In 1937 the last top-level practitioner of the Nanais was dropped into deep water through a hole cut in the ice, with a stone tied to his foot. Of eight arrested among the Khants in

the same period, seven were executed and one survived only by
denying that he was a 'real' shaman.²⁹ More commonly, shamans
were exiled from their homelands, or committed to labour camps,
or forced to make public professions of guilt and renounce their
calling. Their equipment was confiscated and destroyed. Youth
groups and school pupils were incited to expose them to their
communities as charlatans, to report them to officials, and to lam-
poon them in poems and plays.³⁰ A detailed study of the Buryats
has indicated that some shamans at least bore no hostility towards
the Soviet system, accepting it as the will of the deities and venerating
Lenin and other Communist heroes as additional divinities. That
spirit of accommodation was not returned towards them by the
authorities.³¹ By 1980 shamanism was commonly regarded as dead
in Siberia.

The accuracy of that claim will be considered later. For the
present, it is perhaps useful to suggest that the process described
above is, like the Siberian landscape and Siberian ethnography,
susceptible to more than one reading. In the Museum of the History
of Religion and Atheism at Leningrad there hung during the 1980s
a classic Soviet Realist painting entitled 'The Triumph of Enlighten-
ment over Superstition'; it may well hang there still, now that the
city has returned to being St Petersburg. It portrayed an Evenk
shaman, caught in the act of performing an act of magical healing
for a patient lying on a bed in a native hut, cowering defeated
before a Russian flying doctor. The latter has just burst through
the door and is standing, medical bag in hand, young, square-
shouldered, clean-cut and firm-jawed, and dominating the scene
with his physical as well as his professional presence. To some the
scene may be taken as a perfect portrayal of the arrogance and
brutality of western civilization when confronted with native
traditions which challenge it or dissent from it. Others would
add a racial dimension, in taking the Russian as the representative
of colonial mastery and manipulation of indigenous peoples.
Yet others, however – and these included Siberians as well as
Russians to whom I spoke in the 1980s – would take the message
of the work at face value, accepting that the Soviet modernization
of Siberia did represent a replacement of useless or harmful

superstitions with modern sciences or technologies which contributed much to the health and prosperity of the natives. Some commentators would accept a measure of justice in all these readings. In moral terms, Siberian shamanism has been a contested phenomenon ever since records of it begin.

4

The Records of Shamanism

The body of information upon shamanism which is available to scholars is organically embedded in the transformation of Siberia by Russian rule. The nature of that transformation makes it inevitable that much of the information is hostile in nature, and as Gloria Flaherty has pointed out, the nature of that hostility altered in the course of the eighteenth century.[1] Before then, it had expressed a Christian detestation of heathen practices; thereafter it expressed the contempt of modernity for ignorance and superstition. In most cases, if not all, the sentiments expressed were those of the writers, but they also reflected wider pressures and expectations. The earlier authors were producing for a Christian audience, while the later were working under a regime which discouraged shamanism, and for a few decades was led by an empress who had herself written against it.

There are no accounts of Siberian shamans which date from before the sixteenth century, but travellers to the courts of the Mongol Great Khans of the thirteenth century reported figures who were culturally similar. The most famous and most commonly quoted of those travellers was Marco Polo, who described how 'magicians' divined the cause of disease by singing and playing music until a 'devil' entered one of them and spoke through him. Although resembling accounts of the shamans of Siberia, this custom was actually located by Polo in south-west China and not in Mongolia, and there is no precise indication that the magicians concerned entered the altered state of consciousness which is the bottom line of most definitions of shamanism. A much better testimony for scholars of Siberia is that of the Franciscan friar William of Rubruck, who reported in 1254 that a Mongol magician would call a 'demon' to him by singing and drumming in darkness until he began to rave. This signalled the arrival of the spirit, whereupon the magician would make offerings to it and seek answers for specific problems. This is a very close parallel to Siberian shamanism, but was based on hearsay, as no foreigners were allowed to attend these ceremonies.[2]

The earliest known eye-witness description of North Asian shamanism, and the only one made of it as practised by Siberians not yet under Russian rule, was left by an Englishman called Richard Johnson, who visited the coast of north-western Siberia in the mid-sixteenth century. On New Year's Day 1557 he witnessed there what he termed 'devilish rites' among the local Samoyedic-speaking natives, almost certainly Nenets.[3] The primary place of this account in the sequence of evidence makes it worthy of quotation at length:

> The priest doth begin to play upon a thing like a great sieve, with a skin on the one end like a drum: and the stick that he playeth with is about a span long, and one end is round like a ball, covered with the skin of a hart. Also the priest hath upon his head a thing of white like a garland, and his face is covered with a piece of shirt of mail, with many small ribs and teeth of fishes, and wild beasts hanging on the same mail. Then he singeth as we use here in England to halloo, whoop, or shout at hounds, and the rest of the company answer him with this chorus, 'Igha, Igha, Igha', and then the priest replieth again with his voices. And they answer him with the selfsame words so many times, that in the end he becometh as it were mad, and falling down as he were dead, having nothing on him but a shirt, lying upon his back I might perceive him to breathe. I asked them why he lay so, and they answered me, 'Now doth our god tell him what we shall do, and whither we shall go.' And when he had lien still a little while, they cried thus three times together, 'Oghao, Oghao, Oghao', and as they use these three calls, he riseth with his head and lieth down again, and then he rose up and sang with like voices as he did before: and his audience answered him 'Igha, Igha, Igha'. Then he commanded them to kill five olens or great deer, and continued singing still both he and they as before. Then he took a sword of a cubit and a span long (I did measure it myself) and put it into his belly halfway and sometime less, but no wound was to be seen (they continuing in their sweet song still). Then he put the sword into the fire till it was

warm, and so thrust it into the slit of his shirt and thrust it through
his body, as I thought, in at his navel and out at his fundament: the
point being out of his shirt behind, I laid my finger upon it, then he
pulled out the sword and sat down. This being done, they set a kettle
of water over the fire to heat, and when the water doth seethe, the
priest beginneth to sing again, they answering him, for so long as
the water was in heating, they sat and sang not. Then they made a
thing being four square, and in height and squareness of a chair, and
covered with a gown ... The water still seething on the fire, and this
square seat being ready, the priest put off his shirt, and the thing like
a garland which was on his head, with those things which covered
his face, and he had on yet all this while a pair of hose of deers' skins
with the hair on, which came up to his buttocks. So he went into the
square seat, and sat down like a tailor and sang with a strong voice
or hallooing. Then they took a small line made of deers' skins of four
fathoms long, and with a small knot the priest made it fast about his
neck, and under his left arm, and gave it unto two men standing on
both sides of him, which held the end together. Then the kettle of
hot water was set before him in the square seat ... and then it [the
seat] was covered with a gown of broad cloth ... Then the two men
which did hold the ends of the line still standing there ... drew until
they had drawn the ends of the line stiffly and together, and then I
heard a thing fall into the kettle of water which was before him in
the tent. Thereupon I asked them that sat by me what it was that fell
into the water that stood before him. And they answered me, that it
was his head, his shoulder and left arm, which the line had cut off
... Then I rose up and would have looked whether it were so or no,
but they laid hold on me and said, that if they should see him with
their bodily eyes, they should live no longer ... Then they began to
halloo with these words, 'Oghaoo, Oghaoo, Oghaoo', many times
together. As they were thus singing and out calling, I saw a thing like
the finger of a man two times together thrust through the gown from
the priest. I asked them that sat next to me what it was that I saw,
and they said, not his finger; for he was yet dead: and that which I
saw appear through the gown was a beast, but what beast they knew
not nor would not tell. And I looked upon the gown, and there was
no hole to be seen: and then at last the priest lifted up his head with
his shoulder and arm, and all his body, and came forth to the fire ...
And I went to him that served the priest, and asked him what their
god said to him when he lay as dead. He answered, that his own

people doth not know: neither is it for them to know: for they must
do as he commanded.

Not until 1692 can another description be found, in the account of
Siberia left by Nicholas Witsen, which popularized the term
'shaman' among Europeans. Based on his travels in the region,
it included short and pejorative descriptions of the activities of
such practitioners among Tungusic- and Samoyedic-speaking
peoples. It also provided the first known picture of a Siberian
shaman, glossed 'Priest of the Devil' and showing a man dressed in
antlered head-dress and kaftan, beating a drum and chanting. This
has been employed many times as an objective piece of ethnographic
data, and so much of it may be, but it is worth noting a detail of
the figure which is less apparent in some reproductions than in the
original; he has clawed feet. Witsen's shaman is himself a
demon.[4]

In the eighteenth century first-hand accounts multiply, many of
them produced by scientists sent out by the goverment to report
on the human and natural resources of the empire. Their comments
on shamanism are generally brief, and negative according to the
'modern' pattern identified by Gloria Flaherty. Fairly typical in
length and tone are those provided in the book published in 1763
by a Scottish surgeon named John Bell, and based on notes taken
during journeys made in the Russian empire between 1715 and 1738.
In 1720 he crossed the marshy plain of the Baraba steppe in south-
western Siberia, and found that the local Turkic-speaking people
still had many shamans. He and his companions visited the home
of a famous one, a young and 'handsome' woman. On being given
tobacco and other gifts she produced her ritual tools. One was a
shaytan or piece of wood cut into the form of a human head and
adorned with silk and woollen rags of various colours. The other
was a small drum, fixed with brass and iron rings and hung with
rags. She stuck the former in a corner and then beat the latter and
sang for fifteen minutes while her neighbours provided choruses.
When her song was finished she asked for questions and delivered
answers 'with much obscurity and ambiguity'.

Bell was clearly impressed by nothing more about her than her looks, and his attitude remained similar when a famous Buryat shaman was brought to see him on a later expedition into the country south of Lake Baikal. The man was about thirty years of age, grave and dignified, and invited the foreigners to accompany him to a native tent where he was willing to perform for them. They were joined by a group of other local men, and after about thirty minutes the shaman seated himself on the floor near the hearth, his face towards his audience. He then took a staff four feet long in each hand and beat time with them to a song, his companions joining the chorus. As he did so he writhed, until he foamed at the mouth and had red, staring, eyes. He then jumped up and danced furiously until he stamped out the fire with his bare feet. When exhausted, he retired to the door and gave three shrieks to call what Bell termed 'his demon'. Then he returned, sat composed, and answered many questions in ambiguous terms. He then appeared to stab himself with a knife and performed other tricks. Bell concluded that all shamans were 'a parcel of jugglers'.

To another doctor, Daniel Messerschmidt, shamanism likewise consisted of lies and trickery. The botanist Stephan Krascheninnikow thought their deceptions obvious to anyone not 'blinded by superstition'. Another botanist, and chemist, Johann Gmelin, went beyond disapproval to campaign in person against the shamans whom he had set out to study, trying to destroy their reputations among their own people. He considered that their practices were all 'humbug', and wished that he might sentence one old shaman whom he had invited to perform 'to hard labour in a silver mine for life'. The naturalist Petrus Pallas portrayed them as holding the natives in thrall to terror and illusion. He commented in passing on how one famous Evenk practitioner had lost his powers when some European scholars confiscated his ritual costume as an exhibit. Pallas then proceeded to commit just the same action himself, taking away the gown of a shaman who had apparently abandoned his home (with the garment left in it) to avoid being questioned. To another famed academic explorer, Johann Georgi, shamans were 'partly barefaced impostors, partly deceived fanatics', who empowered Satan by making their people serve evil spirits, while to the French traveller Mathieu de Lesseps they were pure charlatans.[5] Those who consented to meet the European scholars of the period were usually cooperating with enemies.

It is easy to imagine, but impossible to establish, how much valuable data must have been missed or distorted by authors filled with prejudices of such vehemence. An ingrained sceptic may be tempted to question the implications even of some of their clear and dogmatic statements. For example, Krascheninnikow recorded that the Itelmens had no shamans of their own, although they used those from neighbouring peoples and regarded old women in general as able to work simple magic and interpret dreams.[6] In the past this has often been taken as a valuable insight into the traditional culture of the people concerned, making them unique in Siberia. It may be worth raising the point that, while Krascheninnikow's observation may have been perfectly correct, by the time that it was made the Itelmens had been subjected for a generation to a particularly traumatic experience of colonial rule. Their numbers were plunging and their social system was being disrupted because of epidemics of European disease, exceptionally heavy exploitation by Russian officials, and desperate and futile acts of armed rebellion. Krascheninnikow himself noted that they were committing suicide in numbers which disturbed the imperial authorities.[7] His account of their customs during the period of his stay may not, therefore, be necessarily true of their aboriginal culture.

The eighteenth-century pattern of hostility and prejudice continued with unbroken momentum into the early nineteenth, when travellers such as Eva Felinska inveighed against shamans as corruptors and parasites in a wholly traditional manner.[8] It remained dangerous for natives to discuss such matters with Europeans. The first account of them among the Nivkhs was provided by a Russian merchant called Ivanov, who opened a school for natives on the Amur in 1855. He gradually won the friendship of a local shaman, who at length allowed him to attend a performance and even to learn how some of the special effects provided in it were achieved. Ivanov rewarded his friend by denouncing him as a fraud, before publishing a report on the episode for fellow Russians.[9]

The century's tendency to nationalism, imperialism and evangelism among Europeans acted to reinforce such attitudes, but that same tendency could operate to a different effect. Its nationalism gave an impetus to the development of folklore studies, and its imperialism to that of anthropology. As the century wore on it became increasingly common for scholars to settle for longer periods among specific native peoples and to concentrate upon studying their culture rather than regarding it as one item among the general human and natural features of a region. Alexander Castren represented the drift towards this development in the middle decades, and G. N. Potanin was one of its most distinguished practitioners in the later part of the century. In a Buryat, M. N. Khangalov, Siberia produced for the first time a native scholar dedicated to the interpretation of his own society. By 1892 there were already enough of these studies for V. M. Mikhailowskii, Vice-President of the Ethnographical Section of the Imperial Society for Natural History, Anthropology and Ethnography, to synthesize them into a general survey of what was known of Siberian shamanism.[10] Three of the most respected and effective of these early anthropologists were men who had been exiled to Siberia for political opposition to the Tsarist state: Waclaw Sieroszewski, Waldemar Jochelson and Waldemar Bogoras. It was as if estrangement from their own government had caused them to identify with the equally marginalized native peoples as most Russians could not. Sieroszewski and Jochelson, in particular, showed a sympathy for the natives, and an imaginative ability to understand the appeal of shamanism to them, which was new in literature. Sieroszewski's prose, in particular, captured the experience of shamanic performances with a vividness never known before. Here is his description of the first part of a healing rite by a Sakhan practitioner:

> When the sun sets and dusk approached, all preparations for the ceremony in the skin tent are swiftly completed; the ground is swept, the wood is cut, and a feast is provided. The neighbours arrive and sit along the wall, men on the right and women on the left, talking quietly and moving softly ... The host chooses the most pliable twigs and forms them into a loop which is placed around the shaman's shoulders and held by one of those present from now on, in case the spirits carry him off. Everyone eats, and relaxes. The shaman, sitting on the edge of the platform of honour, slowly untwists his plaited

hair, muttering and giving instructions. He sometimes shakes hard with a nervous cough; his gaze remains fixed on one point at a time, usually on the fire.

The latter slowly dies down. Darkness creeps into the tent and people speak more and more softly; notice is given that anybody wishing to leave must do so now, because soon the door will be fastened. The shaman slowly takes off his tunic, and puts on his ceremonial kaftan. Then he is given a pipe, which he smokes deeply for a long time; his cough becomes louder, he shakes more violently with it. When he has finished smoking, his pale face leans forward onto his breast, his eyes half closed. At this point his white mare's skin, on which he has been lying, is placed in the middle of the floor. He asks for cold water, and when he has drunk it slowly holds out his hand for a drum made ready for him; he then walks to the centre of the floor, goes down upon his right knee, and bows low to the four cardinal points, dribbling some water from his mouth as he does this.

Now everything is silent. White horsehair is dropped upon the embers of the fire, and in the faint glow of the coals the dark motionless figure of the shaman is still seen for a while, head bowed, drum clutched to breast and face to the south, as is also the head of the mare's hide on which he sits. The fire burns out completely, the audience hardly breathes, and the shaman mutters and jerks for a time, till total silence falls. Then there is a cry like the clanging of iron, then the screech of a falcon and the mewing of a gull, and then silence again. It is broken by a gentle humming noise; the shaman has started to drum.

At first his rhythm is soft and tender, then rough and wild like a breaking storm. As it grows louder and louder, strange cries sound through the air; a crow caws, a grebe laughs, gulls complain, snipes whistle, eagles and hawks screech. The sounds swell to their highest pitch, the beating of the drum becomes more and more powerful, until they combine in a tremendous crescendo, with the clanging of the shaman's metal hangings. It is a cascade of sounds, enough to overwhelm the listeners. Suddenly it breaks off – there are one or two strong beats on the drum and it falls to the floor. All sound ceases for a long moment, and then the gentle humming murmur of the drum begins again.

This sequence is repeated several times ... till at last the drum takes on a new rhythm and the voice of the shaman chants:

> Strong bull of the earth, horse of the steppes
> I, the strong bull, bellow!
> I, the horse of the steppes, neigh!
> I, the man raised above all beings!
> I, the most gifted man of all!
> I, the man created by the Mighty Lord!
> Horse of the steppes, appear, teach me!
> Magic bull of the earth come and speak to me!
> All who will go with me, hear me!
> You who will not obey me, leave me!
> Come no closer than I allow!
> Look carefully, heed me!
> You of the left side, Lady of the Staff,
> If I travel wrongly, correct me!
> Show me my errors and my pathway, Mother of Mine!
> Fly before me! Point out my road!
> Spirits of the sun, mothers of the sun,
> Living in the south on the nine wooded hills,
> Jealous ones! I implore you!
> Let your three shadows stand high!
> In the east on your mountain Lord,
> Forebear of mine, strong-necked, of fearful strength,
> Be you with me!
> And you, old fiery wizard, I ask you –
> With all my dreams comply!
> Consent to my desires!
> Fulfil all! Heed all! Fulfil all!

Now the sound of the drum is heard once more, and then more wild shouts and incoherent words – then all is silent.

The quality of these early ethnographic studies may have been far better than anything before, but it should not be overstated. For one thing, they were devoted to societies which were already significantly altered by contact with Europeans. For another, their own contact with them could be fitful or brief. Jochelson's famous study of the Koryaks was the product of a single winter spent among them, in which he did not have time to learn their language.[11] A third problem was that it was rarely possible, and was not considered necessary, for independent studies to be made of the same people.

As a result, what each scholar was able or willing to perceive of a native culture often remains our only record of it before it was Russianized still further. Many of the general interpretations of shamanism to be published in the early and mid twentieth century were made by working over this same set of studies, again and again, like the reshuffling of a faded set of playing cards.

Fieldwork of this sort continued steadily until disrupted by the First World War and the Revolution which followed. Much of it was now carried out by Finns, who were at once part of the Tsarist empire and developing their own nationalism, which was rooted in a perceived family relationship with Siberian peoples such as the Khants and Mansi. After the Revolution, in the relatively liberal political climate of the 1920s, some of them were encouraged to resume it by a Soviet regime anxious for information about its subject peoples.[12] A White Russian refugee in China, S. M. Shirokogoroff, now worked up his pre-war field notes into the most sophisticated analysis of Siberian shamanism yet made.[13] By 1932 a bibliography of works on the subject in Russian alone listed 650 items, although only a fraction of these consisted of original material.[14]

By then the climate of research had changed. With the advent of Stalinism foreign scholars were no longer welcome in Siberia, and a new generation of Russian ethnographers was going into the field. Exemplified by Arkadiy F. Anisimov, who joined an Evenk group in 1929, they lived with native peoples for long periods, learned their languages thoroughly, and recorded their surviving customs in unprecedented detail. Some of the descriptions which resulted surpassed anything provided before in the drama and colour with which they conveyed the atmosphere of shamanic performances. Here is one which Anisimov wrote of the opening stages of a healing ceremony which he witnessed among his Evenks on the Podkamennaya Tunguska river in central Siberia, during 1931:

> In the middle of the tent a small fire burned. The tent was in semi-darkness. Along the sides sat the clansmen, talking softly. A pervasive feeling of expectation of something extraordinary heightened the nervous excitement, still more strengthening the mystical mood. Opposite the entrance the shaman sat. His pinched, nervous

face pale; he sat silent, alert, irritable, moved his shoulders, gently swaying from side to side. His face twitched, his hands trembled. To the right and left lay the images of spirits – the salmon trout – two pole-knives, fish spears, and a splintered larchwood pole. The fire was surrounded on four sides by shamanistic spirit images, salmon trout. At a sign given by the shaman, his assistant took from the bag the shaman's ritual robes – the gown, the breast-piece, footwear, the cap (for minor shamans, a headband, for chief shamans of clans, besides the cap, an iron 'crown' with a representation of reindeer horns) and mittens. The assistant then got the drum, warmed it over the fire for better sound, and quietly tested it to see that it was ready for action. Then he began to dress the shaman. The clothed shaman sat down on a small wooden platform which represented the shamanic spirits of fish; he held the drum in his left hand, placed it on his left knee, held in his right hand the drumstick, and struck it against the outer side of the drum. The conversation broke off in mid-word. The shamanistic ceremony had actually begun.

The fire was dampened. The drum sounded in the semi-darkness. The clansmen, pressing themselves against the sides of the tent, awaited the shaman's words with palpitating hearts. The most impressionable and those with the strongest imaginations looked with wide-open and protruding eyes at the grim figure of the shaman. Swaying slowly from side to side in time to the drum, the shaman began the invocatory song to the spirits in a quiet melodious voice full of inner feeling.

The invocatory shamanistic songs of the Evenks were always rhymed, rhythmic, full of clear and beautiful metaphors, and always accompanied by a rhythmical refrain. When the shaman had sung a verse of the song, those present repeated it in chorus. Then the shaman beat on the drum at regular intervals, accompanying the sound by the singing of a couplet, and led a rhythmical refrain, matching the note of the drum. Those present joined him. The drum again replaced the refrain. The second verse of the song followed; everything was repeated again in the same order.

In an improvised song of summons to the spirits, the shaman addressed his spirit-helpers, calling them to his aid in the struggle against the spirit of the disease. Addressing each of his spirits in turn, the shaman vividly described for the listeners its form, adorning it with all manner of comparisons, listing its services to the clan and the characteristics of its supernatural power. The shaman related in the song where the spirit was at the time, what it was doing, whether it obeyed the summons willingly or unwillingly, and, finally, how the spirit, submitting to the shaman's demands, left his clan territory and came to the shaman in the tent. At this moment the song ceased and the sounds of the drum were gradually muffled, becoming a soft roll. In the silence following this, the voices of the spirits could clearly be heard: the snorting of beasts, bird-calls, the whirring of wings, or others, according to the spirit appearing before the shaman at the moment ... The sound of the drum was unexpectedly interrupted. The shaman yawned broadly, receiving into himself the spirit which had come, and again struck the drum. Well warmed over the fire, the drum sounded long, filling the half-darkness with sound. Those attending sat there under the impression of the appearance of the spirit, deafened by the incessant rolling of the drum. Then the drumming ceased. The shaman began the invocatory song to the next spirit. Rousing themselves from their torpor, the watchers picked up the shaman's words and everything began again in the same order, until all of the shaman's spirits were gathered.

Having gathered the spirits, the shaman distributed his orders among them ... some he ordered to guard the tent, others to be watchers on all the pathways of the shaman's activity, still others to remain with him to carry out his orders. Among the shaman's spirits, his animal-double filled one of the first places. Under guard of the whole group of spirits the shaman sent his animal-double to the lower world to learn the cause of the clansman's illness. The sound of the drum became thunderous, the shaman's song more agitated. The animal-double, accompanied by the other spirits, headed for the lower world by way of the shamanistic world tree. There he found the chief ancestor-spirit of the shaman, and learned from him everything of interest. In the less important cases it was sufficient for this purpose to turn to the nearest ancestor-spirit of the shaman, most often to the one whom the particular shaman had succeeded on earth. But cases were not rare in which the ancestor proved incapable of establishing the cause of the disease, and the shaman was compelled to send the animal-double for the same purpose to the upper world, to the supreme deity.

The journey of the animal-double to the other world is described in the shaman's songs of such fantastic form, so deftly accompanied by motions, imitations of spirit-voices, comic and dramatic dialogues, wild screams, snorts, noises and the like, that it startled and amazed even this far from superstitious onlooker. The tempo of the song became faster and faster, the shaman's voice more and more excited, the drum sounded ever more thunderously. The moment came when the song reached its highest intensity and feeling of anxiety. The drum moaned, dying out in peals and rolls in the swift nervous hands of the shaman. One or two deafening beats were heard and the shaman leaped from his place. Swaying from side to side, bending in a half-circle to the ground and smoothly straightening up again, the shaman let loose such a torrent of sounds that it seemed everything hummed, beginning with the poles of the tent, and ending with the buttons on the clothing. Screaming the last parting words to the spirits, the shaman went further and further into a state of ecstasy, and finally, throwing the drum into the hands of his assistant, seized with his hands the thongs connected to the tent pole and began the shamanistic dance – a pantomime illustrating how the animal-double, accompanied by the group of spirits, rushed on his dangerous journey fulfilling the shaman's commands. The drumstick in the skilful hands of the shaman's assistant beat out a furious roll. The accompaniment reached its highest point. The voices and snorts of beasts and the like were heard in the tent. Under the hypnotic influence of the shamanic ecstasy, those present fell into a state of mystical hallucination, feeling themselves active participants in the shaman's performance. The shaman leaped into the air, whirled in the tent thongs, imitating the running and flight of his spirits, reached the highest point of ecstasy, and fell foaming at the mouth on the rug which had been spread out in the meanwhile. The assistant fanned the fire and bent over the shaman's stiffened, lifeless body. The latter, representing at this moment his animal-double in the world of the dead, was outside of this seeming corpse. The assistant, fearing that the shaman might not return to the middle world, persuaded him to return as quickly as possible from the lower world, orienting himself by the light of the fire which he (the assistant) had kindled in the tent. The shaman began to show signs of life. A weak, half-understandable babble was heard – the barely audible voices of the spirits. This signified that the animal-double and the spirits accompanying him were returning to the middle world. The shaman's assistant put his ear to the shaman's lips and in a whisper repeated to those present everything that the shaman said was happening at that time to the animal-double and his spirits. The shaman's weak, barely audible whisper, changed into a loud mutter, unconnected snatches of sentences, and wild cries. The helper took the drum, warmed it over the fire, and started to beat it, entreating the shaman (that is, his animal-double) not to get lost on the road, to look fixedly at the light of the tent fire, and to listen more closely for the sound of the drum. The drum sounded faster and louder in the hands of the assistant; the shaman's outcries became ever clearer and more distinct. The drum sounded still louder, calling the shaman, and finally became again the accompaniment of ecstasy. The shaman leapt up and began to dance the shamanistic pantomime dance symbolizing the return of the animal-double and his attendant spirits to the middle world. The shaman's dance became more and more peaceful, its movements slow. Finally, its tempo slowed, the dance broke off. The shaman hung upon the thongs, swaying from side to side in time with the drum. Then, in recitative, he told the onlookers about the animal-double's journey to the other world, and about the adventures that had happened. Freeing himself from the thongs, the shaman returned to his place. He was given the drum. The shaman's song was again heard. the shaman transmitted the advice of the ancestor-spirits as to how the evil spirit of the disease should be fought, put the drum to one side, and paused. Someone from among the onlookers offered him a lit pipe. Pale and exhausted, the shaman began avidly to smoke pipe after pipe. With this the first part of the performance ended.[15]

Much of the work of researchers like Anisimov became available to western scholars in the later twentieth century through the mediation of Hungarian academics, who as members of a Warsaw Pact nation had easier contact with the Soviet Union, and who traced their own ethnic roots back to Siberia. The impetus for this project came largely from one man, Vilmos Dioszegi, who himself made major collections of new data among southern Siberian peoples. Between 1963 and 1997 a series of edited collections of essays appeared wholly or substantially devoted to Siberian shamanism, often based on international conferences and dedicated to making new research accessible to a global academic community and pooling ideas among it.[16] Some of this new research was furnished by fresh expeditions mounted among Siberian natives by Soviet academics, who worked with a care and patience which added greatly to both the volume and the depth of material.

There was, however, an irony to the process which may strike observers either as functional or as tragic. The wave of ethnographers which set out around 1930 was composed of Communist Party zealots, who were studying native culture in detail so that it could be dismantled most effectively. Their role was not merely that of fact-finders but of teachers, equipping themselves to re-educate the peoples under study and to assist others to that end. Their hostility to shamanism was often more bitter than that of their predecessors, and contributed significantly to its destruction. They were recording the last vestiges of societies which were still functioning in something like a traditional manner, as part of the process of annihilating them.

As a result, by the mid twentieth century fieldwork consisted of raking among ashes; of interviewing elderly people and asking them about the world of their youth, in as much as they could remember it and were willing to speak of it. The attitudes of those carrying out the research had altered little; but then neither had the (literal) party line controlling expression of it. Dioszegi declared that 'it is important that shamanism should disappear as soon as possible, but it is just as important that this should not happen without records'.[17] The second part of that statement is most commonly remembered when reviewing the achievements of this great anthropologist; but the first is just as significant. Hostility remained just as blatant, and unrelenting, into the 1980s, and was often most vehemently expressed by experts recruited from the native peoples themselves. The celebrated Sakhan specialist in the shamanism of the Turkic-speaking peoples, Nikolai Alekseevich Alekseev, declared in 1987 that his work was a contribution to the intensification of atheist propaganda ordered by a Communist Party proclamation issued four years before. In 1987 also, a noted Buryat scholar, Taras Maksimovich Mikhailov, published a study of the shamanism of his own people. It concluded by calling for a 'relentless and systematic struggle' against 'shamanistic survivals'.[18]

Anybody attempting to form or base opinions upon the nature of Siberian shamanism has therefore to reckon with three curses which lie over the body of information available. First, not a single shaman working in a traditional Siberian society seems to have left a direct testimony; the words of all, where they are recorded, are mediated through the publications of outsiders. Secondly, virtually no data survives from before a period at which native society was being altered by Russian rule, and the best of it was collected when the traditional ways were either in considerable decline or had disappeared. Thirdly, almost all of the material which we do possess was recorded by people who were at best indifferent to shamanism and often bitterly opposed to it, and that is as true of the twentieth century as of the eighteenth.

PART TWO

WHAT WE THINK
WE KNOW ABOUT SHAMANS

5

What Shamans Did

One consequence of the haphazard way in which westerners got to know Siberia is that the Tungusic term 'shaman' is itself a crude and convenient piece of European labelling. As seen already, it happened to be the one first used of such practitioners in Siberian societies, by the Russian Avvakum and the Dutchman Nicholas Witsen. Its impact on the west was reinforced when Witsen's book was followed after just six years by another which employed the same term, also by a Dutchman. The author was Ysbrants Ides, who had accompanied a Russian embassy to China in 1692–95.[1] Both writers rendered the word as *schaman*, a form especially easy for speakers of Germanic languages, and the prominence of German scholars among those who served the Russian empire in the eighteenth century probably confirmed its ubiquity in the world of international scholarship.[2] It was not the word which would have been used of such figures by the great majority of native Siberians: among the Turkic-speaking peoples the equivalent term was *kam*, among the Samoyedic-speakers *tadibei*, among the Sakha *oyun*, among the Buryats *bö*, among the Koryaks *enenalan*, and so forth.

It is also important to appreciate, especially in view of the western tendency to describe all native Siberian religions as shamanism, that the specialists designated by this range of names were rarely at the centre of traditional social or religious life. In the Even clans it was the old men who decided upon the most propitious places for summer camps, and the shamans who submitted to their choices along with all others. Shamans did not perform the regular sacrifices among the Selkups and were not concerned with normal rites of passage in the Altai. They were banned from the bear festival, the greatest ceremonial event of the Nivkhs, and the Nanais either did

not permit them to accompany hunts or insisted that they put off
their identity as shamans in order to do so; the dominant figure in
a hunting party was an old man who was not a shaman and who
used magic to attract animals.[3]

This last observation impinges on an associated point recently
emphasized by Caroline Humphrey;[4] that all North Asian societies
had other magico-religious specialists alongside shamans, and several
types of shaman. Jochelson noted among the Sakha that individuals
afflicted by illness or uncanny misfortune could turn to the *alhacci*
or 'conjuror'; the *manaric* or 'hysteric'; the *körbüöccü* or 'prophet';
the *ican* or 'sorcerer'; the *oyun* or man who works in trance with
spirits; or the *udahan*, the female equivalent to the *oyun*. The last
two corresponded most closely to the figure which westerners call
the shaman, but the work of the others clearly overlapped and it is
no longer apparent exactly how they were distinguished from each
other. A much more recent analysis of traditional Sakhan society
divides magical specialists into the *oyun*, *udaghan* and '*körbüöchhü*'
(the latter glossed as 'diviner'), plus the *otohut*, translated as 'healer',
the *iicheen*, translated as 'wise person', and the *tüülleekh kihi*, translated as 'dream interpreter'.[5] These lists of practitioners omit smiths,
whose craft was believed among the Sakha to require and confer
arcane knowledge and powers, including those of curing illnesses
and exorcizing spirits. Those who worked with iron were regarded
as more potent than many an *oyun*.[6] The Sakha certainly possessed
a more complex society than some other Siberian peoples, but the
difference was only a matter of degree; among the much simpler
Even clans, people only resorted to shamans after employing other
specialists, such as experts in herbalism and other folk medicine.
Among the Koryaks almost every family included a woman, usually
elderly, who knew magical formulae. Some could summon spirits,
and rivalled shamans in proficiency and prestige.[7] Many people in
Northern and Central Asia employed altered states of consciousness
for spiritual or practical ends, including singers, diviners, midwives,
Buddhist monks and hunters. Shamans used such states to contact
spirits, but not all routines for making these contacts involved
shamans.[8] Western scholars concerned with shamanism are therefore not merely making an intellectual construct but doing so by

arbitrarily selecting, from a complex and intermeshed world of native magical practice, those practitioners and activities which seem most exciting and unusual to them.

Even within the category assembled by this process of selection, there are important distinctions. As Caroline Humphrey has put it,'shamanism is not one thing, but many'.[9] Studying the Daur Mongols of (Chinese) Manchuria, she noted that shamans were rarely regarded as a category, but remembered as individuals.[10] Her perception was anticipated almost two hundred years before by a declaration of Sakha chiefs, required by the government in the 1820s to give an account of their customary law: 'Shamanism is not the faith or religion of the Yakuts [as seen above, the Russian name for the Sakha], but an independent set of actions which take place in certain definite cases'.[11]

To pursue the Sakhan example, the figure known as the *oyun* was classified as 'white' or 'black'. The former operated more like a conventional priest, interceding with deities, especially the 'White-Lord-Creator', to ask for blessings. This sort of practitioner had no special dress or equipment. The 'black' *oyun* possessed both, and worked with spirits to travel in this and other worlds. He cured the sick and had the balancing power to inflict curses. He was, moreover, classified in three traditional categories, *ulahan-oyun*, *orto-oyun* and *kenniki-oyun*, according (in descending order) to the power of the spirits who aided him and the range and difficulty of the magical work which he could effect as a result.[12] All this is complicated enough, if at least intelligible, but there are two further problems. One is that the system thus outlined was one recorded at the end of the nineteenth century, by which time the Sakha had been under Russian rule for almost three hundred years and nominally Christian for a couple of generations. It is possible that the division and cosmology involved, especially the distinctions of 'white' and 'black' and the the cult of the 'White-Lord-Creator', had been to some extent influenced by Christianity.

The other difficulty is that the classification by role and colour is one emphasized by Jochelson, and that according to power by Sieroszewski. It is rare to have two independent scholars commenting on the same people at the same time, and such a difference, though reconcilable, is worrying. Jochelson, indeed, highlighted it by telling his readers that more than one expert had cast doubt on the accuracy of some of Sieroszewski's data.[13] Authors attempting to draw general conclusions about the nature of Siberian shamanism are therefore not merely making arbitrary selections from complex contexts, but are often either selecting from or reconciling different ethnographic accounts in an equally subjective fashion. Another example of this is provided by travellers among the Altaian peoples. A. V. Anokhin, in 1924, spoke of a division of shamans there into 'white' and 'black', but this does not feature in earlier accounts of the same peoples by scholars concerned with their customs.[14]

Similar caveats are suggested by research into the Kets. These were studied by four different expeditions between 1905 and 1962; and, as they have not numbered more than about a thousand individuals during this period, it may be considered that all possible information about their traditional beliefs had been gained. A fifth expedition, in 1970, exploded this surmise by recovering accounts from elderly Kets which revealed that the earlier twofold classification of that people's shamans, into those working with deer and bear spirits, had been quite inadequate. Instead, they had been distinguished as those who were protected by divinities in the form of the reindeer doe, the dragonfly, the mythical *gah* bird, the mythical *kandelok* or bear-man, and the bear. All were respected, although the reindeer-shamans were the most common and the dragonfly shamans were the rarest and most powerful, with the limitations that they could only operate in summer and could not heal. Those who worked with the *kandlok* or bear had their own special costume and operated in the apparent world, rather than in alternative realms as the others did.[15]

A functional division existed among the Nanais, between the *siurinka*, who healed the sick, the *nemanti*, who helped to conduct festivals as well, and the *kasanti*, who led the souls of the dead to the next world.[16] The Nenets had a double set of distinctions, between the various levels of training and equipment which shamans achieved and the range of tasks which they performed. The latter required different costumes, techniques and times of working. In addition all were sometimes divided into those who worked with benevolent spirits and those concerned with the evil variety (which meant, as to many other peoples, that they could call them from the sick and so heal more effectively). Each had a separate name, producing an overall set of eight categories which rendered the overall Nenet term for a shaman, *tadebya*, no more than the vaguest of descriptive labels.[17] The Khants had eleven different words for figures whom scholars would term shamans, and distinguished all these in turn from seven other types of spiritual practitioner.[18] Other Siberian natives used terminologies just as elaborate as those given in example here.

If the shamanism of Siberia was not a single functional phenomenon to the peoples who employed it, neither was it a single social institution. Over the period in which they were studied, the people whom scholars call shamans might serve only their own families, or only relatives and neighbours, or a clan or a tribe, or take on any clients. The pattern was determined by the social composition of the people concerned. Clan shamans were found among the Yukaghirs, Evenks, Evens, many of the Amur peoples, and some of those of the Altai. Family or small-group shamans occurred among the Nganasans, while the Chukchi, Koryaks, Kets, and Nenets combined these with independent professionals. Professionals who served territorial areas were features of the Sakha, Buryats, Tofa, Teleuts, and some of the Evenks.[19]

The existence of the scholarly category of shamanism depends therefore on finding a common set of functions and techniques which transcends the social contexts and local terminologies outlined above. To Shirokogoroff, the work of shamans boiled down to a pair of objectives: to discover the causes of present troubles and to divine the future. Anna-Leena Siikala also characterized them essentially as troubleshooters, dealing with human crises which Siberian tradition blamed on spirits. Mircea Eliade viewed them as concerned with the experiences of the human soul, and especially with the need to defend it against powers of evil. Caroline Humphrey has divided their activities into 'patriarchal', involved in the symbolic reproduction of lineage, clan and polity; and 'transformational', being the resolution of problems on which emphasis has been placed by the other authors cited.[20]

It is plain that some of these formulations are broader than others, and a better sense of what is at stake can best be achieved by surveying what is known of the activities of shamans at the times at which they were recorded. Of all these, there is no doubt that the most widespread and common consisted of healing, by driving out or propitiating the spirits believed to cause illness. It may well be suspected that this function would have become more prominent as shamanism was driven out of the public life of native peoples by Russian hostility and became more of a package of ad hoc services offered to private clients. On the other hand, Marco Polo's testimony proves that healing by transactions with spirits was already very prominent in medieval Asian societies. Witsen's seventeenth-century account of Siberia lays heavy emphasis upon it. As illness has always been one of the most obvious uncanny misfortunes to afflict humans, and as most tribal societies have attributed at least some of it to magical or supernatural agency, this work can be supposed always to have been one of the most important activities of shamans. Treatment of the sick is indeed a major function of traditional magic worldwide; the distinguishing feature of shamanism in this pattern is the emphasis on communication with spirits to achieve a cure.

However, Pallas, in the eighteenth century, noted that those who allegedly possessed this power only employed it as one means among several for the treatment of the sick; they also used natural medicines, sacrifices, and prayers before images of deities.[21] The use of commerce with spirits to effect cures could itself take many different forms. In some, the malady was regarded as caused by an evil entity which had occupied the patient's body, and the shaman would suck it out, seem to cut it out with a knife, blow it out, tempt it out with offerings of incense or blood sacrifice, or drive it out with incantations or fumigation of the sick person. In others, illness was believed to result from the loss or theft of the latter's soul, and the shaman would journey into the spirit-world to retrieve and restore it, or to persuade a deity to effect this work.[22] A range of such responses could be found within the same native people, or indeed deployed by the same practitioner. Clearly only some involved the ability of the shaman to control spirits or to travel into an otherworld, functions which have been used by many scholars as defining characteristics of shamanism itself.

Any attempt to investigate the relationship between shaman and patient, or even to reckon a rough success rate for individual practitioners, is rendered impossible by the lack of available data; the people who collected it were either unable or unwilling to investigate these matters. It is logical that shamans would not have been credited with healing powers were there not some apparent benefit from their actions. It is also logical that in a traditional Siberian society their knowledge of natural medicines would have been effective against some maladies, while their apparent ability to deal with spirits would have had a powerful impact on psycho-somatic disorders and those related to stress. Sometimes, however, the placebo effect – if that is what it was – could be dramatic even in cases of clear physical disease. Jochelson observed the treatment by a Koryak shaman of a patient suffering from syphilitic ulcers of the throat which left him unable to swallow. After the shaman had summoned his spirits to the sick man's aid, the latter immediately felt better and was able to drink two hot cups of tea.[23] Typically, Jochelson was unable to stay longer, and so to discover if the improvement was sustained, let alone whether the illness itself was cured; and it is apparent that at times shamans had their crashing failures, gleefully recorded by hostile European observers. A particularly weak point of the shamanic repertoire seems to have been obstetrics. It was often recorded that shamans were expected to assist childbirth when difficulties occurred. It is easy to imagine, again, that the emotional support rendered by their efforts could be a genuine aid to women in labour; but if there were physical complications then spiritual assistance might count for little. The eighteenth-century traveller Ivan Lepechin recorded how a shaman among the Bashkirs, a Turkic-speaking tribe, worked hard to scare off evil spirits from a woman in prolonged labour, by dancing, screaming, glaring, firing off a gun, and dashing outside to rout his spectral foes with a sword. The woman still died the next day.[24]

The most harrowing story of this sort was recounted to Jochelson by a Russian exile to Siberia called Gebler,[25] and it is worth repeating here because it illustrates not merely the limitations of shamanic

practice but also gender relations among natives, and the fraught
and complex relationship between their traditions and European
culture. Gebler was present when the wife of a Sakhan elder went
into prolonged labour, and a shaman was called to help. The latter
had the woman tied, against her will, to an upright frame of
birch-poles, and tried to squeeze the child out, pronouncing incantations. When this failed, he declared that the baby was being held
inside by a long-tailed evil spirit, and started to pull it out with a
pair of iron tongs. It came out in pieces, whereupon the mother
was untied and left lying in a pool of blood, covered with a fur
coat, while the men drank tea and ignored her. Gebler, fearing for
her life, went straight to the Russian district administrator and
reported the situation. The imperial official acted at once, having
the woman taken to hospital but also arresting the shaman. The
latter died in detention, having gone into a decline when he feared
that he would be sent away to prison at Yakutsk and so suffer exile
as well as confinement. It is not recorded whether the woman
recovered, and having done so was able to resume the same or a
better life in her own society. If not, then the tragedy was complete.

A function of shamanism which was as widespread as healing,
and almost as prominent in the records, was divination, either in
the form of clairvoyance, to trace lost or stolen goods or animals,
or of prophecy, to advise people on how best to prepare for hunting,
fishing, journeying or seasonal migration. To give it this prominence, admittedly, is to contradict the most celebrated western
expert upon shamanism to write in the twentieth century, Mircea
Eliade, who declared categorically that 'these minor exploits are
rather the prerogative of shamanesses or of other classes of sorcerers
and sorceresses'.[26] This judgement was in accord with Eliade's elev-
ated conception of the shaman's role, to be considered later, but he
provided no data to substantiate it, and that now available does not
seem to support his assertion.[27] At first sight, it might seem as if
the issue at stake is the now familiar one of definition, as Eliade
excludes some varieties of native practitioner from his chosen image
of a shaman. Certainly there were specialist diviners in Siberian
societies, as evinced by the Sakhan case examined above; but
divination was also one of the tasks of the figures whom Eliade

considers to have represented shamanism. It was certainly a very
old one; William of Rubruck reported it to be the work of the
thirteenth-century Mongol magicians, and the shamanic rite
observed by Richard Johnson in the sixteenth century was one of
divination. Among the Chukchi those shamans who specialized in
it, the *hetolatirgin*, were the most highly respected of all, and it
features almost everywhere in Siberia as part of the repertoire of
magical practitioners who worked with spirits. They employed,
of course, an even wider range of methods than those used in
healing; the most widespread consisted of communing with spirits
while in trance, but Yukaghir shamans used the bones of predecessors, Sakha sometimes examined a ring or coin in the enquirer's
hand, Buryats read the lines on the burnt shoulder-bone of a sheep,
or watched the flight of arrows, and Khants and Mansi used sacred
boxes, or the motion or sound of an axe.

In addition, among specific peoples shamans had important functions not found in all regions. As seen before, the Nanais had a
special figure, the *kasanti*, whose work was to conduct the souls of
recently deceased tribespeople to the land of the dead, in a long and
elaborate ritual which allowed the bereaved an opportunity to work
through their grief and conclude their relationship with the
dead.[28] A parallel but different task of the Sakhan *oyun* was to
conduct the soul of a sacrificed animal to the deity to whom it was
offered.[29] One specialist category of Nenet shaman, the *sambana*,
was entrusted with the tasks of showing a family in which a death
had occurred the correct place in which to bury the body, and of
purifying the family's sacred objects of any taint left by the proximity
of death. The *sambana* also guided the dead person to the world
beyond, in a manner very similar to the Nanai *kasanti*.[30] Eliade,
while marginalizing the common shamanic task of divination, used
such scattered and disparate examples to suggest that shamans in
general 'always' led the souls of dead humans to the next world. He
noted that other Siberian peoples only expected them to intervene
in matters of death when the deceased remained to haunt the living;
but suggested that this was a 'late innovation'.[31] Once again, the
contrast in emphasis between us shows the different ways in which
scholars may join up the spaces between ethnographic dots.

Certainly the functional elements of shamanism were intrinsically related to broader conceptions of the cosmos, which in turn affected the role of the shaman. The extreme rivalry between many Evenk clans meant that sickness in one was commonly ascribed to the work of an evil spirit sent by a shaman in another. The shaman who cured it had therefore not only to expel the entity concerned but to repair the psychic defences of the community against further attack and perhaps launch a spiritual counter-strike against the other clan.[32] The Nanais, on the other hand, thought that humans suffered illness because of the malevolent powers of bear-spirits, whom the shamans had to fight in turn.[33] Those of the Khants and Mansi, and some Selkups, were expected to make and consecrate all images of deities as a corollary of their ability to communicate with the supernatural.[34]

Likewise, the function of divination could easily shade into the working of magic. This would not merely inform hunters and fishers of the best way to go about their work, but would actively bring them good luck. Before hunts, Evenks held a rite called the *shingkelevun*, in which a shaman travelled out of his or her body to visit the clan's spirit-mistress of the local *taiga* and its animals. He would beg a catch from her, and she usually informed him of the transgressions which the clan had recently made in ritual observances and the measures which had to be taken to propitiate her in return. She would then grant the souls of a certain number of animals, and he would journey on to a greater being, the 'mother of the universe', to have those souls released to the hunters.[35]

Similar rites existed among the Sakha, the *oyun* addressing a spirit which controlled the woods or waters which contained the game, and asking for aid in taking it; sometimes this rite involved the sweeping of the surface of rivers and lakes with burning brands to drive away ill luck. Yukaghir and Selkup shamans made spirit-journeys similar to those of the Evenks, returning to give the chief hunter the soul of the animal granted by the guardian deity of its terrain or species.[36] Outside the area of central Siberia occupied by these peoples it is hard to find parallel activities for shamans, although those of the Khants and Mansi apparently thanked spirits when a kill was made, and Buryat legends suggested that shamans among that people may once have engaged in hunting magic.[37] Among the Nanais, as we have seen, they were specifically banned from it.

A few native groups gave shamans responsibility for offering sacrifices, the most spectacular and best-documented example being that of the Buryat *tailgan* ceremony, described earlier. Behind this role and some of those cited above may lie glimpses of more general functions for shamans as spiritual and social leaders, which had atrophied or disappeared under Russian rule. They seem to be clearest in the case of the Yukaghirs, who had believed that every clan was ultimately descended from a shaman, and honoured living shamans as representatives of clan identity. This is at any rate what Jochelson asserted, although he also stated that this situation had disappeared by the time at which he visited the people concerned, and he did not explain how he had reconstructed it.[38]

This, then, is a summary of the assemblage of information available upon the activities of Siberian shamans. A cautionary note has already been sounded as to how it may be used by scholars, even in the case of such a distinguished one as Eliade. The most recent exercise in working it up into a grand explanatory scheme has been provided by the French anthropologist Roberte Hamayon.[39] In this, the main function of the shaman in most archaic Siberian societies was to obtain good luck for hunters; it was a much more basic one than healing, and the only regular duty which shamans performed. It often represented the only major seasonal rite of the tribe. When these societies took to stock-breeding, however, the archaic worldview of exchanges with spirits was transmuted into a more complex one of transmission and production. Shamans were devalued, being subordinated to clan law and confined to a few specific rites, especially those involving the safeguarding of the fertility of the community.

This meta-narrative is certainly one that can be proposed from the material set out above, but some objections to it may already be apparent from the nature of that data. Shamans can only be proved to have been involved in hunting magic in a minority of Siberian societies, concentrated in the central region, and were actually prohibited from it in some others. Even among those in which they supplied it, it was not always their preserve; Jochelson noted that clan elders conducted it as well as shamans among the Yukaghir.[40] Nor is it clear that the *shingkelevun* of the Evenk hunters gave the shaman a more central role than the *tailgan* of the Buryat farmers. The apparent overwhelming prominence of healing and divination in the records cannot be argued away so easily. Once again, ethnographic records are being ordered in a pattern which creates certainty and neatness where neither exists in the primary material. By the time that the latter was gathered, the function of the shamans as troubleshooters, dealing with uncanny problems in the present and attempting to prevent them in the future, is dominant; in this sense, the definitions of Shirokogoroff and Siikala, cited above, stand up best of all. Evidence for a more central and priestly role in regulating relations between human and divine is more localised and fragmentary.

6

Shamanic Cosmologies

Another major characteristic of the figure of the Siberian shaman, as conceptualized by scholars, is that he or she worked with spirits. This could in itself be a complex matter. Shirokogoroff, writing of the southern Tungusic-speaking peoples alone, observed that five different categories of spirit were involved: those who had served local shamans from time immemorial; those who had recently been obtained from other ethnic or linguistic groups; those who had recently been subdued by local practitioners; the ghosts of ancestors; and the ghosts of other dead humans, or of animals.[1] The component parts of this system were widespread in Siberia, in different combinations and bound up with a classification of the uncanny world into entities which were naturally hostile to humans and those which were benevolent or could be made to serve human beings. All took their place in a series of local cosmologies which had three very common features of special significance to the operation of shamans: the beliefs that even apparently inanimate objects were inhabited by spirit-forms; that the world was structured on a number of different levels; and that living beings possessed more than one 'soul' or animating force.

The first concept was summed up neatly by one of the Chukchi shamans interviewed by Bogoras:

> All that exists lives. The lamp walks around. The walls of the houses have voices of their own. Even the chamber-vessel has a separate land and house. The skins sleeping in the bags talk at night. The antlers lying on the tombs arise at night and walk in procession around the mounds, while the deceased get up and visit the living.

Bogoras had spelled out to him the emotional implications of living in such a world: 'We are surrounded by enemies. Spirits always walk about invisibly with gaping mouths. We are always cringing, and distributing gifts on all sides, asking protection of one, giving ransom to another, and unable to obtain anything whatsoever gratuitously'.[2] It seems that the relationship of the Chukchi with their environment was more than usually adversarial, but the sense of an animate universe provided in these statements has been recorded among all Siberian peoples. Just as common was the notion that certain especially powerful entities controlled, or 'owned', particular mountains, forests or stretches of water, responsible not merely for the lesser spirits within them but all the living flora and fauna also. For humans to exist in, on or near these places, and exploit their resources, it was necessary to negotiate with such beings, as well as with the still more potent forces or personalities who operated throughout the cosmos and had the status of deities.[3]

The second belief, in a world constructed on a series of levels, has become fairly well known among western scholars in the form depicted by Eliade. According to him, Siberians in general conceived of three levels, of which the middle one was represented by the earth itself, the upper one by heaven, and the lower one by an underworld. All were connected by a central axis, which could take the form of a world pillar, tree or mountain, and the 'pre-eminently shamanic technique' was the ability to travel in spirit-flight from one level to another.[4] Such a scheme has an obvious familiarity to westerners, corresponding as it does to the Christian cosmos in particular. It was also certainly employed by some Siberian natives, such as the Evenks studied by Anisimov.

To represent it as a standard component of Siberian tradition, however, would be a considerable oversimplification. The Chukchi believed in a stack of nine worlds, with deities dwelling at twenty-two points of the compass in the human one. The Samoyedic-speaking peoples conceived of a heaven in six tiers, and the Khants imagined one in seven. The tribes of the Altai spoke variously of three, seven, nine or more levels in the sky alone, with more beneath the earth, but also sometimes imagined the world as a disc supported by a giant fish. The Buryats portrayed a heaven with ninety-nine provinces, and a separate realm in the north for evil spirits. Most or all of these other worlds consisted of physical landscapes mirroring those of the earth, the roof of each one being the floor of the next. Those shamans who did travel to them often had to reckon with an elaborate geography in each. Sometimes their spirit-flight involved moving up or down onto these other cosmic levels, and sometimes sideways into alternative worlds upon the terrestrial plane.[5]

The third significant belief was that in multiple 'souls'. To the Khants, every limb and organ of a human being, and each person's shadow, had its own individual spirit. The Sakha thought that everyone was born with three life-giving spirits, and died when the last was destroyed or lost. Throughout Siberia, it was very commonly accepted that dreams were caused by a person's spirit-double, or one of them, wandering as she or he slept, and that illness was often the result of the inability of this entity to return to the person because it had become lost or captured during its travels. One aspect of a shaman's work was to restore health by retrieving it.[6]

All these concepts were also found among native peoples outside Siberia, including some which did not have figures like shamans. None, moreover, are in themselves preconditions for the existence of shamanism. Although it does seem to have been a defining characteristic of shamans that they worked with a spirit-world, this did not have to take the form of a cosmos in which even chamber-pots had indwelling spirits, and (as will be seen) they did not have to make spirit-flights into other levels of the cosmos to perform their work. As said earlier, the retrieval of souls was only one method employed by them to cure the sick. These beliefs represented, rather, major conditioning factors in the context in which Siberian shamans operated.

Cosmology, however, impinges on the study of those shamans in a different way, because an analysis of it has sometimes been used to draw conclusions about the historical development of shamanism itself; Shirokogoroff was one of the most distinguished of the scholars to attempt this method. The problem with it is that Siberian cultures were so mobile and dynamic, and shared a continent with some of the world's most elaborate and expansionist religious systems. Jochelson recognised that the Koryaks, in their remote corner of the north east, had elements of mythology and ceremony

which were clearly derived from Eskimo sources, others which had
a Mongol or Turkic provenance, and many which were identical
with native American traditions. He found that the Yukaghirs had
stories which he could trace to roots in Evenk, Russian, Sakhan and
Chukchi folklore.[7]

Much native Siberian belief is harder to unscramble. Even where
relationships between traditions are clear, the same is seldom true
of the date at which the transmission of ideas took place. For
example, by the late nineteenth century some Altaian peoples had
a version of the tale of the expulsion from the Garden of Eden very
similar to that in the Book of Genesis, but connecting the misfortune
to the fruit itself rather than to disobedience to the divine will.[8]
This could be a garbled reception of the biblical story resulting from
recent contact with the Russians. It could, however, have been
transmitted by the Nestorian Christians who spread through Central
Asia in the middle ages; or could equally well represent the original
form of the myth from which the account in Genesis itself derived,
and which had travelled up from the Fertile Crescent thousands of
years before.

The same consideration relates to many other motifs which
Siberian mythology shares with Judaeo-Christian, Islamic or Indian
tradition; they could have been the product of relatively modern
contacts with Russians, Moslems or Chinese, or of very ancient flows
of ideas across Asia.[9] Likewise, it has often been suggested that the
existence in some Siberian traditions of powerful devil-figures or
dominant creator-gods located in the sky, was the product of Christian or Islamic influence.[10] This is a reasonable enough assumption,
but the lack of any accounts of those traditions before contact with
the missionary religions concerned makes confirmation of it impossible.

Similar problems attend assessments of the influence of Buddhism
on native Siberians. One observer described the native religion of
the Soyots of Tuva in the late nineteenth century as 'a strange
mixture of Lamaism and shamanism'. Shirokogoroff demonstrated
that, in his expression, the cultures of south-eastern Siberia were
'saturated' with Buddhist elements.[11] What is much more difficult
is to determine whether these elements extended beyond the

superficial – the addition of specific figures and images – to remodel the fundamental nature of native belief. Once again, there are no records which predate the advent of Buddhist influence to enable that fundamental nature to be reconstructed. Moreover, Buddhism, like shamanism, is itself a scholarly construct, made by westerners who imposed a framework on a variety of Asian belief systems which had not possessed any sense of belonging to the same family.[12] Any attempt to gauge the Buddhist impact on Siberian shamanic practices is further vexed by the fact that, on their journey north from India, Buddhist ideas absorbed Tibetan Bon-po traditions which had much in common with shamanism. The result is a classic riddle of chicken and egg. The Buddhism which entered Siberia from the seventeenth century onward was already a complex faith made up of many different cultural origins, and impacted on native beliefs which were probably themselves almost as complicated and as diverse in their origins.[13]

All this makes it at least strongly arguable that the relationships between Siberian shamanism and spirit-worlds can only be analyzed in the forms which they took at the time in which they were recorded; effectively, in the late nineteenth and early twentieth centuries. These records reveal that all over Siberia shamans were believed to depend for much of their work on the superhuman powers of spirit helpers. The latter were usually regarded as having the characteristics of animals. There seems to be a straightforward fuctional explanation for this: that the great spirit-guardians of mountains, rivers, lakes and forests were at once too powerful and too static to be put to work by shamans. What was required was a set of lesser entities which could take mobile shapes endowed with particular qualities which would enable them to traverse different environments and tackle differing challenges.

The result was usually a highly personal combination varying from one shaman to another. One Chukchi practitioner was assisted by a reindeer fawn (the function of which was not specified), a wolf (for attacking evil spirits), a raven (for devouring illnesses), and a leather bucket (for covering the heads of game animals and so blinding them to make them easy prey). A Khant shaman called up entities in the form of an owl, a hoopoe, ducks and a squirrel, while a Koryak one worked with a hare, a cuckoo, a stork, an owl, a diver, a wolf, a bear and a dog.[14] Symbolic power was often valued over physical strength or fierceness: the frog, which can live in three different elements, was a popular assistant spirit to shamans among the Turkic tribes around Minusinsk.[15] Particular forms were preferred in particular localities; the most common among the Chulym Turks of south-western Siberia were hare, weasel, fox, stoat, marten and various birds, while Koryak shamans most commonly worked with wolf, raven, bear, gull and eagle.[16] None the less, the precise combination of forms everywhere varied between individuals. Scholars of Sakhan shamanism are agreed that there was a hierarchy of preference, with the bear being a spirit-form associated with the greatest practitioners and the dog being left to the least respected. The detail of the rest of the list, however, differs according to the ethnographer making the report.[17]

Some peoples believed that each shaman was assisted by one or two spirits in particular. With their love of elaborate systems, the Sakha held that every proper *oyun* should be served by an *amagyat* (an indispensable personal guardian), a *ye-keela* (a favourite animal spirit) and *yekyua* (the rest of the spirit-helpers, mostly animal but sometimes dead shamans, and controlled with the aid of *amagyat* and *ye-keela*).[18] Nivkh shamans all had two particular helpers, *kekhn* and *kenchkh*, without whom they could not deal with any other supernatural entities.[19] Some Nanais, Buryats and Teleuts were fortunate enough to have guardians who appeared to them in dreams as beautiful members of the opposite human sex, and became their lovers.[20] Evenks and Enets thought that shamans each had an animal-double, often in the form of a reindeer or boar, who acted as a special assistant; it was one of these which featured so vividly in Anisimov's description of a performance quoted earlier.[21] In the Altai this role of special partner or protector was usually taken by the ghost of a former shaman.[22]

Regional traditions were further melted down, and the range of potential for individual variation increased, by the opportunities for travel and contact produced by the Russian empire. It may be remembered that one of the categories of spirit described by Shirokogoroff among the southern Tungusic-speakers was that of entities recently acquired from other peoples. One shaman inter-viewed by Jochelson was a Koryak who worked among the Yukaghirs and had acquired a Sakhan spirit as his principal helper, who spoke through him in the Sakhan language. Another operating among the same people was an Even who had been trained by a Koryak and still invoked spirits in his teacher's language, of which he himself understood nothing. His own favourite assistant was the Russian saint Athanasy. Shirokogoroff observed that the shamans of the southern Evenks would always take on new ways of working from other peoples if they seemed effective.[23]

Another statement by Shirokogoroff has received much more attention, and started a long controversy: that the hallmark of a shaman among the southern Evenks was the ability to summon and expel spirits at will. This power clearly distinguished shamans from people who were possessed by spirits, and were controlled by them. To be recognised as a shaman, a person had to be able to command supernatural assistants.[24] Eliade took this definition and applied it to shamans across the globe, to separate them from other classes of spiritual practitioner such as mediums. His dictum has sometimes been questioned in the context of other cultures.[25] May it be more straightforwardly applied to Siberia?

Shirokogoroff's formula certainly has some general relevance, in that throughout Siberia shamans were expected to be conscious and active agents in their dealings with what westerners would call the supernatural. They had to negotiate and mediate with a spirit-world rather than act as passive vessels or mouthpieces for its inhabitants. It does seem, however, that, even in the Siberian context, the formula cannot be widely applied as it was stated by Shirokogoroff and repeated by Eliade . It may have been true of the southern Evenks, but it cannot be extended even to other peoples speaking Tungusic languages in south-eastern Siberia. Among these were the Orochi, who were studied in Shirokogoroff's generation by Ivan Lopatin. He has left a detailed eye-witness account of a rite carried out by a shaman of that people, to re-establish contact with her principal spirit after a period of personal crisis. She began by singing a slow complaint to her spectral helper, to a gentle drumbeat, and went on to dance and drum wildly around a fire. She interrupted this to sing to the spirit again, inviting it to sample foods of various kinds laid out in dishes on a table. After some more dancing, her eyes closed in ecstasy, and she begged her guardian again to accept the gifts of food, weeping passionately. The food was then thrown in the fire and, after a libation of vodka as a further offering, the ceremony concluded. From start to finish it represented a process in which the shaman clearly featured as suppliant and the spirit as patron.

Lopatin also witnessed a healing rite carried out in the same community by a different practitioner. The tone was still very much one of cajoling and persuading a spirit-helper, who had no need to obey, into pursuing and defeating an evil entity which had stolen the patient's 'soul'. The spirit concerned was implored at considerable length to take pity on the sick person and to accept the promise of a splendid feast in return. There is no sense in either account of that absolute control of shaman over spirits which Shirokogoroff declared to be definitive among the Evenks. Among another Tungusic-speaking group bordering the Orochi, the Nanai, a shaman remembered how his guardian spirit first introduced herself to him with the words, 'If you don't obey me, too bad for you – I shall kill you.'![26]

A survey of Siberia as a whole reveals a spectrum of relationships between shamans and their otherworld helpers. The Chukchi seem to have regarded spirits as being groups of efficient but untrustworthy thugs. Those serving a single shaman would commonly quarrel amongst themselves, and would punish with death any human master or mistress who shirked the duties of the shamanic vocation. In effect, they were ultimately in charge, and this was apparently just as true among the neighbouring Koryaks, where the shaman was seen as the servant of his or her spirits.[27] The Sakha also seem to have had the sense that to be a shaman was to ride a whirlwind, commanding entities who could be dangerous, or even lethal. Sieroszewski met one old man among them who had once been an *oyun*, but had become convinced by Christian teachings that his vocation was sinful. He told how he had therefore abandoned it, and how his spirits had blinded him in revenge.[28] By contrast, the Enets and Khants of the north west were famed for fearing their spectral assistants less than other peoples, so that shamans bought and sold them like slaves.[29] Shirokogoroff himself noted that Evenk shamans formed a variety of relationships with their spirits; sometimes trusting, and sometimes watchful and domineering.[30] Throughout Siberia, it seems that an important distinction lay between the lesser entities which attended a shaman and her or his principal, guardian spirit – where belief in such a being existed. The latter was often regarded with much more respect, affection and solicitude. Enet shamans may have put some of their helpers on the market, but could never do that with their animal-doubles, which were attached to them for life. Likewise, a Sakhan hoped to be united with her or his *amagyat* at the moment of death, and to become a heavenly being who might assist living people in turn.[31]

Shirokogoroff declared that a shaman's spirits were in reality altered states of mind, which made her or him able to perform, while their evil equivalents, against whom performances were aimed, were conditions of psychic disfunction. This view has recently been echoed by Piers Vitebsky, who has suggested that shamanic spirits can be viewed as the practitioner's own alter ego or projections, scattered aspects of his or her self, or else extra aspects of that personhood which made a shaman more significant than ordinary people.[32] Such an interpretation has much to commend it. It makes sense of many of the phenomena concerned and – perhaps more important – it translates them into a terminology which modern westerners are likely to find both meaningful and sympathetic. It also has two drawbacks. One is a qualification provided by both the scholars cited: that it is not of course how things would have seemed to native Siberians themselves. What are characterized here as matters internal to the mind were regarded by those natives as an exact opposite: relationships with an external world as objectively real as the physical one. In Siberian cosmologies, spirits were fully integrated with the natural and human environments; indeed they were an aspect of them. The second objection is that ultimately the psychologizing of Siberian spirits is itself a statement of faith, resting upon no ultimate proof. It makes sense to modern westerners of otherwise uncanny or repugnant phenomena; but in its different way the native explanation made equal sense, and with as much claim to objective demonstration of evidence.

7

Shamanic Apprenticeship
and Equipment

The relationship between the shaman and the spirit-world on the one hand, and the shaman and the human world on the other, can be explored in more depth by examining the evidence for the selection and training of practitioners. Here again earlier observers were either unable or insufficiently interested to gather data, and virtually all that we have refers to the period between 1850 and 1930. It represents a field in which Eliade's genius for schematization scored a notable success, for his tripartite division of the apprenticeship of a Siberian shaman – discovery of vocation, training for it, and acceptance by a wider community – stands up to analysis. It has recently been replicated by another outstanding authority on the subject, Anna-Leena Siikala, with some differences of emphasis: retirement and training, spiritual crisis and initiation, and proving of worth to the community.[1] Almost inevitably, however, the reality was more complex than these broad patterns would suggest.

One aspect of Siberian shamanism which was downplayed by Eliade and in much of the subsequent literature is that it was generally hereditary. Siikala has recognised this as being true among the peoples of the south, and those in which clanship was strong,[2] and the evidence bears her out. Most shamans among the Buryats, the various Tungusic-speaking groups and the Turkic-speaking tribes of the south and south west, and all among the Yukaghirs, were descended, often immediately, from other practitioners. Ulla Johansen has pointed out a practical reason for the phenomenon, found among many of these peoples, that the shamanic vocation often appeared in alternate generations; children were often effectively barred from shamanizing because they had a parent serving

their community in this capacity. It was therefore left to grand-
children to fill the gaps as the oldest generation died or retired. What
is worth emphasizing here is that the hereditary pattern obtained
across much of the rest of Siberia as well. Among Khants the calling
passed from father to son, and when a Sakhan *oyun* died, his spirits
would seek out a relative. The Samoyedic-speaking peoples of the
Arctic similarly expected that a shaman would be the descendant
of others. The principle was less articulated among the Chukchi,
but this may have had much to do with the fact that low-level
shamanizing was found in virtually all families, and about a third
of the population claimed to be able to perform for others. Inheritance of the gift was therefore remarkably easy.[3] In some respects,
Siberian shamanism was a craft, and in traditional societies crafts
often run in families.

The hereditary principle was, however, universally subject to two
major qualifications. One was that the commodity being inherited
consisted of spirits, and they had to consent to the transaction or
(more often) take the initiative in propelling a new shaman into
the vocation. The other was that the spirits regularly chose
individuals who were not from families in which shamanism had
formerly manifested, especially if for some reason there was no
prospective shaman available who had a hereditary claim. In
essence, shamans were perceived as people chosen by the superhuman world. This is an aspect of their identity which has been much
emphasized and investigated by scholars, from M. N. Khangalov and
V. M. Mikhailowskii in the late nineteenth century to Vladimir
Basilov and Piers Vitebsky in the late twentieth.

In north-west Siberia there was a widespread notion that the
spirits had to be enticed to a prospective shaman. Kets who wanted
to acquire shamanic powers cooked a flying squirrel, ate most of it
and left the rest on the ground, and returned to the place each day
for a week, to walk around the piece of animal. At the end of that
time the ability to shamanize might come to him or her. A Khant
wishing to inherit spirit-helpers could make a wooden image of his
father's hand, symbolizing the ability to control them. A would-be
Selkup shaman retired alone to a tent on the tundra to drum, chant
and invite entities to come. One young Enet was simply blindfolded

by two veteran shamans and beaten about the head by them until he was dazed enough to see spirits![4]

Across the rest of Siberia, from the Chukchi and Koryaks in the north east and Nanais, Orochi, and Nivkhs in the south east, through the Arctic regions of the Nganasans and the central territories of the Sakha, Evenks, and Buryats down to the Turkic-speaking peoples of the south west, there was a consistent tradition that the spirits came unbidden. Their contact with a prospective shaman was marked by the onset of physical or mental illness in the person concerned, which was relieved when she or he began to work with them and to shamanize. Future shamans were usually chosen young. Among the Chukchi most were still living in the parental home, and it was very rare for somebody to be 'called' past the age of forty. Among the Soyots of Tuva, the spirits came to girls aged between ten and twelve and boys of twenty to twenty-five.[5] A more impressionistic indication of youth is given in the reports from other areas.

Basilov and Siikala have both suggested that the 'shamanic illness' was generally psychosomatic, a product of cultural expectations,[6] and some of the data bears out their view. Among the Soyots, the symptoms consisted of headaches and nausea, in the Altai they took the form of cramps, and among the Koryaks of fits;[7] all of which could be hysterically produced. Prospective Buryat shamans also suffered from fits, or became dreamy, withdrawn and prone to visions, as did those among the Chukchi. Those of the Sakha frequently went through periods of apparent derangement.[8] It is also clear, however, that some of the illnesses were very real, such as smallpox,[9] and that some of the periods of madness followed terrible personal experiences, such as the deaths of the person's whole family in epidemics or famines.[10] Whether genuine or psychosomatic, the great variation in the time for which people had to endure the initiatory sickness, from a few months to a decade, suggests in itself that more was involved than a simple adherence to a cultural expectation.[11]

Some of the individual stories bring home this point vividly. One Soyot *kam* told Dioszegi how, as a young man, he had gone hunting and come across a crow standing unmoving in the road. When the animal did not react to his approach he hit it on the beak with a stick, and on doing so he fell into a madness which gripped him for nine years. He only recovered when he began to shamanize.[12] A parallel tale is that of Savone, an Enet woman who went berry-picking in the forest when a girl. She was found there days later, wandering about demented with a tale of how she had been attacked by a forest god. As she proved to be pregnant, and produced a stillborn child, it may be presumed that she had been raped by a stranger. Her trauma-induced madness persisted, until her family handed her over to a Ket shaman who persuaded her that she had been chosen by the spirits for his vocation, and that the god's attack on her had been the first sign of this. With that realization she began to recover her wits, and under the old man's training gradually turned into one of the most famous shamans of her people in the early twentieth century.[13]

The part played by the Ket in Savone's story brings us on to the second stage of a shaman's development in Eliade's scheme: the period of training for the work. Among many Evenk clans, the Soyots and the Sakha, this process was the straightforward one found among the Enets and Kets of Savone's homeland, whereby the novice was educated by an experienced practitioner.[14] Other Evenk groups, and the Buryats, Koryaks and Chukchi, expected the young shaman to withdraw from human society, either to the wilderness or into an inner room, and to be educated by the spirits themselves, in visions and dreams.[15] The education which they underwent, even from these apparently non-human sources, would still have been heavily conditioned by the customs of their people; they would, after all, almost certainly have observed shamans at work, and probably have grown up with one in the family or community. It is significant that Evenk clans gave human instructors only to those trainees who did not come from families which had already included shamans.[16]

Some of the dreams and visions were culturally stereotyped, although that did not make them any less vivid and traumatic for those on the receiving end. Buryats and some Evenks were expected to be contacted by a shaman ancestor in their first such experience. Among the Sagays of the south-western steppe, those in the grip of the initiatory illness were expected to make a spirit-journey to

find the ancestor, often involving the crossing of a menacing landscape in which they faced a series of ordeals. The latter commonly
consisted of getting round or across a giant kettle of boiling tar,
finding the correct way at a crossroads, traversing a fast river on a
plank, or passing between clashing rocks.[17] A common theme across
a swathe of central Siberia, from the Sagays through the Evenks and
Sakha to the Nganasan, was that the novice underwent the terrifying
dream-experience of being physically dismembered and then reconstructed. This was a component of one of the best-known and
most elaborate accounts of a shamanic initiatory vision ever recorded, that copied down by the Soviet ethnographer A. A. Popov
from the recollections of a famous Nganasan *nga* or shaman, Sereptie Djaruoskin. In this, the young Djaruoskin found himself
guided by a spirit in human form through a tunnel into an underworld, where he entered a series of tents. In each his guide asked
him the meaning of what he saw, and he instinctively gave the
correct answer: that he was meeting the spirits of various diseases
and so acquiring knowledge of how to cure them. His reduction to
bones came in the seventh tent:

> People were sitting around the fire, men on one side and women on
> the other. I went in, not as a man but as a skeleton; I don't know
> who gnawed me off, I don't know how it happened. As I took a close
> look at them, they did not look like real human beings but like
> skeletons which had been dressed. At the bottom of the tent, there
> was a seven-bladed anvil. I saw a woman who looked as if she were
> made of fire. I saw a man holding [a pair of] pliers. The woman had
> seven apertures on her body. From these, the man pulled out iron
> pieces from the fire, placed them on the anvil and struck them with
> the hammer. When the iron cooled down, the man replaced it in the
> aperture of the woman's body as if it were fire ... The man took a
> piece of iron, placed it on the anvil and hit it with the hammer which
> consisted in reality of seven small hammers on a single helve ... My
> companion asked me: 'What do you think, what tent have we entered?'
> 'I don't know', said I. 'However, it must be here that the pendants of
> the shaman's clothes are forged and it is probably these people I have
> to ask [for pendants] for my clothes. The man [shaman] descends
> from many places, this is surely one of them.' ... I tossed my head
> back and began to look at the smoke hole. 'What are those seven

figures in the upper part of the tent?' I asked. 'They are the spirits of your future saw-toothed pendants', he said. 'Do you give me those pieces of iron?' 'No, the time has not yet come for it' they said. I began to feel uneasy. 'Then why do you make me guess?' 'Who are those two beings, the man and the woman; are they humans?' 'So that is the origin of the shamans', I said. 'Indeed.' This is my fate – to lose my mind. 'Whenever you become a shaman, ask them for permission to make yourself clothes and a drum. Ask them also to to give you reindeer for your clothes; if you come to this tent they will provide you with the necessary things. The sparks are birds, catch them, imitate them, we have birds, geese made from them, on the back of the dress.' When I entered as a skeleton and they forged, it meant that they forged me. The master of the earth, the spirit of the shamans, has become my origin. When a shin-bone or something else is hit and the sparks fly, there will be a shaman in your generation.[18]

Eliade used parallel examples from other parts of the world to suggest that a visionary experience of death and rebirth was intrinsic to the making of a shaman,[19] but it does not seem to have been universal even in that tract of Siberia in which it is recorded, or known in other parts. The truly universal pattern was that the prospective shaman underwent a period of withdrawal in order to develop her or his skills and knowledge.

In the classic manner of a rite of passage, this period ended with the new shaman's reacceptance into society as a qualified practitioner. In Siberia this took two different but overlapping forms: recognition by existing shamans; and recognition by prospective clients. The Buryats, who were noted for long and elaborate ceremonies, honoured these processes with particularly complex rites. In one account of these, they lasted three days and nights, and involved the sacrifice of nine animals and the felling of fifty-four birch trees to make a sacred space for the action. An old shaman conducted them. In other reports, they were divided into an initiation ceremony which admitted the novice to the rank of shaman, and a dedication one which presented him or her to the community. Both were conducted by a 'father-shaman' with nine assistants, and were very detailed; indeed, the accounts differ over the exact procedures followed.[20] These discrepancies should warn scholars against treating any as a standard one. Predictably, the Sakha also staged impressive public spectacles, led by an experienced practitioner. In one record, the initiate was stood in an open field or on a hill, with nine youths on one side and nine maidens on the other, invested with the shamanic costume and made to repeat an oath of loyalty to his *amagyat*. He then sacrificed an animal, and the company feasted. Khants had a much simpler and more private version of this process, in which the new shaman stood facing west while the old one called on spirits to aid them, and made the initiate repeat a prayer to them and offer a sacrifice.[21] Some at least of the Sagays held a two-stage process of ceremonial feasts. At the first the initiate recited the names of the clan's former shamans, and at the second he or she was invested with ceremonial gear.[22] Some Evenk shamans were awarded their first spirit in a public rite, but for most of them, the other Tungusic-speaking peoples, and the tribes who spoke Samoyed tongues, the ceremony of recognition seems to have consisted simply of the first full shamanic performance by the new practitioner. It launched a process by which gradually the shaman added to her or his repertoire, costume and number of spirit-helpers while increasing in power and prestige.[23]

The process of becoming a Siberian shaman can thus be characterized as having been produced by three successive effects. Two were general and one specific; two were cultural and one functional. It began with a general, culturally-induced, condition: that a shaman was somebody who worked with spirits to assist others. Once this was created, the triple sequence of the call by the spirits, the period of training and the process of acceptance as a practitioner was dictated more or less by practical circumstance; it was a functional approach to a need which was again general. The exact forms that each of these stages took, however, varied greatly across Siberia, and no one such form can be treated as normative for the region, let alone for shamanism worldwide.

Even less generalization can be made about relations between shamans and clients or host communities, other than the single statement that such relations were crucial to the functioning of a shaman. To a disturbing degree, perceptions of the personae of shamans themselves varied according to the ethnographer making the observations. Shirokogoroff emphasized that the southern Evenks expected a shaman to conform to certain requirements: to be an impressive public performer, to have a good general knowledge, and to satisfy the community's moral standards. He commented that this people contained many individuals who claimed to shamanize but who were never recognized by others as having this ability. In general, one shaman was accepted to serve each clan. Shirokogoroff went on to emphasize that they displayed between them a tremendous range of personality types, including the patently mad and the perfectly sane, the dedicated and the half-hearted, the affable and the withdrawn, the eccentric and the socially conventional. In a series of vivid cameos he drove home the point that they displayed between them most of the character-forms which a human society can produce. A Soviet scholar, writing about the Evenks at approximately the same time, went to equal pains to stress that constant battling with spirits made all their shamans distinctively reticent, secretive and distrustful, often living in seclusion from other humans.[24] Both cannot be right.

Similar problems attend the reports from the north east. Jochelson made a stark contrast between two shamans whom he found among the Yukaghir, the one calm, rational and self-possessed, the other deranged and violent. To him they represented two extremes of personality. In the same period, however, Sieroszewski claimed to be able to distinguish a Sakhan *oyun* at a glance; whereas the Sakha in general had impassive faces, those of shamans were always mobile, with frightening eyes, and they were also distinctively spry in their movements. Bogoras echoed this view when describing the Chukchi; he declared that most of the shamans whom he met among them were hysterics, and that some were crazy.[25]

To some extent these accounts may reflect genuine cultural differences; the eighteenth-century scholar Pallas contrasted the general composure of the Buryats and Turkic-speaking peoples with the sensitivity of the Khants and Samoyedic-speaking tribes, and the hypersensitivity of the Sakha and Evenks.[26] Those contrasts were, however, themselves dependent on a particular cultural standpoint, and it is hard to resist the conclusion that the differences between the records cited above to some extent reflect the individual attitudes of those who made them. There is no doubt that the Soviet scholar was more hostile to traditional Evenki culture than Shirokogoroff, or that Bogoras was worse-disposed towards shamanism than Jochelson. Bogoras indeed extended his opinion of Chukchi shamans into the assertion that shamanism in general was a form of mental illness, a theory which enjoyed some popularity among scholars in the early twentieth century but was abandoned by the 1950s as patently untenable. What seems harder to refute is Sieroszewski's perception that shamans were somehow different in kind from the rest of their society. It was repeated long afterwards by Vilmos Dioszegi, after his work among former practitioners in various ethnic communities of southern Siberia. He stated that they all had some distinctive trait, being introverts, invalids, psychopaths or misanthropes.[27] Such first-hand research must be treated with respect, but how it accords with Shirokogoroff's characterization of shamans as spanning the spectrum of social types, and how much it reflects the experiences of Dioszegi's interviewees under Stalinism, now seems impossible to say.

It is just as hard to make confident generalizations about relationships between shamans. The Soviet ethnographer Anisimov reported that among the Evenks, whose clans existed on terms of intense rivalry, they were expected to give spiritual battle to each other on behalf of their respective communities. Shirokogoroff, however, asserted as confidently that only ill-natured Evenk shamans waged war in this fashion, and became unpopular and neglected as a result.[28] Perhaps they were speaking of different tribes – Shirokogoroff's people were further south – or perhaps, again, Anisimov's overt hostility to shamans coloured his portrait. A strong Soyot *kam* was expected to have the power to employ his spirits to kill a weaker one, and to capture the latter's spirit-helpers to reinforce his own. A child of his victim who wished to be a shaman in turn would have to destroy the murderer and regain them. There is no indication in the record of how commonly this was supposed to have taken place. Among the Sakha such duels were rare, and somewhat different in form; the *amagyat* of each was supposed to fight the other until one died, whereupon the shaman attached to the vanquished one perished as well.[29]

The Buryats seem to have been unique in the intensity of the manner in which they distinguished between shamans who worked with good and with evil spirits. This was a distinction made elsewhere in Siberia, but without any particular stigma being attached to the latter. The Buryat *bö* declared his or her allegiance at a glance, for those whose spirit-helpers were evil wore darker robes. It was rare to work with both kinds. The two varieties of shaman were expected to dislike each other and, whereas both were respected by their communities, those associated with good were generally loved and the others were generally feared. Whereas the former could only heal and divine, the latter could blight and kill as well, and were sometimes hired to attack the enemies of their clients. When one such practitioner died in the nineteenth century, her fellow villagers put her corpse into a coffin of aspen, an 'unclean' wood, and nailed her into it face-downward with aspen stakes, to prevent her ghost from walking.[30] Nothing so lurid is recorded outside the Buryat lands, and in general shamans seem to have got on with each other as well as personal relations and vocational competition permitted, and with their public according to their powers and their personalities.

A further universal characteristic of the Siberians whom scholars have termed shamans, alluded to in many of the passages above, was that when performing they had some ritual costume or equipment which distinguished them from other people on sight. Shirokogoroff's statement concerning the southern Evenks, 'there is no shamanism without paraphernalia', may be applied to every other native culture in the region. Much more recently the great Hungarian authority on the subject, Mihaly Hoppál, provided a different formulation of the same truth: 'symbols make a shaman'.[31] Once again, however, a legitimate generalization covers an enormous range of practice.

Across most of Siberia, shamans put on a special form of dress. This rule was weakest at both of the region's geographical extremes. Among a few Turkic-speaking peoples in the south west, such as the Shors and Teleuts, they simply wound a cloth about their heads. An eighteenth-century description of a performance among their near neighbours, the Baraba Turks, mentions no particular dress at all, although the general rule held, as the shaman carried a heavily-decorated spirit-image and drum.[32] In the same broad area, the Chulym Turks shamanized only with a white kerchief tied over their eyes (after its being waved to invoke spirit-helpers) and iron-shod boots (stamped to drive away evil spirits).[33] In the north west some Khant shamans wore no special clothes, and the Samoyedic one who performed for Richard Johnson in 1557 had just an elaborate head-dress; in the nineteenth century this was still the distinctive garb of Nenet shamans.[34] In south-eastern Siberia Shirokogoroff found that the less prestigious of the Evenk shamans put on only a bronze mirror pendant; and, further east along the Amur, the ordinary Nanai practitioner sported a copper disc on the chest, to ward off spectral darts. The greatest Nanai shamans wore a tall fur hat crowned with metal prongs, symbolizing the roots of the world-tree.[35] In the north east, Jochelson could find no ritual dress among the Koryaks, and the custom of the Chukchi was only that shamans should wear a coat and cap of some unusual type, including those obtained from American sailors.[36]

Across the whole of central Siberia it was normal for shamans to perform in an elaborate ceremonial dress, consisting of a gown or kaftan which was usually ornamented with embroidery, tassels or metal pendants, and a headpiece decorated with hangings, iron-works, feathers or fur. The most ornate clothing and headgear could combine all these forms of decoration, so that the most lavishly embellished of all the Evenk garments weighed forty kilogrammes.[37] Such costumes were also recorded among some of the Turkic-speaking peoples of the south west, especially in the Altai and Sayan mountains, and along the Amur at the other end of the southern frontier of Siberia, among the Orochi, Nivkhs and other peoples. Some Khants and Nenets also wore them. Virtually all of those preserved in museums date from the decades around 1900,[38] but they were drawn and described by the European travellers of the seventeenth and eighteenth centuries,[39] and so were well established by then. There was a common tendency for the richest costumes to belong to the most important shamans, and for practitioners to acquire and elaborate them in measured stages as their expertise increased.[40] The richest Altaian *kams* had over a thousand figures of snakes woven onto their gowns, plus iron and copper pendants, owl feathers, and skins of ermines and squirrels.[41]

The analysis of these costumes has generated an extensive scholarly literature, but no comparable space will be given to it here, where the emphasis is on Siberian shamanism as a whole. As seen, many shamans operated without these special garments, even among peoples such as the Evenks where they were common. The Sakha likewise were famous for them, but not every *oyun* troubled to obtain one. Those who did had no common framework of symbolism for their decorations, and every practitioner strove to invent some distinguishing peculiarity. Shirokogoroff recorded of the southern Evenks that 'there are no two absolutely similar cases of paraphernalia observed in the individual cases of shamans, even within the same ethnical unit'.[42] Dioszegi observed that the Tofa of the eastern Sayan mountains numbered no more than 440 people at any known point up to the 1950s, but were traditionally divided into five clans which each had a distinctive shamanic costume. Here also the precise elements of the latter varied between individuals.[43]

A case-study of the problems consequent on using costume to elucidate the meaning of shamanism is provided by the tradition, recorded in parts of Siberia, that the ornaments upon the gown represented a human or animal skeleton. Eliade fastened on this as further justification of his characterization of a shaman as 'one who has been dead and has been returned to life'. More cautiously, Dioszegi suggested that such ornamentation was found only in a few groups – the Nenets, Enets, Selkups, Tofa, and Soyots of north-east Tuva – and proved an ancient ethnic and cultural connection between them, based on a common former identity as speakers of Samoyedic languages.[44] The existing data does not easily support either claim. Dioszegi was perfectly correct to emphasize that the costumes which represented skeletons were found in a restricted geographical range, making Eliade's generalization doubtful. He also noted that, even among the peoples where such costumes were most common, some shamans wore different decorations.[45] His own theory is weakened by the fact that the Sakha, who are fairly clearly unrelated to the peoples in his cultural group, also believed that the ornaments on a shaman's gown sometimes represented 'spirit-bones'. Jochelson, who lived among them for a decade, discovered that this was only one interpretation made of the same sorts of iron pendants. To other shamans, they were armour against the attacks of hostile spirits, or feathers which could give powers of spirit-flight, or a map of cosmic geography.[46] All this suggests that the skeletal motif was found across a belt of central Siberia from the Sayans northward to the Arctic, and represented just one which the shamans of that region could adopt. It elucidates no universal principles; and, while it may be a relic of ancient ethnic identity, this is not susceptible of proof.

As well as a distinctive mode of dress, Siberian shamans were marked out by the use of special implements or objects, of which by far the most widespread was the drum, made of animal skin stretched over a round or oval wooden frame. This was associated with shamanic performances across almost the whole of the region, and had been since records of them begin.[47] Its prominence did not mean that it was a universal and essential accessory. Even among peoples to whom it was a regular part of shamanic practice, such as the Sakha, there were some shamans who worked without it.[48] Most Buryat shamans did not use drums, nor did many of those among the Kets, Khants and Altaians, and all of those among the Lebed and Chulym Turks.[49] Eliade, so often intent on generalizations, was sensitive to the wide variation in the form of these instruments; the most obvious regional tradition was that most of those employed among the Turkic-speaking groups of the south west, and among the Selkups, Sakha and Evenks, were decorated with painted figures. He also pointed out that there was no common agreement upon what the drum represented. To some shamans, it was a steed or vessel to carry them into an otherworld, while to others it was a receptacle into which spirits might be gathered before being set to work, and to yet others it was a means of scaring away evil entities. There was some tribal tradition behind these beliefs – the notion of the drum as a steed was especially strong among the Sakha, Evenks and Altaians – but they could vary within the same people.[50] The only point at which Eliade may have yielded to the temptation to ignore the complexities of the evidence in this respect is in his declaration that the painted drums mostly depicted the otherworld journeying which he felt to be the main hallmark of a shaman. It seems to have been very rare for an owner to explain the meaning of such decorations to an ethnographer, so most interpretations rest on guesswork.[51]

Given the variation in its perceived spiritual significance, the dominance of the drum in Siberian shamanism may be attributed to functional factors; it was apparently the most common musical instrument among the peoples concerned, and its powerful rhythmic capacity could easily induce altered moods. Among the Lebed Turks, and the Altaian groups who shamanized with stringed instruments, the latter seem to have been more highly regarded in general.[52] The main shamanic accessory among the Buryats was a staff or pair of staves, made of wood or iron and usually heavily decorated with carvings, bells, ribbons, animal skins and metal pendants.[53] These were also essential equipment among the Soyots of north-east Tuva, where the use of the drum was considered optional. The Soyot shamans of the western part of this small territory, however, never used staves, and regarded the drum as their definitive possession.[54] Both groups sometimes employed rattles, and these were the prime shamanic accessory of the Chulym Turks, made of wood with metal rings fixed in it. They were also almost as common as drums among Khant shamans, but some of the latter also used stringed instruments, axes or boxes as magical tools.[55]

This impression of diversity is borne out further by local traditions of how the paraphernalia should be made and treated. Koryak shamans had no drum of their own but borrowed that owned by the household in which they were performing at the time. Among the Nenets, Enets and Nganasans some made their own drums, while their marital partners kept out of the way. Others insisted that the special gown be sewn by the wife of a male shaman or a woman friend of a female one, and the drum presented by the shaman's teacher.[56] New Sagay *kams* designed their own dress and drums, while the staves used by those of the north-eastern Soyots were made by the veteran shamans who trained them. In some Evenk groups shamans made drumstick and drum-frame for themselves, but the skin of the drum was obtained and sewn for them by their clan.[57]

All this powerfully suggests that what Shirokogoroff found among the southern Evenks holds good for all native Siberia: that special dress or equipment was essential to shamans, but that its form was subject to both local custom and individual taste. The most touching illustration of how important it was to shamans to have some sort of paraphernalia with which to perform was provided by Dioszegi's interviews of former practitioners in the 1950s. These old Sagays, Tofa and Soyots had been in voluntary or enforced retirement for many years, and had long disposed of or forfeited their ritual gear. All of them, on being invited to recreate a performance for his researches, still found it necessary to hold a special object in order to do so. All that was available to them was a stick with a rag tied to it, or a cloth gripped in their hands; yet, once it was there, they were shamans again for a moment.[58]

8

Shamanic Performance

The final characteristic shared by all the practitioners whom scholars have placed in the category of Siberian shaman is that they were all performing artists. If shamanism was partly a craft and partly a spiritual vocation, it was also an aspect of theatre, and often a spectacularly effective one. Dioszegi may have felt that all the former shamans whom he met were misfits, but he also credited each with exceptional skill as a performer: one was a great singer, another an expressive dancer, another had exceptional dramatic skills, another was an evocative raconteur, and so forth.[1]

It was precisely this feature of shamanism which had drawn the attention of earlier European travellers, and impressed them with the sense that they were encountering something not found at home. Their reactions were generally unfavourable; lacking any sympathy with the belief-systems which conditioned the actions concerned, they almost always saw something either baffling or barbaric. One of the few exceptions was the scientist Johann Georgi, writing in the 1770s, who credited the performers with real artistry; but another hundred years was to pass before a foreign observer could express enthusiastic appreciation. This was Sieroszewski, who wrote of Sakhan shamans that

> some of them dispose of light and darkness in such a masterly manner, also of silence and incantation; the modulation of the voice is so flexible; the gestures so peculiar and expressive; the blows of the drum and the tone of them correspond so well to the moment; and all is intertwined with such an original set of words, witty observations, artistic and often elegant metaphors, that involuntarily you give yourself up to the charm of watching this wild and free evocation of a wild and free spirit.[2]

The detailed accounts of shamanizing provided by ethnographers who witnessed them during the following half-century often conveyed the spectacular excitement of the experience, whatever the genuine or affected disapproval of the author. The Stalinist missionary Anisimov may have been not merely a proponent but an agent of the destruction of shamanism, but his description of an Evenk rite, quoted in part earlier, remains one of the most powerful and evocative portraits of a shaman ever written. He admitted to having been caught up in it despite his own beliefs.[3] Working in the afterglow of the tradition, recording the song of an old former practitioner among the western Soyots, Dioszegi noted that 'the voice of the shamaness had not become louder, she did not raise it at all, her recitation did not even become faster. And, in spite of that, the atmosphere was filled with tension.' At a demonstration of skills by another retired shaman, in south Tuva, he observed that the baby children in the watching group of villagers ceased to suckle or cry, but became caught up in the same rapt attention as the adults.[4]

Because of their colourful and semi-public nature, performances were the aspects of shamanism which were most commonly and fully recorded by travellers and ethnographers. The resulting descriptions (a selection of which was provided earlier) make plain that they consisted in essence of a summoning of spirits and the direction or persuasion of them to accomplish set tasks, by a process of which the possible component parts were song, dance, chanting, playing of music (usually drumming) and recitation. The more elaborate performances were held after dark, both because the community tended to be home from work by then and because a more evocative atmosphere was created. They usually depended upon a slow crescendo of pace, sound and tension, rising to a dramatic climax. It is also obvious that no two shamans performed in exactly the same way. Jochelson watched two in action among the Yukaghirs, one an old man and the other his son-in-law. The former sang himself into trance softly and with deep feeling, making smooth rhythmical movements and inducing an atmosphere of quiet sadness before lying motionless on his stomach as his spirit apparently travelled into the otherworld. The latter screamed and leaped about like a madman for two hours, with grinding of teeth and fierce facial contortions, terrifying the watching natives. In this fashion he called his spirit-helpers into his own body and became one with them. At the end his wife banged him repeatedly over the head with a plank to make them leave, and he grew calm. Both in theory and practice, they were totally different ways of shamanizing.[5]

Such contrasts need to be borne in mind when considering the theories which scholars have based on the performance techniques of Siberian shamans. To Mircea Eliade, in 1951, the defining characteristic of a shaman was the apparent ability to make a spiritual journey into alternative worlds and realities: 'from the earth to the sky or from earth to the underworld'. In 1996 Caroline Humphrey affirmed that this trait was the essential one. A year before, Piers Vitebsky had accepted this 'journey of the soul' as the 'narrow' means of distinguishing shamans from magicians, sorcerers and tribal healers. His 'broad' definition consisted of anybody who could control their own state of trance, but he himself preferred to concentrate on those who undertook soul-journeys: 'what those shamans do is so special that they deserve a term to themselves'.[6] The problem, which Vitebsky implicitly recognised but could not resolve, is that they haven't got one.

In 1987 Anna-Leena Siikala identified seven stages as normative for what she termed the 'rite technique' which defined the Siberian shaman: preparation; calling of spirit-helpers; their arrival; encounter with the spirit causing the problem; the shaman's soul-journey; the banishing of the spirit-helpers; and the conclusion. Five years later, however, she emphasized that the spiritual journey was only one mode in which shamans had operated, although it was still one which distinguished shamanism from other mediumistic traditions. In doing so she was making a point first advanced by Johann Reinhard in 1976: that Siberia itself had produced clear evidence of both a 'soul journey shamanism' and a 'possession shamanism', in which the practitioners took spirits into their own bodies and appeared to speak for them. These were, of course, the two techniques which Jochelson had recorded in use simultaneously, and by near-relatives, among the Yukaghir. Siikala now went further, to suggest that three devices were employed by Siberians for the essential business of communicating with an alternative reality. Among the peoples of the north west, the soul-journey was the most common, while in the centre and east of the region, the 'possession' technique was more normal. At opposite extremes, among the Chukchi and among the Turkic cultural groups of the south west, shamans summoned spirits and carried on a dialogue with them.[7] What can be made of all these scholarly positions?

The short answer is that Reinhard's is patently correct, and that the scheme which most closely fits the apparent data is the threefold division proposed by Siikala; but that the data itself is just not good enough to sustain the regional pattern with which she associated it. Instead, all three modes of operation are recorded across Siberia, but records are too sparse to provide a realistic estimate of the relative frequency with which any of them were employed. The spirit-journey appears to be the most widely distributed, and in that sense it deserves the prominence given to it by Eliade, although arguably not the significance. It is recorded among the Chukchi, Yukaghirs, Evenks, Sakha, Buryats, Nanais, Enets, Nenets, Nganasans, Kets, Khants, Altaians, Soyots and some of the Turkic-speaking peoples of the steppes; in other words, across almost the whole of Siberia.[8] In the majority of regions the symbolic process by which the journey was undertaken varied from shaman to shaman. Some fell to the floor and lay motionless during the experience, recounting the progress and events of their adventures in the other worlds – if at all – when they revived. Others sat or danced throughout their apparent time of spirit-travel and provided a running commentary for onlookers.

It was relatively rare for ethnographers to note down the details of these narratives, even when they perfectly understood the local language, but the few descriptions which survive indicate that they could be quest romances of the highest quality. One Khant shaman sang of how he was climbing to an upper world by means of a rope let down from it, pushing aside the stars which blocked his way. Once in the sky, he boarded a boat and floated across the heaven in it before sailing down a star-stream to the earth again, the wind rushing through him. He then released his craft and sank below the ground, to a world of shadows where he asked a dark spirit for a

cloak of power (at that moment one of his audience, primed for
the moment, threw a real cloak over him as a stage-prop). At the
other end of Siberia, in the Altai, a *kam* danced and drummed
around a tent, describing himself as riding a spirit-horse over the
local mountains and across the desert of Chinese Turkestan beyond.
Having thus passed the limit of his people's geographical knowledge,
he spoke of journeying over a succession of strange steppes of
different colours, to the Iron Mountain which reached from earth
to sky. Its slopes were littered with the bones of shamans who had
failed to climb it, but he rode over the top and through a hole into
an underworld. He crossed a subterranean sea by a bridge made of
a single hair, seeing the skeletons of more failed shamans in the
water below. On the other shore he found the place where dead
sinners suffer fearful punishments. He reached the dwelling of Erlik,
god of the nether worlds, where he dismounted and appeased the
gatekeeper with presents of food, drink and skins. Three times he
approached the throne where the god sat, looking furious, and
offered him wine (at this point he put real wine into a tambourine
and mimed out the actions). Erlik at length accepted the drink
(the shaman imitating the god's swallowing and belching). The
practitioner then presented him with an ox, which had been sacrificed before the ceremony, and with furs and fine clothes hung up
in the tent where it was performed. He acted out the growing
intoxication of the god, and imitated his slurred speech pronouncing
a blessing upon the community. He then described his return
journey on a spirit-goose, walking about the tent on tiptoe as if
flying. Then he sat down, and the drum was taken from him. He
carried on beating time with its stick upon his hands and chest for
a while, until that too was taken, and then he stopped, rubbed his
eyes, and seemed to be awakening from sleep.

The technique whereby shamans absorbed spirits into their own
bodies was also clearly widespread, but more common in the central
and eastern parts of Siberia as Siikala suggested; it is recorded among
the Orochi, Nanais, Buryats, Evenks, Koryaks, Yukaghirs, Sakha and
Chukchi.[9] That of summoning the spirits and then interrogating
them or carrying on a dialogue with them was found almost as
widely as the soul-journey; the Khants, Altaian peoples, Evenks,

Nenets, Yukaghirs, and Chukchi all practised it.[10] Sometimes a
shaman would send off a spirit-helper on a journey, and report
bulletins of its progress.[11] The three basic ways of working could be
combined sequentially; one Evenk shaman took his spirits into
himself at the opening of the performance, then questioned them,
and finally flew with them.[12] All three were, moreover, well established by the eighteenth century at latest, for they feature in the
accounts left by early travellers.[13]

Once again, two points need special emphasis. One is that,
although work with spirit-helpers was a hallmark of the Siberians
whom scholars have grouped under the term of shaman, even those
engaged in this work employed other techniques of healing and
divination at times. The other is that every shaman was an individual
performer, with a personal mode of operation which could be varied
to suit each occasion. Shirokogoroff noted that 'in almost every
shamanizing there is something new'. He also got the impression
that most of the shamans whom he met enjoyed performing,
although it was so exhausting that they had to pace themselves
carefully.[14] The vivid contrast between the two practitioners
observed by Jochelson among the Yukaghir could be repeated from
the work of several other ethnographers. A classic parallel comes
from the Altai and was observed by the famous scholar and explorer
Potanin. On the Taldu river he met a young *kam* who danced
'writhing like a snake', while the rags hung upon his costume 'made
lovely waving lines'. He drummed with equal grace and dexterity,
producing many different sounds, and carefully varied the pace and
volume of his singing. At the settlement of Uriankhai he watched
an old woman perform, throwing away her drum and dragging
herself towards the spectators, baring her teeth and stretching out
clawed fingers. She then fell to the ground and tried to chew the
hot stones around the hearth.[15]

The variation in costumes alone ensured different movements
and tempos of dance, and the pattern of harmonics on Siberian
drums could be extremely complex.[16] A Soviet Russian study of
Sakhan shamans' dances concluded that they were essentially
improvisations, having a clear rhythm but no strict composition. In
the earlier stages of performances they tended to imitate animals,

the special spirit-shapes of the performer's helpers, but developed into free form as the event moved towards its climax.[17] Likewise, Dioszegi reached the opinion that shaman chants or songs had no standard texts except the refrains at the beginning and end; ethnic signature-tunes to which spirits were expected to respond. The rest was improvised, often on the spot.[18] Another Soviet ethnographer made the valid if polemical point that Siberian shamanism was not necessarily a tradition of 'the people' at all, but a creation of individual artists.[19]

Some shamans clearly collapsed under the strain of maintaining their reputations and meeting public expectations. Others worked on into extreme old age and the natural end of their days.[20] Survival depended partly, as Shirkogoroff perceived, on avoiding over-exertion. Among the Evenks whom he studied, the elaborate presentations of dancing, invocation and trance were reserved for evenings, and relatively infrequent. 'Small' performances, consisting of a prayer followed by singing and drumming, were much more common, and were carried out at any time of the day.[21] Chukchi shamans never did more than drum and sing to achieve trances, and their spirit-journeys often lasted about fifteen minutes. Among the Turkic-speaking groups who became the Khakass nation, a great kam would sometimes perform for up to six hours, but more usually the practitioner would leave the company and return with an account of a spirit-journey undertaken in solitude. For small assignments a Sakhan oyun sat on a chair in the middle of a room, holding a branch ornamented with white hair, and went into trance in this (literally) sedate fashion.[22]

The most elaborate performances required their own sacred spaces, and tended to be for the general benefit of communities. One class of these was represented by the offering of sacrifices. Among the Sakha, a line of posts was set up to mark the path which the oyun was to take to the upper worlds, with the spirit of a beast offered to their deities. A rope was strung between them at a rising angle, with a rag hung between each and the sacrificial beast tethered at the lower end. The equivalent rite among the Evenks required the erection of a large lodge for the shaman's dance and entrance-ment, with several carved images of spirits.[23] The importance of the

Buryats' sacrificial ceremony conducted by shamans, the *tailgan*, has
been described. An ornate tent was constructed and decorated for
the three-day Altaian festival in honour of the celestial deity
Bai-Yulgen. On the first, the *kam* dedicated the soul of the horse
given in sacrifice; and, on the second, he made a spirit-journey to
the god in order to present his people's compliments. Sometimes
complex rites such as these were employed for the treatment of a
sick person, especially where the latter was important or (as in the
case of some Evenk clans) the illness of an individual represented
a psychic attack on the whole community.[24]

When performing, shamans often relied to some extent on support from two different sorts of people. One consisted of assistants,
who were used by practitioners across most of Siberia. Some were
apprentices in training, like the three pupils who helped an old
Buryat *bö* set up a rite of divination by gazing into burning
wood-chips, witnessed by a nineteenth-century German scholar.[25]
Others were themselves highly-trained specialists, who worked with
shamans but were themselves unable or unwilling to take up the
vocation. Shirokogoroff observed among the southern Evenks that
in some tribes it was not the custom for shamans to be assisted,
while in the others it was a matter of personal preference. Some
practitioners worked alone, while others employed several helpers.
They tended most often, though not always, to be male, and their
work varied from setting out the shaman's equipment and warming
the drum-skins to taking a lesser part in actual performances. Good
assistants were highly valued.[26]

The second sort of support came from the audience at performances. In Caroline Humphrey's deft phrase, the shaman was 'a
relational being',[27] who worked for and before others, and required
a response from them. This is true of most performing artists, but
often more literally so of Siberian shamans, because the onlookers
were expected to contribute directly to their presentations by
chanting or singing refrains.[28] This feature of performances is
very obvious in the selection of them reported earlier, from that
witnessed by Richard Johnson in the sixteenth century on.
Shirokogoroff felt that the sense of bonding between Evenk shamans
and their audiences, expressed most obviously when the latter

functioned as a chorus, was vital to the success of shamanizing. He noted that if men were more prominent as assistants, women were more commonly the singers of refrains. He also recorded, however, that audience reaction to individual performers varied from enthusiastic approval to outright scepticism. The latter had been much strengthened by his own time because of the influence of Christianity and Buddhism, and of Russian and Chinese attitudes. None the less, most Evenks still enjoyed a shamanic presentation, and good performers continued to win confidence and admiration. It may be remembered that Anisimov, working slightly later among another group of Evenks, observed that the general atmosphere at a performance was one of 'nervous excitement' and a 'mystical mood', with 'palpitating hearts'. The more impressionable clanspeople had 'wide-open and protruding eyes', and by the time that the event was well under way had entered trance themselves. They were experiencing personally all the actions described by the performer in the spirit-world.[29]

The sensitivity of shamans to their settings varied enormously between practitioners. One Nganasan would call off a performance if anybody present made a noise or a movement. At the other extreme, the Altaian *kam* Mampyi was invited by an ethnographer to shamanize before a Russian audience at the big provincial capital of Tomsk in 1909. He was working on stage before a large and strange crowd of people, many of whom could be expected to be sceptical, mocking or downright hostile, and yet he became so entranced that repeated efforts were needed to persuade him to stop.[30] Bogoras noted that Chukchi shamans tended to be very nervous before going to work, but elated and often boastful afterwards;[31] this is a sequence of behaviour familiar to virtually every performing artist who has pleased a live group of people. If Siberian shamanism was a form of spirituality, and a form of therapy, it was also a form of entertainment.

The question of whether the shamans' spirits were in any sense real entities is one which should not much trouble many contemporary academic practitioners of anthropology or religious studies. The consensus among these is that belief systems need to be understood in their own terms, without the need for judgements on the part of the scholar carrying out research into them; in other words, the spirits can be supposed to have reality to the people under study, even while the academic making the supposition has no personal belief in their literal existence. Such an attitude would have been utterly foreign to most writers upon Siberian shamanism between the thirteenth and nineteenth centuries. To the earlier generations of these, the spirits were real because they were demons, and cooperation with them represented an objective act of evil. To the later generations, the spirits were illusory, and the shamans were tricksters, and it was important to make as many people as possible aware of these facts. Both perceptions were sharpened by the phenomenon that shamans, throughout their recorded history, were commonly expected to give practical demonstrations of the powers conferred on them by contact with superhuman entities, by accomplishing marvels not supposed to be humanly possible.

It may be recalled that in the first known account of Siberian shamanism, that of Richard Johnson, the performer appeared first to run himself through with a sword and then to have his head pulled off together with an arm and a shoulder.[32] Such feats were also witnessed by several eighteenth-century authors – those recorded by Bell were also cited earlier – and served to fuel the vehemence with which the latter denounced shamanism as imposture, trickery and illusion. Sometimes it was; one Evenk performer showed the scientist Johann Gmelin how he pushed arrows through his ceremonial coat, piercing a bladder filled with blood as he did so to give the impression of having run it through his own body. As Gmelin especially delighted in exposing shamans as frauds, this was a very dangerous admission to make.[33] Such real or presumed conjuring tricks remained a staple component of descriptions of shamans in action in most parts of Siberia until the twentieth century.

By the end of the nineteenth, some ethnographers were starting to discover that a crude dismissal of them as impostures was not as straightforward a business as it had seemed. Jochelson watched a Koryak shaman bring his performance to a climax by taking the Russian's knife and thrusting it into his breast through the opening of his jacket. He then pulled the opening apart to reveal blood on his skin. Jochelson himself could see that the blood could have been painted on before the presentation, and that the knife was turned downwards as the blow was delivered, to slide harmlessly between jacket and body. He also noted, however, that not only was the native audience deceived by the action but that the shaman himself, on some level, apparently believed that the knife had really entered his body. Furthermore this same trickster effected the apparently miraculous cure – or at least the soothing – of the man with the ulcerated throat, cited earlier.[34]

At the same time, Jochelson's friend Bogoras was having parallel conceptual problems in the Chukchi Peninsula; but with a difference. Whereas Jochelson had detected a fraud but realized that it had genuine cultural significance and value, Bogoras was all too ready to dismiss some aspects of shamanizing as staged illusions, but sometimes found it difficult to obtain the necessary proof. He described how he watched in broad daylight as a Yupik (Eskimo) shaman took a stone the size of a human fist in her hands and appeared to wring it out. A stream of small pebbles fell from it and piled up on a drum placed below, while the original rock remained intact. The Russian was convinced that he was watching a conjuring trick but could not see how it could be managed; she could not have hidden the pebbles in a jacket or coat because she was naked to the waist.[35]

The complexities of the issue were brought home further to Bogoras in encounters with a (male) Chukchi shaman called Scratching-Woman. The latter told him that 'there are many liars in our calling. One will lift up the skirts of the sleeping-room with his right toe and then assure you it was done by "spirits", another will talk into the bosom of his shirt or through his sleeve, making the voice issue from a quite unusual place'. Having thus done his best to give his visitor a bad impression of shamans, he proceeded to compound it personally by attempting to steal some of Bogoras's clothes from a washing-line. Scratching-Woman, then, was a scoundrel. He was also a superb performer, and the ethnographer made pioneering use of a phonograph to record him in action. On playing back the result, Bogoras discovered an eerie effect. The voice of the shaman himself remained at a distance from the machine, proceeding from where he was sitting, drumming and singing in a dark room. The voices of the spirits whom he was presumed to be imitating, however, seemed to be coming directly into the speaker of the phonograph. Scratching-Woman himself had as good as given the answer to this conundrum – ventriloquism – but Bogoras was still puzzled as to how exactly such a remarkable result could be achieved.[36]

He encountered more examples of the voice-throwing effect from other shamans, and a range of further unsettling phenomena during performances; in the dark huts or tents where the latter took place, objects would seem to levitate, poles shake, stones and pieces of wood rain down, the recognizable voices of the dead converse with the living, and so forth. Bogoras was armoured against belief in a superhuman origin for any of these experiences; he perceived them all as staged by the shaman, perhaps with collaborators. Neverthe-less, he had to concede that, if they were tricks, then they were very impressive tricks. He made a significant cultural comparison: to the Spiritualist seances which were then attracting considerable attention and controversy across the western world and which were celebrated for the same kinds of phenomena. To Bogoras the reference was damning, for he was equally convinced that Spiritualist mediums were frauds.[37] In some cases he was certainly correct, but it is worth pointing out that a blanket condemnation of all is historically unsupportable, and ultimately the same doubt, coloured by conflicting prejudices, hangs over the accomplishments of mediums as over those of shamans.

Other scholars have approached the problem in different ways. Sieroszewski put it in perspective by pointing out that among the Sakha an *oyun* who never produced any such special effects could be deeply respected, and another who had many of them could be little valued. Much more recently, Piers Vitebsky has suggested that shamanic performance 'transforms the inner reality or conscious-ness of a whole range of people who are involved in a number of different ways. It is this which makes the question of trickery irrelevant'. This is the conclusion approached by Jochelson, and it was subsequently reached by Shirokogoroff, with a more specific formulation: that shamanizing was a form of hypnotherapy. In his

view, 'self-suggestion, suggestion and hypnosis' were the 'fundamental methods' of shamanic technique. The illusions produced by
the performer could succeed because the audience was to some
extent in an altered state of consciousness; but then so was the
shaman who was performing them.[38]

In the 1980s this idea was taken forward by a Soviet academic,
Vladimir Basilov, who braved the problem that not all the accomplishments recorded of shamans could be explained away in terms
of conjuring tricks.[39] The Soyot *kam* Shonchur was old and very
feeble when an ethnographer asked him to perform, but became
fast and agile in his movements once he had begun to do so.
Full-scale performances often required several hours of dancing,
drumming, singing and reciting – effectively an entire night – and
thus demanded tremendous powers of endurance from individuals
who, like Shonchur, were often no longer young. Shamans could
also show an almost preternatural immunity to cold. The Soviet
scholar A. A. Popov once got frostbite in his fingers while taking
photographs of an Nganasan shaman at work in the open air in
temperatures below –50 degrees centigrade. The shaman himself
wore only a thin leather garment, whereas Popov was warmly clad,
and yet he danced for twenty minutes without any ill effects. Even
allowing for the native's greater familiarity with such extreme
temperatures, and for the effects of the dance on circulation, this
was remarkable. Basilov ascribed all these feats, tentatively, to a state
of self-hypnosis which suspended normal physical reactions to
fatigue and exposure.

He then went further, to suggest that training in perception and
sensitivity, and the heightening of both by a hypnotic trance, could
enable shamans to understand instinctively the nature of a sick
person's ailment and the means by which a cure could be effected.
He linked this speculation with his previous theorizing about the
use of hypnotherapy to support physical endurance, and gave no
sign that in recognizing this further possibility he was dealing with
something different in kind. In fact, he had just stepped across a
conceptual boundary, to credit shamans with a power remarkably
close to what has traditionally been termed magic. It was actually
easier for a Russian academic of his generation to take such a step,

without risk to reputation, than it would have been for a colleague on the other side of the Iron Curtain. He was not, after all, arguing for the agency of superhuman entities but for the expression of powers concealed within human beings. The former notion would have been directly contrary to Soviet dogma, but the latter was wholly conformable with it – the study of what is commonly called parapsychology was far more respectable in the Soviet Union than in the nations grouped in NATO. None the less, the fact that a highly-regarded modern scholar could make such a suggestion is a sign that the achievements of Siberian shamans might indeed have exceeded those which can be explained in terms of conventional mental and physical training, and the tricks of the stage conjurer and illusionist. This line of enquiry ends, after all, not in an irrelevancy but in a disturbingly open question.

9

Knots and Loose Ends

This analysis of the work of Siberian shamans may be wound up by considering a set of minor aspects of the subject. One concerns the payment which they received for their services; in which there was a predictably wide variation according to the communities in which they operated. Shirokogoroff stated unequivocally that, among the southern Evenks in the early twentieth century, the job was its own reward. Shamans never got money from anybody, and their only material profit consisted of a share of the meat from a sacrificed animal, if one was offered, and the occasional gift of an extra decoration for their costumes. They were accordingly often poorer than the average member of their tribe or clan. He contrasted this situation with that obtaining just over the Chinese border, among the Manchu shamans, who could charge fees to clients outside their communities, and those of the Daur Mongols, who expected payment from everybody and could therefore make a living from their vocation. A Soviet scholar, G. M. Vasilevich, bore out his statement concerning the Evenks, with the qualification that by the end of the nineteenth century their shamans received regular gifts of meat and could take on external clients for cash rewards. Both were, however, contradicted by the Stalinist ethnographer Anisimov, who recorded with disapproval how pampered Evenk shamans had been; they were never contradicted in opinions, were given help with their hunting and fishing, and received at least one reindeer for every performance as well as regular gifts. Anisimov had a vested interest in representing shamans as an oppressive social and economic elite, the removal of which was essential for Communism. He explicitly classed them with the *kulaks*, the wealthy former peasants who were prime villains of government propaganda. His data must therefore be treated with caution; but it cannot be dismissed.[1]

Sieroszewski recorded that Sakhan practitioners usually got a ruble and a good meal for their services. Bogoras just stated that their Chukchi counterparts attempted to extort as much as they possibly could, and made the largest demands for a soul-journey. He added, however, that their takings were never large enough to represent a livelihood, so all of them shamanized to supplement more regular work. Among the Khants and Mansi some were paid money, while others received gifts in kind. The Turkic-speaking groups who became the Khakass had shamans who asked no payment, but were always given something, often fixed by custom, to prevent them from taking offence and working vengeful magic upon ungenerous clients.[2] Little data on the subject seems to exist for other peoples, and that collected here suggests once again that the attitudes of observers might count almost as much as actual customs in determining what was recorded.

The few records available are nevertheless sufficiently in accordance to invite the conclusion that by the early twentieth century Siberian shamanism was still a vocation rather than a profession. Across the region, many shamans were now paid in cash or a regular tithe of food, but many others – especially those that served clans or other well-defined social groups – had to be content with an entertainment on the night of a performance and the respect and gratitude of their communities. According to Shirokogoroff, they generally were contented. Shamanism was supposed, after all, to be a spiritual compulsion, not a choice of career.

The second issue concerns the relationship between shamanism and drugs. In the tribal societies of the Americas, and especially in the Amazon basin, the trance states of magical healers and seers are frequently induced by the taking of hallucinogens. As the recent upsurge of academic interest in shamanism has been, as seen earlier, largely powered from the United States, it is natural that these American models should often be treated as normative for it. This tendency has converged with a homegrown European scholarly tradition of ascribing the performances of Siberian shamans to drug-produced states. It was launched in 1939 by a Swedish academic, Åke Ohlmarks, who pointed specifically to one substance: the fly agaric mushroom, which contains a poison capable of inducing hallucinations if taken in sub-lethal quantities. This, he claimed, was used by shamans all across northern Siberia. His ideas were extended in the 1960s by the Hungarian scholar J. Balazs, who suggested that Siberian shamans in general had depended on mind-altering substances for their trances. This notion was repugnant to Eliade, as it wrought havoc with his exalted concept of the shaman's role as a controller of altered mental states and master technician of the soul. He therefore declared roundly that drugs, when used at all, were a late and degenerate addition to the shamanic repertoire. He has been supported by Siikala, who pronounced with equal certitude that hallucinogens and other intoxicants were not 'essential to or even a vital factor in the shaman's trance technique'.[3] Who is correct?

In answering this, it must first be made clear that, in his determination to prove shamans drug-dependent, Balazs swept into the category of mind-altering substances many things which are so mild in their effects as scarcely to belong to it. For example, he noted that the performer watched by Richard Johnson in the 1550s sat at one point by a boiling kettle, and suggested that to inhale steam can affect the senses. Those who worked in tents or huts with a fire burning could be assumed to be inhaling smoke. The aromatic herbs used by some to perfume a space before working were deemed by Balazs to have narcotic properties, rather than the same consecratory function as church incense. By the late nineteenth century native Siberians had become very fond of tobacco, and there are several descriptions of shamans smoking before performing, as their nerves wound up; Balazs treated nicotine as a mind-altering drug. The same might be said, with more justice, of alcohol, and he seized upon accounts of performers who drank some before commencing, to suggest that they were dependent on it. None of these cases can be treated as very convincing; at best, all these substances seem only to have enhanced an effect created far more obviously by the dynamics of the performance itself.

Fly agaric, however, is in quite a different class, and comparable to the hallucinogenic plants of the South Americans. It is therefore important to check carefully the sources which associate it with shamans. There is no doubt that Ohlmarks was right to emphasize

its importance in northern Siberia, where many native peoples
employed it as an intoxicant. This is not, however, the same thing
as proving that it was used for shamanizing. The prime piece of
evidence cited by Balazs was taken from a Finnish ethnographer,
K. F. Karjalainen, whom he quoted as finding that the Khant shamans along the rivers Irtysh and Tsingala employed the mushrooms
to achieve trance. He did not, however, go on to cite the comment
with which the Finn himself had glossed this information: that it
seemed to be a recently-adopted and inessential technique.[4] Another
Finnish scholar working in north-western Siberia, Kai Donner, said
much the same thing of the Selkups, but with a reversed chronology.
He had heard that their shamans used to eat mushrooms before
performing, but the practice now seemed to be rare. Among the
Kets, he found that fly agaric was reputed to be employed as a test
of prowess by some practitioners; they ate it to prove that they could
consume poison and survive.[5] Bordering these peoples to the north
were the Enets, and another ethnographer recorded of them that
their shamans sometimes used the mushrooms.[6]

Three detailed studies may serve to put this information in a
clearer perspective. One is that made by Bogoras, who stated that
the performances of Chukchi shamans required considerable concentration, skill and energy, and that the special diet which they
employed in preparation consisted therefore of abstention from rich
and heavy foods. The second is that by Jochelson, of the Koryaks,
among whom he observed that ordinary people took fly agaric in
the hope of gaining visions normally vouchsafed to shamans, who
apparently did not need it. The third is the most comprehensive
survey yet made of shamanism among the Khants and Mansi, by
Z. P. Sokolova, who concluded that it did indeed sometimes include
the use of mushrooms, but only as one option among a range of
techniques for trance induction which also included drumming,
dancing, smoking, smoke inhalation, and staring at a candle, the
sun or a fire.[7] It seems therefore that fly agaric played a minor part
in shamanic performances in one area of Siberia, the north west.
Eliade and Siikala were right; drugs were not the central features of
North Asian shamanism that they have been in South American
ritual practices.

The third issue concerns the ability of shamans to shift shape; that is, to transform themselves into the shapes of animals or to make their own spirit-bodies take on animal forms while journeying into other worlds. This significance of this, like the shamanic use of drugs, is conditioned by cross-cultural assumptions and will shortly be made clear. For the present it is sufficient to note that relatively few accounts have been preserved of the spirit-journeys undertaken by Siberian shamans,[8] and these almost always suggest that the practitioner is travelling in his or her normal, human, form. There are occasional exceptions, such as the Buryat *bö* who some-times took the form of a hawk to hunt for a missing soul of a sick person in spirit worlds, but in general the need to shift shape was rendered superfluous by the assistance of spirits which took the natures of various beasts and birds. Some confusion may have been caused here, however, by the tradition recorded among the Sakha, Evenks and Enets, and noted earlier, of a special guardian spirit which sometimes or always took the form of a particular animal, and is commonly called in translation the shaman's 'animal double'.

The fourth issue is powered by a debate among non-academic writers. It is rooted in the twentieth-century British tradition of ley-hunting and earth mysteries, which flowered during the 1990s into a suggestion that in many parts of the world shamanism is associated with the concept that spirits travel along accustomed routes, set in straight lines across the physical landscape.[9] This incorporated Siberian material into its supporting data, mostly quoted from Eliade. The hypothesis has been challenged from within the same community of writers, and again the use of data from native Siberia has played its part in the controversy; a critic of the theory has declared that the examples used were few and arbitrarily selected from a complex mass of native cosmology which contains many more indications that the paths of spirit-worlds were as prone to wind as those of the apparent one.[10] Who is the more correct? Is there good evidence of a widespread Siberian tradition of straight spirit-tracks which can be assimilated to parallel beliefs elsewhere in the world?

Shirokogoroff stated unequivocally that all the southern Evenks enacted rituals in which spirit-roads were symbolized by posts between which strings and thongs were stretched; classic straight tracks. The same tradition is recorded among the Sakha, by two different observers: for the sacrifice of an animal to the celestial powers, three posts were set up and decorated, with a rope stretched between them. This was to represent the highway to the heavens taken by the animal's spirit, and the *oyun* danced between them as if flying, to function as a symbolic escort for it. Among the Buryats, there is a single description of a healing ceremony in which the *bö* tied a red silk thread from a tree outside the sick person's tent to an arrow beside the sickbed. He then entreated the patient's missing soul to return to its owner along this path.[11] All this is good evidence for the straight-track hypothesis.

Against it may be set two reflections. The first is that no such traditions are recorded outside these three major peoples of central Siberia: the physical use of a rope or thread to symbolize a spirit-path seems to be peculiar to them, and it may well have originated with just one of them. The descriptions of shamanic performances and soul-journeys recorded in other areas of Siberia give no sense of a standard motif of straight travel.[12] More disturbing is the publication by Anisimov of a detailed drawing made by an Evenk to illustrate a spiritual battle between shamans, as the paths shown in it are sharply curved; not surprisingly, as their purpose was to sneak spirits past the psychic defences of rival clans.[13] This raises the uncomfortable possibility that, even among these central peoples, the straight ropes, cords and threads tied in ritual did not correspond to a view of the cosmos; they were simply the easiest way in which to indicate an aerial path in three dimensions. As its stands, therefore, the evidence can be regarded as inconclusive.

From many of the records cited earlier, it must be very clear that Siberian shamans could be of both sexes. In 1751 the German scholar Johann Gmelin invented the word *schamanka* to distinguish a female practitioner, by cobbling together the Tungusic term with the usual Russian suffix indicating the feminine.[14] This is sometimes employed in modern studies, apparently because of a belief that it is a more 'authentic' rendering than the English translation of 'shamaness'. The latter has its uses in highlighting issues of gender, but as the original Tungusic word *shaman* has none, it has been used here to indicate practitioners of either sex.

What is very clear is that female shamans were found throughout Siberia; the problem here is to attempt some sense of their relative numbers and social standing. Those figures which do exist suggest that, naturally enough, shamans in general always represented a minority of the population of their respective communities, but the size of that minority could vary considerably. As seen, Bogoras recorded that nearly a third of all the Chukchi claimed the status. This situation seems to have been unique, but they were still clearly plentiful wherever they were not persecuted. In the nineteenth century every western Buryat village was said to have anything from one to five of them in residence, and censuses of the Sakha taken in the seventeenth century, when shamanism was still legal, suggest that *oyuns* made up 3 per cent of adult males. In 1900 two Teleut villages about seven miles apart contained six practitioners. The Evenks east of Lake Baikal numbered over two thousand in the 1910s, among whom Shirokogoroff managed to identify fourteen working shamans. A survey was taken of the Soyots of Tuva in 1931, during a period when Tuva was an independent republic. This found 725 shamans active within its borders, amounting to 1.1 per cent of the population. They were, however, concentrated in the more remote and mountainous parts of the territory: 20 per cent of households in the reindeer-rearing valleys of the north east admitted to including a shaman. Furthermore, Tuvan shamanism had been submitted to harassment by the newly-installed Communist regime in 1921, so people living closer to the captial may have been less willing to reveal its presence in their midst.[15]

Such data as there exists suggests that women made up a large minority of practitioners in most areas. Of those 725 Soyot shamans identified in Tuva in 1931, 314 were female. No other such precise figures appear to survive, but Shirokogoroff stated that 'less than half' of his sample of fourteen among the Transbaikal Evenks were women. Jochelson met or heard of four male shamans among the Yukaghirs, but no females.[16]

If women seem generally to have been less common as shamans, then there is some evidence that they were also less valued. Among the Chukchi, Bogoras noted that they were regarded as receiving the gift of shamanism more frequently than men. This should have meant that they dominated as practitioners, but Bogoras went on to record that they did not because they were also thought to make inferior shamans. Jochelson found something similar among the Koryaks; almost every family contained a woman who knew magical formulae, and some could call spirits, but the people identified as shamans were men. The Yukaghirs, also, seemed to regard shamanism as essentially a male business. Women attended performances and sang refrains at them but were not allowed to touch a shaman's gear while menstruating or soon after childbirth, which was thought to destroy its efficacy. A scholar of Selkup shamanism has stated that the greatest shamans, those who interceded between the human and spirit worlds, were always male, while women were confined to simple healings and divinations.[17] On the other hand, Savone of the Enets, a closely-related Samoyedic-speaking people, was a *budtode*, a practitioner of the highest rank who had earned the full ceremonial kit and contacted celestial spirits. In the eighteenth century, Gmelin encountered Evenk women who were thought to be superior shamans to men.[18]

The Sakha illustrate particularly well the problems which can beset this issue. One nineteenth-century observer of their customs, Soloviev, stated confidently that the *udahan*, or female shaman, was regarded by them as inferior to the *oyun*, or male one, and only called in if no male was available. Female shamans, he reported, were mostly confined to finding lost or stolen things and telling the future, and only preferred in cases of mental illness. Another well-qualified authority, Sieroszewski, declared with the same determination that the *udahan* was generally thought to be more powerful than the *oyun*. About a century and a half before, Gmelin had met a twenty-year-old *udahan* who was held in deep respect by older male practitioners. The leading Soviet Russian academic Nikolai Alekseev, himself a Sakhan, has opined that, although the seventeenth-century censuses do not allow us to estimate the number of *udahans*, the latter may have been more numerous than *oyuns*.[19] One possible way out of this pool of cross-currents is to suggest that Soloviev may have been wrong. Another was provided by Jochelson, who noted that some Sakhan folklore attributed a higher status to the *udahan* than the *oyun*, but that he had not actually found a single female shaman still active among the Sakha.[20] Nor, it seems, had Sieroszewski; when speaking of them he, too, may have been repeating tradition. It may be, therefore, that the *udahan* had formerly been very important but was dying out by the late nineteenth century; or it may be that legend had inflated her original standing. Another Russian scholar working at the time of Jochelson and Sieroszewski, V. F. Troschanski, developed the former possibility into the theory that all Sakhans who provided shamanic performances had once been female, but that men had intruded into the vocation and supplanted them.[21] As was recognised almost immediately,[22] there is no means by which this suggestion can be either substantiated or refuted.

The Buryats raise some of the same problems. Two recent academic authors, Roberte Hamayon and Caroline Humphrey, have agreed that the male shaman, or *bö*, was a more common figure than the female one, or *udgan*, and more respected. Women were discouraged from entering the vocation, and if they did they were confined mostly to divination. They could not touch the ritual equipment of a *bö*, while the latter had no inhibition about handling their gear. They were also far less trusted, and more vulnerable to suspicions of working evil; it is no coincidence that the dead shaman who was staked with aspen wood had been a woman. At the same time, Buryat legends sometimes attributed great magical power to women, although admittedly they were usually portrayed in this role as the opponents of male heroes, and defeated by the latter. Mythology is a slippery commodity for the historian. In this case the stories may reflect a time when women did wield greater influence as shamans, or they may have been concocted to justify male supremacy.[23]

What can stated with confidence is that, whatever the limitations upon their exercise of it, the role of shaman afforded women a rare or unique opportunity to wield public authority in native Siberian societies. It was usually the single means by which they could transcend the constraints which custom placed on their gender; in effect, by which they could behave like a man.[24] In considering gender relationships in traditional societies, a modern western academic has to try to avoid the twin injustices of undervaluing the extent of female influence, authority or independence, and concealing the extent to which women were oppressed. It is important not to impose Eurocentric perceptions, and to avoid citing hasty conclusions drawn by (usually male) European observers. Given these caveats, it seems permissible to state that no Europeans who travelled among native Siberian peoples reported that women in the latter enjoyed a higher social status or more public power than those in Europe during the same period. Some, indeed, noted the exact opposite. Sieroszewski commented that Sakhan women were especially degraded and exploited, with wives being treated as household labourers. Buryat scholars have recorded that women's work was not socially honoured, that they were prohibited from entering shrines or attending major religious ceremonies such as the *tailgan*, and were not allowed to touch smith's tools or hunting weapons; there were no corresponding prohibitions on the men. Jochelson witnessed how Koryak women had to eat separately and were allowed only the food remaining after the men had taken the best pieces.[25] As among many traditional peoples, menstruation and parturition provoked particular awe, fear and disgust, with consequences which were sometimes uncomfortable for women. An ethnographer working among the Nivkhs in 1885 noted how an expectant mother was always banished from the family home, to the open air in summer or a purpose-built hut in winter. She could be attended by other women, but her physical situation was often very uncomfortable, especially in winter as the hut was unheated. A female Soviet academic made a close study of comparable customs among the Mansi. She found that a menstruating woman was treated as dangerous, and exiled alone to a small hut, always unfurnished and usually unheated, until her courses ended. Worse, one who had given birth was expected to 'purify' herself by exposing her naked body to biting insects in summer or frost in winter. No comparable rites of pain or discomfort seem to have been expected of the men.[26]

Again, such data has to be interpreted with care. It is possible that women treated such ordeals as a means of gaining status, and entered into them with pride; though none of those interviewed or observed seems actually to have said this. It must be significant that, when it abolished the traditional restrictions on women in native Siberia, the Communist regime won a disproportionate amount of support from the female members of those societies. In 1931 about a quarter of all deputies of the soviets in the theoretically auto- nomous republics of the region were female, representing the first political leadership by women among Siberian peoples in their recorded history.[27] It must therefore be reiterated that shamanism had provided women with exceptional opportunities to undertake public roles; another clear indication of the importance attached to it and the high degree of personal talent and skill required for the calling. It tended to manifest in, or to attract, exceptional individ- uals, and there was simply not a large enough supply of those with the necessary gifts among most native male populations.

Issues of gender leave us with one further question regarding Siberian shamanism: that of its relationship with transexuality, bisexuality, lesbianism, homosexuality and transvestitism. Again, this is a cross-cultural issue, powered by the clear connection between these attributes and the figures whom scholars call shamans in parts of native America. It seems certain that there is also such a connection in Siberia, but confined to those peoples who were geographically and culturally closest to American natives. The most important and celebrated case is that of the Chukchi, who had a special class of shaman, the 'soft man', who was commanded by his spirits to dress and behave as a woman. Some got married to other men, but usually they only changed their outward behaviour and continued to live with their wives, while also taking a spirit as their 'husband'. Bogoras recorded that public opinion was always hostile to them, but his own distaste is so apparent in his writings on the subject that he may have been projecting it; certainly he added that such men were commonly believed to have exceptional shamanic powers. He heard that women were sometimes transformed in the same way, but never met one who had been.[28]

Among their neighbours and relatives, the Itelmens and Koryaks, Jochelson found stories of shamans who had behaved like the Chukchi 'soft men', but no living examples of any. Not even the stories existed among the Yukaghirs and Sakha, a stage further west, but their male shamans sometimes donned female dress. Sieroszewski interpreted this as another proof of the exceptional regard accorded by the Sakha to female shamans, while Jochelson preferred to regard it either as an echo of the 'soft man' upon the final inland frontier of that tradition, or else, more functionally, as yet another means of satisfying the expectation that shamans should have some distinctive dress.[29]

Some conclusions may be proposed from the analyses made above. It seems fairly clear that although Siberian peoples were ethnically, linguistically and culturally very heterogenous, and although most had various different kinds of religious and magical specialists, virtually all contained a sort of figure whom Europeans found disturbingly strange, and therefore interesting. Such people appeared to communicate with spirits, and sometimes to journey in spirit-worlds, in the service of others. They did so in a dramatic performance witnessed and often assisted by those for whom they were working, and wore a distinctive costume or used specialized equipment which marked them off from others in their community. Their most important functions at the time when records of them were collected were as healers and diviners – the classic twin pur-poses of magical specialists serving traditional societies the world over – but they sometimes interceded with superhuman entities on behalf of the general economic activities or spiritual wellbeing of their communities. Most were male, but women made up an important minority of these practitioners and could be as highly esteemed among them as men. In most, and perhaps all, cases, their performances involved their entry into an altered state of conscious-ness, but there is no firm evidence that this always occurred, or was deemed to be necessary; the notion of a 'state of consciousness' is in itself a western scholarly concept. The crucial requirement to Siberian natives was that these people were believed to be working with spirits to achieve practical ends in the objectively perceptible world.

PART THREE

SIBERIA
IN THE SHAMANIC WORLD

10

The Discovery of a Shamanic World

It remains now to be seen how the characterization of Siberian shamans suggested in this book matches the use which has been made of them by historians and anthropologists, with special reference to the study of the European past. The first part of this examination should concentrate on what can be said about the historical development of Siberian shamanism itself, and here there are two opposed scholarly models. One was first suggested by Johann Georgi back in the 1770s: that this shamanism was a very ancient spiritual practice which had heavily influenced the development of major Asian religions such as Buddhism and Hinduism. The opposite theory was first fully articulated by Shirokogoroff: that shamanism developed in Siberia only in what Europeans call the medieval period, as a result of the blending of native traditions with those of Buddhism.[1] How ancient was it?

The whole drift of this book has been against any decisive resolution of the question. As has been said, there are no known descriptions of Siberian shamans dating from before the sixteenth century, and references to apparently similar practices anywhere in northern or central Asia take us back only to the thirteenth. The dubious utility of oral tradition and mythology, in taking the place of written sources, has already been suggested. It is quite possible that a systematic and comprehensive collation of all the apparent records of shamanism made before (say) 1800, in European, Chinese, Persian, Korean and Mongol documents, would produce some valuable new insights; but such an enterprise has never been undertaken. The Hungarian scholar Voigt, publishing in 1984, could declare that 'there is no history of shamanism in Siberia',[2] and this still seems to be true.

Nor is there a prehistory, for magical and religious practices are notoriously hard to deduce from material remains alone. A partial exception to this rule is provided by works of art, and in the Siberian context these are represented by petroglyphs, carvings on rock-faces which exist in large quantity in parts of the region. They can only be dated by association with other archaeological data, and this test suggests that the Siberian figures vary from a century to a few thousand years in age. Since 1950 they have been the focus of considerable interest on the part of Russian scholars, who have produced several hundred books and articles upon them. Some have been interpreted as representations of shamanism, especially anthropomorphic beings shown dancing or with animal heads. However, the only clear images of shamans, as identifiable from their costume, activities and social setting, are among the carvings produced in the last two hundred years. The older art is much more enigmatic, and its apparently shamanic figures could be spirits, deities or disguised dancers at festivals. They cannot take the place of written evidence.[3]

Another scholarly device for reaching behind the appearance of writing is the study of linguistics, but here again the particular case of Siberian shamanism presents a conundrum. It centres on the fact that the word for a Buddhist monk in Pali, the basic textual language of Buddhism, is *samana* or *shamana*. The second-century writer Clement of Alexandria, citing cases of barbarian philosophers who could equal those of the Greeks in sophistication, included the *samanaoi* of Bactria. The latter region was substantially the area of modern Afghanistan, where both written and material evidence amply attests the presence of Buddhist activity at this time. There is by contrast none for the existence of shamanism of the Siberian sort, which would in any case make less sense as a comparison for Greek sages. Clement's *samanaoi* were therefore Buddhist holy men, and it seems equally safe to make the same identification for the use of similar words by other Greek writers, Megasthenes and Strabo, to characterize the same sort of figures in Bactria and India.[4]

Further north, the confusion begins. The Chinese word for a Buddhist monk is *sha-men*, derived directly from the Pali and virtually identical with the Tungus *shaman*. Thus, when a twelfth-century Chinese inscription refers to a *sha-man* as a worker of wonders, it probably denotes a monk, but may be the oldest known record in Asia of shamans of the Siberian sort. The linguistic problem vanishes if the Tungus word is actually the Pali one all along, taken into Siberian tribal cultures. If this were the case, then it would provide some convincing support for Shirokogoroff's argument that Buddhism had a decisive influence on the development of shamanism in Siberia; for otherwise, why was it necessary to borrow an Indian term for a native institution? The linguistic issue is, however, far more complex. The most widespread Siberian term for a shaman, after all, is *kam*. This has a long historical provenance of its own, appearing in the annals of the Tang emperors of China (618–906) to describe the sorcerers of the Turkic-speaking Kirgiz people of extreme south-western Siberia; figures who may or may not have operated like the later shamans. It was also used by the Persian historian Rashid-eddin, in 1302, for those same Mongol magicians of whom William of Rubruck had written, fifty years before, as employing methods which seem unmistakeably shamanic. Furthermore, it is used for shamans by the Nivkhs, the cultural and linguistic group whom archaeology identifies, tentatively, as the original one to inhabit the Amur basin. The word *kam* may therefore be an ancient Siberian term for a shaman, and the word *shaman* itself may have derived from it. Its resemblance to the Buddhist term could be entirely coincidental.[5]

If so, however, then it is a coincidence of a size almost to challenge belief. The cautious way out of accepting it is to suggest that *shaman* derived from a convergence of the native word with the Buddhist one. The radical way is to reverse the whole sequence of derivation, and propose that *kam* itself is ultimately descended from the Pali term. The problem in supporting any of these theories is that, whereas there is ample literary and archaeological evidence for the impact of Buddhism on southern Siberia from the seventeenth century onward, there is none of comparable certainty for an earlier such influence in the first millennium. It is possible to argue – or at least to assert – that there was one,[6] but the conclusive data is missing. In the absence of any, the linguistic argument chases its own tail.

The fact that there is no history of Siberian shamanism has not, of course, stopped scholars from trying to write histories of it. Indeed, it was virtually incumbent upon academics in the USSR to do so. Marxism, even more than most political philosophies, rests upon a view of the past, and the Soviet campaign to eradicate shamanism demanded a historiography. It was important that the traditions under attack should not be regarded as part of the original and 'natural' condition of Siberian natives, but as part of systems of abuse and exploitation which had evolved historically and were now ripe for destruction. The result was a series of publications by Soviet scholars which often offered theories incompatible with each other, and upon which no consensus was ever achieved.[7]

Arkadiy Anisimov declared that shamanism had evolved out of ancient totemism, as a result of changes in modes of economic production which inspired a more hierarchical form of society. Shamans were thus an embryonic priesthood, which could be classed with churchmen, and their appearance had been part of the process by which primitive Communism had been destroyed, He took Evenk myths which suggested that the first shamans had been old women as proof of the former existence of matriarchy, according to the scheme laid down by Friedrich Engels. Equally schematic was I. S. Vdovin, who argued that among the peoples of north-eastern Siberia shamans had been the priests of an ancestor-cult, and that they had declined into healers and diviners with the coming of Christianity. Taras Mikhailov produced a dogmatically-asserted sequence of evolution for Buryat shamanism through one phase of socio-economic change after another from ancient times onward, based on the historical vision of Marx and Engels.[8]

Other Soviet authors were more subtle and tentative. The orientalist L. N. Gumilov proposed a history of south Siberian religion, whereby a native belief in a single celestial god and a single deity of the earth was destroyed by the arrival of Islam and Buddhism, and shamanism developed as syncretic forms of all three. The ethnographer L. P. Potapov suggested that it was preceded in the Altai by a cult of sacred mountains linked to clan territories and functioning as sites for ancestor-worship. It therefore appeared as clans decayed, and as responsibility for religious practices was vested in a new specialist, the shaman. S. I. Vainstein agreed, proposing that shamanism appeared latest in societies in which the clan system lasted longest. N. L. Zhukovskaya also saw shamanism as arising because of the need for a greater specialization of social function, but identified the change as occuring at the transition from kin networks to feudalism.[9]

What all these theories had in common was that they attempted to portray shamanism as a relatively late development associated with the decay of a simpler and more equal society. As Caroline Humphrey has pointed out,[10] none of them has amounted to more than speculation, but all have the merit of attempting at least to relate shamanism to specific systems of thought and society, and to credit it with a capacity to develop over time. They recognize that religious change is commonly associated with social change, and Humphrey herself has shown very persuasively that the different religious allegiances of the western and eastern Buryats were founded in social contrasts. In the period between the seventeenth and nineteenth centuries, the western group had a stagnant economy and an ancestor-based view of society which validated land owner-ship and ranked social status. This was well suited to shamanism, which venerated ancestors and land-spirits, and produced practi-tioners tied to clans. The eastern group had an expanding economy in which kinship was weak and hierarchy more monolithic, and that better suited the Buddhist world-picture. Humphrey went on to show ways in which the imperial rulers of the Mongols and Manchus used concepts or practices taken from shamanism in order to vali-date their rule, and either discarded or redeveloped these as their states became more formalized.[11]

These were, however, classic examples of how North Asian shamanism might be studied with the benefit of written records. There is no doubt that its social relationships, and even more markedly its relationships with state systems, have altered signifi-cantly during the periods from which those records survive. What is apparently both lost and irrecoverable is its history before the appearance of such texts. Richard Johnson's report shows us a Siberian shamanism in the mid-1550s which is already, in essentials, fully formed. All the details of his description reappear in subsequent observations of other shamans at work right up to the twentieth century. The thirteenth- and fourteenth-century descriptions of Mongol and Chinese magicians prove that very similar, if not identical, techniques were employed in North Asia three hundred years before Johnson's encounter. That is as far as the North Asian evidence can take us.

In moving beyond that point, Soviet scholars relied partly on ideological prescriptions, but also upon a technique which was employed by some of their Russian predecessors and by some foreign academics: of comparing the social context of shamanism among different Siberian peoples and attempting to decide which represented its oldest and 'purest' form. This comparative method has the virtue of challenging theories raised on too narrow and localized a basis of evidence. It also, however, has severe limitations of its own. This are apparent even when dealing with the easier of the two tasks to which it may be applied: of criticizing general hypotheses. A major example here is Shirokogoroff's suggestion that shamanism had been created by the impact of Buddhist mysticism. At first sight this is left virtually untenable by a Siberia-wide perspective, for shamans were just as important among northern peoples whose cultures showed no trace of Buddhist influence as in the south where such influence was obvious. Closer inspection, however, reveals that motifs could travel into regions in which their original context had been lost; for example, the snake was found as a motif on shamanic costumes in areas too far north for the animal itself to exist.[12] It is entirely possible that an idea or practice could be adopted and applied by peoples who had taken on no other aspects of the culture with which it had been associated.

The comparative method is even less effective in its other usage: of constructing general theories. A classic example consists of the forms of shamanizing found among the Koryaks, which were divided between individuals who could be hired by any client and approximated to professional practitioners, and those who served only particular families and were associated with their domestic shrines. To Jochelson, the latter represented the original, and 'primitive', nature of shamanism, from which the latter had evolved. So it might have been, but it is equally possible that Koryak 'family' shamanism represented a local democratization of a role which had formerly been the preserve of a few specialists as in most of Siberia. Family-based shamanism was even more common among the neighbouring Chukchi, and when considering them Eliade dismissed it as 'a plagiaristic aping' of the real thing: the precise opposite to Jochelson's view.[13]

It therefore remains possible that this phenomenon found among the far north-eastern peoples represented either a relic of the ancient form of all Siberian shamanism, lingering in a corner, or else an idiosyncratic and geographically marginal development from the older and normal pattern, of the specialist individual serving a clan or a district. A similar problem attends the varieties of shamanism found in western Siberia, among the Khants, Mansi, and some Turkic-speaking groups such as those on the River Chulym. Compared to the peoples of the central and southern parts of the region, these tended to be much simpler, with minimal costume and ceremony and a much looser sense of common identity and training among practitioners. The scholars who have worked in these areas were left baffled as to whether they were studying an older and less highly-evolved form of shamanism or a late and degenerate one.[14] By the time that Caroline Humphrey wrote on the subject in 1980, she could remark that it was 'well-known' that to try to construct a history of the shamans of Siberia on the basis of ethnographic reports was a doubtful exercise.[15]

Seventy years of Soviet scholarship therefore served to add large quantities of valuable fieldwork to the corpus available, to increase knowledge of the recorded history of Siberian shamanism, and to produce a set of different hypotheses regarding its origins and early development. The common characteristics of this scholarship were an ability to explore the subject on the ground and in depth. What it most obviously lacked was a dimension of space. The early diplomatic isolation of the USSR, and the siege mentality of the interlinked regimes in the later Warsaw Pact, tended to make Soviet research relatively self-contained and self-referential. Its main scope for comparison in studies of shamanism lay in relations with one ally and satellite state, Hungary, and these, as suggested earlier, did prove fruitful. They were also necessarily limited, and the world beyond was largely over the horizon of Soviet experts in the subject.

It was this other, global, perspective, which was to be most heavily exploited by western scholars, and largely because of the lead taken by one of them, whose name has recurred constantly in the present study: Mircea Eliade. For a quarter of a century he dominated the field, and his influence on West European and North American academic and popular cultures is still very obvious. By contrast, he was almost completely ignored inside the Soviet bloc, and this differing treatment of his work did much to widen the gulf between Russian and American studies of shamanism, with important implications for the subject.[16]

It may have counted for something that Eliade was personally a mortal enemy of the Soviet Union and of the Warsaw Pact. He had been involved in right-wing politics in his native Romania during the Second World War, and fled to the West when the Red Army overran his homeland. He remained a refugee for the rest of his life, first in Paris and then in Chicago, where he settled down to become America's leading figure in the comparative study of religion. All of this, however, would probably have mattered little if Eliade had not been so completely committed to a view of religion which was thoroughly at odds with that embedded in Soviet ideology. To him, the propensity for religious belief was one of the most admirable and fascinating aspects of humanity, and he devoted his academic career to exploring it. As part of this project, he represented shamans as exemplars of an ancient form of spirituality which had been of crucial importance to the development of religion worldwide. As such, he treated them as worthy of respect, and even of admiration.

Eliade wrote his great study of shamanism in Paris in the first years of his exile, between 1946 and 1951. It was published in French in that latter year, and translated into English in 1964, after which it completed its transition into being the most heavily-read text on the subject in western scholarship. As said earlier, the idea that shamanism underpinned some of the world's greatest religions, such as Buddhism and Hinduism, had been around since the eighteenth century. Eliade suggested that it underlay most if not all religions, and buttressed this claim with the undeniable fact that traditional societies in many parts of the world had figures similar to the shamans of Siberia; specialist practitioners who contacted spirits in a public performance in order to obtain benefits for other humans. The tactic of employing ethnographic data to construct general theories of the history of religion had been well known to the nineteenth century, its most celebrated expression in English being Sir James Frazer's *The Golden Bough.* Since the 1910s it had been abandoned by anthropologists because of doubts concerning the basic validity of its method; of selecting apparently similar phenomena from very different societies widely separated in time and space, and lumping them together in order to propose universal schemes for human development and behaviour. It had, however, persisted among scholars of comparative religion, and Eliade now employed it on a grand scale.

He began by restating the importance of Siberia and neighbouring parts of North and Central Asia as the 'classic' homeland of shamanism. He emphasised that even there shamans were not the only important figures in native spirituality, but insisted that they were dominant in it, as 'its privileged adherents', with access to mystical experience of prime importance. For Eliade, this hinged on two abilities: to control spirits instead of being possessed by them; and to journey into spirit-worlds. In essence, his shaman was 'the master of ecstasy'. This figure could exist within a considerable number of religions, 'for shamanism always remains an ecstatic technique at the disposal of a particular elite'. Membership of this elect group was obtained by an intense process of initiatory experience, of which the essential one was that of 'suffering, death, resurrection'. Although Eliade fully recognised that Siberian shamans were believed to journey into nether worlds and upon the same cosmological plane as the apparent one, as well as into celestial realms, his book gradually gave primacy to the heavenly missions. In its final pages, he declared that the original underlying ideology of shamanism had been 'belief in a celestial Supreme Being with whom it was possible to have direct relations by ascending into the sky'. Furthermore, his shamans were champions in a timeless holy war, consoling and comforting their communities by defending the 'psychic integrity' of the latter against 'what we would call "the powers of evil"'. This was their fundamental and universal role.[17] Both the religious mysticism and the elitism of Eliade's writing

make it easy to appreciate why this book was so coldly received in
the Soviet bloc, but also why it made such a dramatic impact upon
many western readers.

To support his argument with Siberian material, he deployed
tremendous diligence and industry, and an equally remarkable talent
for languages, locating the first-hand accounts of shamanism left by
travellers and scholars and mining them for data. He selected and
arranged the latter with a ruthlessness on which comment has been
passed repeatedly in the preceding sections of this book. At times,
as has been suggested, he perceived what seem to have been genuine
common features, and at others he was sensitive to variations in
overall patterns. For the most part, however, he highlighted material
which supported his arguments, and disposed of the rest. Sometimes
the latter was simply disregarded. It has been noted that Waldemar
Jochelson was careful to provide examples of the very different styles
and methods used by shamans in north-eastern Siberia. Eliade
simply declared that not all of the performances recorded in
Jochelson's work were 'interesting',[18] and so consigned to the
rubbish heap some of the labour, and a large part of the argument,
of this most scrupulous of early Russian ethnographers. At other
times he took account of variant material, but never accepted that
this might necessitate a qualification of his general model; instead
he repeatedly declared that the variants represented 'a late innovation', 'a recent technique', 'minor exploits', phenomena that 'could
not be regarded as properly shamanic', or simply 'decadence'. All
were dismissed as outgrowths from the genuine shamanism which
he was identifying, or else as irrelevant to it. Occasionally, if he read
two different accounts of practices which in themselves did not
support his argument, then he would splice them together to create
a single one which did.[19]

None the less, the sheer quantity of information which he provided, and the verve with which he interpreted it, was exhilarating
for readers who had previously known little about Siberia. Even
more impressive, and audacious, was the manner in which he linked
it to ethnographic data from outside the region. It is absolutely
correct, as has been stated, that phenomena similar to Siberian
shamanism have been recorded in other parts of Asia, and other

continents, and Eliade made a survey of those examples provided in the literature of his time. The result was a curious map, for his shamanism was found in recent times among some peoples in South-East Asia, Polynesia, Australia, Africa, and North and South America. The last two continents were the most prolific in examples, and South America provided more cases similar to the Siberian material than any other.[20] There were two obvious explanations for the apparent common identity of activities scattered, often with wide separations, across a wide expanse of the globe. One was that they were examples of how humans beings could evolve the same sorts of technique independently to cope with particular needs. Eliade gave this no time at all, putting the whole thrust of his book behind the other, which was that the shamanism which he had characterized had once been a worldwide phenomenon. Areas of traditional peoples such as Melanesia, which seemed to lack any trace of it, but which lay between regions in which his 'shamanic tradition' had apparently been recorded, were assumed by him to have lost it at some point in the past.[21]

In building up this picture, Eliade was reproducing most of those methodological devices which had already been rejected by anthropologists and which had become so discredited in the work of precursors such as Frazer. He was imposing an ideal type on a very diverse and complex set of phenomena. It was both a free-floating and a static model, lacking much sense of either specific social contexts and specific historical development. It was an image of direct, transformative and socially powerful religious experience, disassociated from institutions or dogmas and represented as more ancient, fundamental, universal and ancestral than they. It was both an inversion of the modern western experience of religion and of the modern western tradition of rationalism. All these qualities gave it a considerable romantic appeal. That appeal could only be enhanced by the fact that much of what Eliade had to say fell upon ground already prepared to receive it. After all, the concept of the shaman as a spiritual warrior against the forces of evil, empowered by a personal relationship with a celestial god, was hardly foreign to western culture. If in some ways it was an inversion, in others it was an extrapolation. Furthermore, the identification of the Siberian shaman as the archetype of the primitive worker of magic, opposed to western norms of religion, was as old as the first European contacts with shamans. As Eliade had noted, since the opening of the twentieth century the word 'shaman' had already become widely applied by academics to figures in tribal societies otherwise known as medicine men, witch doctors, sorcerers and magicians. He just gave this application a new sense of excitement and importance, and an apparent new precision.

The reception of his work itself varied from one culture to another within the western world. In 1971 a distinguished British anthropologist, Ioan Lewis, observed that American scholars were especially prone to study religion as a universal phenomenon, with its own patterns of belief and symbolism. They treated it as a thing with a life of its own, independent of social frameworks, as Eliade himself did; it is no coincidence that he had settled among them. Lewis noted that this was also the attitude taken to religion by religious believers, and 'reflected the abiding strength of the American preoccupation with culture rather than society'. He drew attention to the popularity which the term 'shaman' had enjoyed in the United States ever since the publication of Eliade's book, and to the looseness and variety of ways in which it had become used there. The broadest one was that of 'inspired priest'. This was, of course, to contravene the boundaries within which Eliade himself had tried to confine the word.

Lewis accompanied these reflections with other on his own academic culture. He noted that British anthropologists had an opposite set of priorities: that they had 'studiously avoided paying much attention to anything that could be called spirituality'; that they rarely employed the term 'shaman'; and that they tended to show more interest in the social nexus in which beliefs and symbols were expressed. He himself set out to break with that tradition, by extending the definition of shamanism to any practice by which an individual gained a special position in society by an apparent controlled communication with spirits. He explicitly included those who claimed to be voluntarily possessed and used as mouthpieces by those entities, whom Eliade had as explicitly excluded. In part, this was a result of geographical distinctions. One further reason for the natural accordance between Eliade and the United States was the fact that the Americas contained more apparent parallels for the shamanism which he had defined than any other parts of the world outside Siberia. Conversely, Africa contained the fewest, although it had preserved a very large number of tribal societies. As Africa was also the favourite hunting-ground of twentieth-century British ethnographers, this was another reason why the latter had not found Eliade's formulation seductive. It did, on the other hand, include many cases of culturally-sanctioned spirit-possession, and Lewis now brought all of these into the shamanic family.

He did so, moreover, with a rhetoric of approval and admiration which at times outran anything written by Eliade. To Lewis 'the shaman' was the symbol of

> independence and hope. Through him the otherwise unfettered power of the world beyond human society is harnessed purposefully and applied to minister to the needs of the community. If by incarnating spirits he embodies the most profound intrusion of the gods into the realm of human society, his mastering of those powers dramatically asserts man's claim to control his spiritual environment and to treat with the gods on terms of equality.

Lewis concluded by spelling out the implications of this for modern religion. In his view, 'shamanistic religions' avoided the 'mistake' of Christianity, of setting up an all-powerful god who came to seem diminished by human advances in science and technology. 'They assume from the start that, at least on certain occasions, man can rise to the level of the gods.' Thus shamanism

> celebrates a confident and egalitarian view of man's relations with the divine, and perpetuates that original accord between God and man which those who have lost the ecstatic mystery can only nostalgically recall in myths of creation, or desperately seek in doctrines of personal salvation.[22]

The floodgates of the academic imagination were now open. There was a widespread impression that shamanism was something important, and exciting, and global in its scale, and relevant to contemporary concerns, and that in some way the template of it could still be located in Siberia. There was no agreement as to what

it actually was. During the 1980s and 1990s more and more was
published upon it, with the recurrent observation that no consensual
definition was being achieved of even the main features of what was
being studied with such fervour.[23] Entire continents may appear in
or be deleted from the ledger of admissible data according to the
personal decisions of individual scholars. To Eliade, and more recently Piers Vitebsky, there was important evidence of shamanic
practices among native Australians; to an equally respected authority
on the subject, Åke Hultkranz, there was not. All three scholars are
in agreement that shamanism is apparently missing from most of
Africa; but, according to Ioan Lewis's definition, African material
is centrally important.[24] By the 1990s a widespread impression had
grown up among western scholars, apparently fuelled by Eliade's
emphasis on its archaism and former universality, that shamanism
(whatever it was) was primarily associated with simple hunting and
gathering societies. This went against the clear fact that most native
Siberians had been pastoralists, herding reindeer, cattle, sheep or
horses. It also sat oddly with the apparent prevalence of practices
which most scholars called shamanism in agrarian economies such
as those of the Koreans and several South Asian ethnic groups.
Furthermore, it begged the question of why Australia and Africa,
which between them contained such a large proportion of the
world's surviving hunter-gatherers, should have such a doubtful
status in the study of the subject. Where Siberia fitted into all this
was by no means clear. In most generalizations it was still treated
as the homeland of the classic, normative, examples of shamanism.
Hultkranz, however, felt it necessary to point out that, far from
being typical of what was now commonly grouped under that term,
the Siberian examples were unusually institutionalized, ritualized
and sophisticated, and far more dominant in their societies.[25] This
did beg the question of whether they should then be regarded as
the most developed form of it, or something different enough to
be distinguished from what was called shamanism in the rest of the
world. It is not a question to which any resolution has yet been
made.

Meanwhile the problem of origins has continued to bubble away
in the background of studies, as the choice faced and made by Eliade

remains as stark as ever to those willing to take notice of it. One such has been Hultkranz, who has settled for Eliade's theory of diffusion; that the fact that shamanism was apparently found across the world, among peoples who had not been in contact with each other for many millennia, argues for the belief that it is a legacy of ancient hunting culture. Specifically, he has called it a hallmark of the 'old Palaeolithic culture' of Eurasia, and so spread east and south from that.[26] This notion certainly gets round some of the problems of distribution, but it raises others to which there is no apparent answer: why it spread only to some peoples within its recorded range; or else why others lost it; and why it should have reached the furthest limit of South America but had a less obvious impact on Africa, Australia and Melanesia. When it is appreciated that the San, the oldest known inhabitants of South Africa, have practices closer to Siberian shamanism than any of the various peoples between, the whole theory of dispersal begins to look very shaky. The obvious way of disposing of it is to adopt the alternative idea, which Eliade rejected, of an independent development of similar techniques and practitioners by widely separated and very different cultures. Vitebsky approached this by suggesting that the propensity of particular individuals to contact spirit-worlds (or to be contacted by them), while in an altered state of consciousness, is an experience of individuals found throughout humanity, but that in only some peoples did it become formalized in the figure of the shaman.[27] While getting rid of all the difficulties attendant on the diffusionist hypothesis, this concept does raise the parallel one of why only certain groups developed (and perhaps in some cases lost) such a figure.

In the course of the twentieth century research into shamanism came to follow different models on respective sides of the Iron Curtain; but each had two important characteristics in common. Both resulted in the collection of large quantities of valuable new data, and both produced a set of speculative suggestions regarding the origins and nature of shamanism which failed to achieve any consensus. The result in each case was confusion, but that on the western side of the division was far more comprehensive.

11

The Discovery of a Shamanic Past

It remains now to consider the specific implications of the scholarly interest in shamanism for the history and prehistory of Europe. To the south west, the boundaries of the Siberian shamanic province have been fairly well defined since the end of antiquity. In Russian Turkestan and Kazakhstan shamanic practices were assimilated into Islam. Practitioners were devout Moslems who had no special costume and sent their assistant spirits to combat demons which caused illness instead of travelling into a spirit-world themselves. They began performances by calling on Allah, and then on Moslem saints, and only after that upon their own spirits.[1] The overlap with Siberian techniques is very clear, but their application was equally clearly made within a different cultural context, and whether they represented surviving native traditions, or ideas imported from Siberia itself, is impossible to tell. Although Islamic societies further south and west had mystics who entered trance, none of them have possessed in historic times figures as close to shamans as these in what became Russian Central Asia.

It is possible, however, that traces of ancient shamanism may be found in the religions of the Near and Middle East; something which Eliade suggested, drawing in turn on the work of previous twentieth-century scholars. The keenest debate in this field has focused on Zoroastrianism. During the 1930s a German expert, S. H. Nyberg, proposed that North Asian shamanism had exerted a decisive influence upon the formative ideas of that faith. His theory attracted critics, of whom W. B. Henning was the most prominent, and it remains controversial. The key questions concerning it are, as usual, those of definition: whether traditions in which heroes or saints visit Heaven, Hell or comparable theological otherworlds should automatically be regarded as shamanic, and if so whether

they can then be treated as the results of Siberian influence. At
present they seem insoluble in this context.[2]

Similar problems attend the relationship between shamanism
and the ancient Greeks. During the early 1940s the famous British
classicist Francis Cornford wrote an essay in which he compared
the Greek tradition of inspired poets with Siberian shamans.
Cornford's work was known to a younger colleague who achieved
equal eminence, Eric Dodds, and in 1951 Dodds went a step further,
to suggest that Greek concepts of the soul were influenced directly
by shamanism, brought to them by the Scythian tribes which roamed
the region north of the Black Sea. By this argument, philosophers
like Pythagoras and Empedocles, and legendary heroes such as
Orpheus, all became shamans. Three decades later another leader
of the discipline, the German professor Walter Burkert, added
Heracles to the list. The hero's feats mostly concerned dealings with
extraordinary animals, and included a visit to an Underworld, and
he was associated with sacrifices. It could therefore be postulated
that his character was created out of an accumulation of tales
'marked by shamanistic hunting ritual'. Suggestions such as these,
made by such respected scholars, ensured that the influence of
shamanism on early Greek culture became widely accepted. In 1983,
however, a Dutch classicist on his way to achieving comparable
distinction, Jan Bremmer, pointed out that there was in fact no
evidence whatsoever that the ancient Scythians had shamans, and
that all of the Greek customs for which Dodds had suggested
shamanic roots could have other, equally or more plausible, origins.
He concluded that 'no convincing evidence exists for shamanistic
influence on Archaic Greece'.[3] With that, the apparent orthodoxy
melted into indeterminacy.

In Western Europe, the same sorts of difficulty hang over the some
of the earliest remains of human activity: the painted and mobile
art of the Palaeolithic. It was a major prop of the respective theories
of Eliade, Hultkranz and Burkert that such art could be taken
as good evidence of shamanic practices even at this remote period.
Old Stone Age evidence has, indeed, underpinned most assumptions and assertions that shamanism is one of the most archaic of
human spiritual techniques, if not the oldest of all. The argument

has tended to be circular, as the art is interpreted in the light of such beliefs, and this interpretation reinforces the beliefs in turn; though circularity is not in itself a sign that the original idea was wrong. The debates over it have gone on longer than those over related issues in the history of Greek and Middle Eastern religion, have involved many more scholars, and dominate their subject to a much greater degree.

It seems to have been Eliade himself who got them rolling, because the publication of his book on shamanism in 1951, emphasizing its antiquity and ubiquity, was immediately followed by a set of studies by German scholars which sought to identify Palaeolithic evidence for it. They suggested that certain scenes in cave paintings represented shamanic trances, and that some tools had been shamanic equipment. In a perfect demonstration of the circular effect noted above, when Eliade published the English edition of his book in 1964, he added the assertion that these researches had 'clearly brought out the "shamanic elements"' in Old Stone Age European culture, and that the antiquity of shamanism now seemed 'certain'.[4] A full-scale debate over the matter was precipitated by the English translation of a book by another German, Andreas Lommel, which took this apparent proof further to suggest that western art, as well as western religion, was rooted in Palaeolithic shamanism. The German edition appeared in 1965, and the English one two years later (in the United States), allowing a set-piece discussion of it in an American journal in 1970. The result was that, although some experts accepted the idea, most of them felt that it was neither proven nor could be proved. The three crucial problems with it have already been stated above, in other contexts: that there is no necessary connection between shamans and hunting societies; that the very term 'shamanism' is ill-defined; and that it is very difficult to use material remains to reconstuct beliefs.[5] With that, interest in the issue ebbed away.

It came flooding back in 1988, with the publication of an article by two South African archaeologists, David Lewis-Williams and Thomas Dowson. They brought two new and important pieces of evidence in support of shamanic practices as a 'significant component' of Palaeolithic rock art. The first was that the art of the San

provided a case in which designs could actually be interpreted by
recorded testimony from people who had made or used it. Those
witnesses identified much of it as representing shamanic transform-
ations; and these designs were similar to many found on the walls
of European caves. The other evidence was gained from psychology,
which had suggested that human beings entering 'entopic states'
(trances or drug-powered visions) commonly see the material world
disintegrate into a sequence of images from the apparent to the
abstract to the geometric, and all these forms were represented in
the Old Stone Age paintings of Europe. Both scholars developed
these arguments further over the following ten years, and a book
published by Lewis-Williams in the United States in 1998, in partnership with Jean Clottes, summed them up in a form accessible and
attractive to lay readers.[6]

By then the theory had attracted reactions at every point of the
critical spectrum. Some South African specialists replied that San
art itself embodied a range of cultural meanings, of which shamanism was only one. Experts in native Australian rock art doubted
that the latter was 'entopic', while those in the Central Asian equivalent were undecided as to whether that could better be interpreted
in terms of shamanism or of Indo-Iranian religion. Some Palaeolithic images could be explained more readily in terms of hunting
magic, others in those of fertility magic. Not only was shamanism
not intrinsic to hunter-gatherer cultures, but figures which blended
human and animal forms, and geometric patterns of the allegedly
entopic kind, were painted by surviving traditional societies who
did not practise it (or anything defined by scholars as it).[7]

What is attractive about the argument of Lewis-Williams and
Dowson is that it seems to account for certain forms of Palaeolithic
art better than any other. Lewis-Williams and Clottes went to
pains in their book to emphasize that the diversity of concepts,
subjects and techniques found in the art of France and Spain
alone made it 'naïve to hope for one complete explanation'.[8] Their
theory does explain why that art is often found hidden deep in caves
which could only be entered with effort, and often consists of a
careful combination and composition of images, creating spaces for
the performance of different rites. If the cave wall was seen as a

membrane between real and other worlds, then much of the patterning and location of figures makes sense, while entopic states provide one easy explanation for the mixture of animal and geometric art. There are good ethnographic parallels for all these points, especially among the San. The problems are that, in the very nature of archaeological investigation, ultimate proof will always be missing, and that it is equally impossible to demonstrate conclusively that the art concerned is specifically the relic of practices which scholars call shamanism. There are many examples in history and anthropology of initiatory and mystery religions which did not involve control of, or possession by, spirits.

If the Old Stone Age hunters of Europe really did have shamans, then the question arises of when the latter disappeared. After all, they flourished in the pastoral societies of Siberia, and such economies have dominated large areas of Europe from the New Stone Age until the present. Nor, as has been said, are they incompatible with agrarian systems. If the Khants and Mansi had cultures more or less identical with several in early medieval northern and eastern Europe, and a flourishing shamanism, then there is no intrinsic reason why the shamans of the European Palaeolithic should not have survived into periods well recorded in history. Some scholars have indeed discerned evidence for them in later times. Jeremy Dronfield has suggested that the abstract art carved on the stones of Neolithic passage graves in Ireland also reproduced the tell-tale signs of entopic states. His thesis was submitted to a formal debate in a British journal by eight experts in 1996, and the majority opinion was the predictable one that the hypothesis was possible but not susceptible to proof.[9] From time to time prehistoric burials excavated in Western Europe and found to be associated with unusual ornaments or personal possessions have been identified as those of shamans. The logic involved is the shaky one that, if Siberian shamans were marked out by a special costume or equipment, then any prehistoric person marked out in this way would probably have been a shaman.[10]

Early historical sources, and especially medieval Irish and Welsh texts, have also been used as evidence for shamanism in North-Western Europe. The classicists Cornford and Dodds were influenced in their treatment of Greek material by the work of a British colleague, the deeply respected expert in Celtic literatures Nora Chadwick. In 1936 she published an article which drew the attention of specialists to the importance of accounts of Siberian shamanism for the interpretation of ancient spiritual practices in Northern Europe.[11] This theme was followed up in her later works, most especially a book published in 1942,[12] where she united a span of figures from the druids and bards of the Celtic-speaking lands to the shamans of Siberia in a common ancient Eurasian tradition of inspired poets, seers and healers who communed with spirit-worlds. As part of this work she made specific associations, such as that between the feathered cloaks and head-pieces worn by druids or poets in a few Irish tales and the feathers sewn into some Siberian shamans' gowns and caps,[13] which were to recur in works of popular Celticism in the late twentieth century. Her ideas were drawn upon by Alwyn and Brinley Rees for their book on Celtic tradition, aimed at and reaching a mass audience, which appeared in 1961.[14]

They tended to disappear among British experts in Celtic studies during the second half of the century, and to feature instead – occasionally – in the work of North American counterparts. One such was Daniel Melia, who in 1983 claimed to have detected sha-manic elements in the biography of a celebrated Irish saint, Adamnan. The essential part of these was that Adamnan went through physical ordeals in order to win divine intervention in a worthy moral cause, and obtained greater personal spiritual power and standing in the process.[15] Behind this characterization is dis-cernible Eliade's definition of the shaman as one of a spiritual elite who passes through a traumatic initiatory experience of death and rebirth; but even this (as seen) was not true of all, or even perhaps of most, Siberian practitioners. It is, furthermore, all that Melia's shaman-saint has in common with them. Two years before Melia published, Joseph Nagy had provided a template to enable scholars to determine whether characters in medieval literature were 'sha-manic'. Such people had to travel freely to and from otherworlds; have a primary function to protect members of their society from malignant external forces; inform that society about worlds beyond it; and be vulnerable to the powerful supernatural forces which they sought to control. Working to this checklist, Leslie Ellen Jones was able to identify Owein ap Urien as 'the ideal shamanic knight', and Taliesin as one of the best examples of the 'Celtic poet as shaman'.[16] Indeed, Siberian shamans did have all these characteristics, but they also had others which these literary personalities lack, and which were arguably more striking, distinctive and definitive. No figure in early Irish or Welsh literature provides a human audience with a dramatic performance of singing, drumming and dancing, in the course of which she or he works with an established group of attendant spirits.

To say this is not to suggest that the applications of the terms 'shaman' or 'shamanic' made by these scholars are incorrect or illegitimate. The lack of any accepted academic definition of them renders such an exercise futile from the start. A different and at first sight more viable question – whether the stretching of the Siberian term to cover such different phenomena produces any useful new insights or progress in knowledge – founders on the near certainty that specialists in different disciplines, based in different national cultures, would provide conflicting answers. What seems difficult to argue away is the sense of regret that a set of words and concepts which might so usefully have transcended national and disciplinary boundaries has been productive instead of so much confusion and incoherence.

A single textual example may serve to point up some of the difficulties of comparison. Not a single record has been left, in either literary or inscriptional form, of a ceremony carried out by the druids of ancient north-western Europe. The closest thing in existence is a description in an Irish story, *Togail bruidne Da Derga*, which survives in a twelfth-century text. This means, of course, that it may well represent what medieval Irish monks or courtly entertainers believed that the pagan Irish had done, rather than what the latter actually did, but the belief is still significant. The rite in question is the *ta-bheis* or bull-feast:

> a bull was killed, and one man ate his fill and drank its broth and slept, and an incantation of truth was chanted over him. Whomever this man saw in his sleep became king; if the man lied about what he saw in his sleep he would die.[17]

Some might instantly recognise 'shamanic elements' in this custom. Others, among whom the present author is one, would be more impressed by the utter disimilarity with the means by which a Siberian shaman would obtain access to the same sort of information – by summoning spirit-helpers in a performance before an audience.

It is worth emphasizing now that not only did European visitors to Central Asia from the thirteenth to the eighteenth century find such performances unfamiliar and alien, but that none of them seem to have had any sense that a tradition of these activities had existed in their own societies. All the researches of historians and archaeologists to date have not succeeded in proving them wrong. It is therefore worth mapping the discernible European boundaries of the Siberian shamanic province during recorded time. They certainly did not coincide perfectly with the modern continental boundary, for the territories of the Khants and Mansi once overlapped the Urals, until the advance of the Russians pushed them back onto the eastern side. Moreover, one at least of the native tribes in the eastern parts of European Russia had an equivalent figure to the Siberian shaman. This was the Votyak, and the figure was the *tuno*, a man who told fortunes, healed diseases, found lost or stolen property and decided on the right form of sacrifices. He discovered the will of the gods by visiting their shrines or going into trance. Sometimes the latter was achieved by dancing with a sword and a whip to the music of a psaltery, until he cried out the answers to questions in delirium. The vocation was mostly hereditary, although very gifted individuals might take on this role without such a qualification. Spirits or gods appeared to trainees at night to instruct them. A lesser functionary in the same tribe was the *pellyaskis*, who could be male or female and carried out the duties of the *tuno* without being able to communicate with supernatural entities. The *vedin* was a *tuno* who was prepared to work harm, for hire or personal satisfaction.[18]

None of the other tribes of this region, however, had such functionaries. The Cheremises included the *kart* or *muzhan*, diviners who operated by casting beans or gazing into vessels of water. The *muzhan* put on a special blouse to work. The Chuvashes had the *iemzya*, who were of both sexes and healed with herbs, told fortunes and spoke charms against diseases. The Mordvins had people who specialized in communing with the dead, and old men who put on white robes at festivals to bless food.[19] Save for the marginal detail of the special costume for the *muzhan*, none of these are much like shamans. The food-blessers of the Mordvins resembled priests, while all the others belong to the tradition of practitioners well recorded from the Urals westward to the Atlantic, and known in English most commonly as wise-folk or cunning-folk: workers of spells, herblore and forms of divination who did not commune with spirits in a performance for their clients. We have moved into a different world.

That sense of contrast is strikingly reinforced when considering the one European people who have, in historic times, possessed a shamanism of exactly the sort recorded in Siberia; that known to itself as the Saami, to the Russians as Lopar, and to other Europeans as the Lapps. Since records begin its territory has consisted of the north of Scandinavia, divided among the four modern nation-states of Norway, Sweden, Finland and Russia. Until the early modern period, the Saami had specialist practitioners who served others by drumming and chanting themselves into trance, during which their spirits were believed to venture forth from their bodies to discover the requisite information or effect the necessary work. They had spirit-helpers and their drums were distinctive pieces of magical equipment, often elaborately painted. They represent in effect a westward continuation of the Siberian shamanic province along the Arctic coast of Europe. Archaeology has given their history some back-projection by revealing that ornaments associated with the historical shamanism are present in graves and on settlement sites in Saami territory which date from the beginning of the eleventh century onward.

Just as in Siberia, it did not die naturally. In the seventeenth century the monarchies of Denmark and Sweden partitioned northern Scandinavia between them and launched campaigns to convert the natives to Christianity. The public practice of shamanism was suppressed in a series of persecutions between 1671 and 1724, the period in which the Russian monarchy turned upon it in Siberia.

The methods used were as or more brutal, involving floggings, fines and at least one execution. Rumours of its private continuation persisted for another two hundred years, and the tradition of magical healers who go into trances to effect their cures has never died out among the Saami. Furthermore, just as Siberian shamanism was reflected on its geographical margins in the practices of the Votyaks and the Moslems of Russian Central Asia, so that of the Saami had a buffer zone amongst the Finns. In the nineteenth century the farming people of south-eastern Finland still had a variety of folk magician called the *tietaja*, who was a healer, visionary, diviner and worker of protective magic. In many ways these practitioners corresponded to the European cunning folk, but with the crucial additions that they went into trances before their clients, recited or sang invocations to spirits in these performances, and sent out special spectral helpers in the form of dogs to do battle with evil entities. This package relates them very clearly to the shamans of the Saami and Siberians.[20]

The much greater depth of documentation in European history – even in the north – allows a dimension of study to Saami and Finnish shamanism which is missing in Siberia. The oldest certain reference to Eurasian shamanism in the world seems, indeed, to be an entry concerning Saami magicians in the *Historia Norvegiae*, a Latin text written at some point between 1170 and 1190 by somebody familiar with eastern Norway. It is an account given by Norse merchants among the Saami who observed performances intended to restore a woman sick to the point of death. The first of them was by a man carrying a magical instrument, who sang and danced until he fell down in a trance. After he had lain a while, his stomach burst open, and he died. The Norse were told that his spirit had gone forth from his body, and taken to the sea in the shape of a whale. The latter had been torn open by colliding with some stakes, destroying both the spirit-body and its human host. The second performer did succeed in healing the woman, using a sieve-shaped instrument (almost certainly a drum) painted with whales, reindeer, skis, sledges and a small boat with oars; images representing the vehicles by which his spirit could range the world once he had entered trance.[21] The essential uniformity of this account with both later Saami and later Siberian shamanism should be obvious, and has important implications for both. As seen, the text was written in the later twelfth century, and may have been composed then, but the entry in question may have been a hundred years older. It thus proves that a shamanism of the Siberian sort was already functioning in northern Eurasia at least a century before William of Rubruck visited Mongolia and four hundred years before Richard Johnson reached the Nenets. The origins of Siberian shamanism can therefore be fairly securely pushed back to the opening of the second millennium, and the theory of a Buddhist origin for it becomes considerably weaker; the Saami are a very long way from Buddhists, even if the latter can be proved to have had any impact on Siberia at that remote date. On the other hand, the lack of a definite archaeological context for Saami shamanism before about the year 1000 makes it difficult to argue conclusively that it had not developed, or arrived from the east, a century or two before the Norse recorded it. What seems definite is that while Siberian material is often cited as having importance for the study of European spirituality, the reverse is also true.

The richest source of information on magico-religious traditions in the Scandinavian world consists of thirteenth-century Icelandic literature, and this confirms the high reputation of Saami magicians among the Norse. One text, *Vatnsdaela Saga*, features a prophetess and three diviners of that people, who are hired by Norse chieftains. The diviners were asked to trace a missing amulet, and did so by going into trance for three days and nights, in which time their own spirits wandered abroad and found it. Saami or Finnish trance-magic also features as a distinctive, exotic and potent kind of sorcery in *Ynglinga Saga*, *St Olaf's Saga* and *Fostbroeda Saga*. At times, the same literature portrays the Norse themselves as using similar techniques. In *Harvardar Saga* a warrior skilled in magic is overcome by drowsiness, and lies on the ground covering his head with a cape. His spirit then leaves his body to duel with that of an enemy until he obtains the victory. *Eirik's Saga* contains a detailed portrait of a seeress called Thorbjorg, who had allegedly served the Norse settlements in Greenland three centuries before. She is invited to feasts by those who wish to know the future, and arrives in a distinctive costume: a blue mantle adorned with precious stones, a necklace of glass beads, a black lambskin hood lined with white cat's fur, a belt with a large pouch containing charms, calfskin shoes with long laces, catskin gloves lined with white fur, and a staff tipped with a brass knob studded with more stones. She sits on a platform amid a circle of women, one of whom sings set words to call spirits to her so that she can commune with them.

This is very clearly a shamanic performance, of a sort to which there are close parallels right across Siberia; but there is nobody else like Thorbjorg in this whole body of literature. The other example, of the warrior engaging in a spirit-duel, is only an echo of the practices of Saami or Siberian shamans. His action is apparently not voluntary, and the trance which overcomes him is not induced by a process of performance. None the less, it is a good deal closer to shamanic workings than anything else in the Icelandic texts, except the portraits of the Greenland seeress and of the Saami and Finns themselves. The nearest comparable episode in the Celtic literatures is found in a medieval Irish tale, *The Siege of Drum Damhgaire*, where two druids serving rival kingdoms fly up into the air to fight each other. One wears a striking costume of a feathered cap and leather cloak. The bodies in which they fly are, however, their normal physical selves, transported into the air by magic; the warrior in the Icelandic saga stands midway between the two different traditions, and combines elements of both. Whether all should be seen as aspects of shamanism, positioned at points on a common spectrum, or whether the Saami and Siberian tradition of spirit-flight is the 'truly' shamanic one, is a matter for individual choice. It is important here merely to note that there are differences.

In general it seems true that the Icelandic literature, and the pan-Norse world which it reflects, lies in a frontier zone, or a cross-roads, of distinct magical cultures. The clearly shamanic element was only one of several reflected in it, and not the most important. Magic is a major theme of many sagas, and worked in many different ways; most often by chanting spells, by carving symbols, or by unleashing innate or acquired spiritual power. One means of effecting it which does have relevance to Siberian practice is that of shape-shifting, usually employed by evil characters who are destroyed while attempting to harm others. It takes two forms in the sagas: either the person alters the shape of her or his physical body into that of an animal, or sleeps while his or her spirit goes abroad and assumes an apparently solid animal shape. Both afford the opportunity for a sorcerer or witch to roam at speeds, into places, and with powers, not possible to a human body.[22] This ability is known across the rest of Europe, in both literary and folk tradition and from ancient times to the present, as one of the characteristics of a worker of powerful magic; above all, of the maleficent kind. Its similarity to Siberian and Saami shamanism is obvious, but so also should be its difference: shape-shifting is conceived of as a technique used in the normal, physical, world, without any association with spirit-helpers, trance-states or performances before audiences, and is intended for the private benefit of the magician or of people who have secretly hired the latter. It is essentially a separate phenomenon although, as in the case of the unfortunate Saami magician in the *Historia Norvegiae*, it can overlap with shamanism of the Siberian sort.

The two magico-religious complexes are dramatically differentiated in another way: native Siberians do not seem to have believed in witches. As shown, they attributed uncanny and capricious misfortune to the operation of malevolent spirits which were a part of the natural order. If these were directed at all by human agency, then this was thought to be the work of shamans employed by rival clans, or else by enemies within the same social group who had hired a shaman to carry on a personal feud by magical means. What is apparently lacking is the presence of a stereotypical figure found in many parts of the world, to whom the English gave the name of witch. This person uses what are believed to be supernatural means to harm others, working in particular against other member of the same community. She or he is either inherently evil or in the grip of an evil force, and motivated by envy and malice rather than the lure of straightforward material gain. This person operates in a tradition, either by inheritance, training or initiation, and does not represent an isolated or unique phenomenon. It is possible to oppose and thwart the witch-figure, by using counter-magic, or by forcing him or her to rescind spells, or by eliminating her or him directly.[23]

Although the 'black' shamans of the Buryats corresponded in some respects to this stereotype, they differed in their public and recognized formal status, and in the fact that their powers were regarded as having some potential utility, at least for some members of their communities. They had something of the ambivalent character of many of the wise-folk or cunning-folk of Europe, who were likewise credited with the potential both to heal and curse, and with similar local magicians across the world. By contrast, the witch-figure worked in secret, and when detected had either to be neutralized or removed. It is true that English translators have sometimes found 'witches' in the traditional stories of the Buryats and some Turkic-speaking peoples, but these are always superhuman females, overcome by heroes in creation legends.[24] When Siberians felt themselves or their dependents to be the victims of uncanny bad luck or illness, they resorted to shamans to remove it by defeating or propitiating the spirits responsible. The shamans did not operate by detecting and accusing other other human beings in the same community, who would be held directly responsible for the affliction concerned and forced to lift it, or else be removed themselves in order to break its power at source. There is no structural reason why they should not have done so: the figures whom scholars have called shamans in the Arctic zone of North America specialized in witch-finding, assisted by their spirit-helpers in classic shamanic performances. This tradition has been found from the Tlingit of Alaska eastward across the whole continent to the Eskimo of eastern Greenland, but it did not obtain in Siberia. This is one of the ways in which the Bering Strait represents a genuine cultural division, despite the many similarities between the peoples on the opposite shores of the divide. Belief in the witch-figure is another feature which marks off the Siberian shamanic province to the west, for that figure is found in ancient or early medieval European texts and, notoriously, was made the focus of sometimes sensational legal persecution in the early modern period. It does not seem to feature in Saami tradition; but it does, strongly, in Finnish folk-beliefs and in the Icelandic literature, alongside the elements of shamanism. Once again, Norse and Finnish cultures can be seen to exist in a boundary zone. According to all these criteria, shamanism of the Siberian sort can be identified confidently among the Saami, Finns and Votyaks, but only traces of it can be detected among the other peoples of northern Europe, from the Urals to the Atlantic, and those are the groups immediately neighbouring to the Saami themselves.

What of southern Europe? Here two diferent academic traditions, with separate geographical starting-points, have produced diametrically opposed suggestions. One is rooted in Hungary. The major part played by that nation's academics in studies of Siberian shamanism has been described earlier, together with its its motivating force, the need to define more securely a national identity for their state. The Hungarian race, the Magyars, migrated into Central Europe from the east in the tenth century. Their language proves them to have been kin to the Khants and Mansi, and it seems logical that their culture may have once have included other traits in common with the tribes of north-western Siberia. One of these was of course shamanism, and indeed Hungarian popular tradition had contained a figure, the *taltos*, who could be equated with the shaman. Just as in Siberia, this practitioner was only one of a number of different magical specialists to operate within local society, and the special distinction awarded to him or her by modern scholars has been a reflection of their preoccupations rather than those of the people under study. Although mentioned in seventeenth- and eighteenth-century Hungarian documents, the *taltos* is mostly recorded in folklore collected in the last two hundred years. Common features perceived between this figure and Siberian shamans are to be born with a remarkable distinguishing feature (such as teeth or an extra bone); to undergo an initiatory experience in childhood (a convulsive illness, a mysterious period of disappearance, or a dream of being dismembered); to acquire unusual powers thereafter (such as those of vanishing at will, changing shape into that of an animal, or duelling with enemies in spirit-flight); and to use special equipment (such as a feathered or horned head-dress, a drum or a sieve). Vilmos Dioszegi found this sufficient to declare that the *taltos* was the Magyar shaman, brought in the migration from Siberia. If this were the case, then the Magyars represent a southern parallel to the Saami, an isolated example of 'classic' shamanism of the Siberian sort which had some influence on the other European peoples around.[25]

The other tradition is rooted in Italy, and in the work of Carlo Ginzburg. This outstanding historian first made his name by revealing to the modern world the former existence of the *benandanti*. These were individuals once found in the north-eastern Italian province of Friuli, born with cauls and believed to have the ability to send forth their spirits from their sleeping bodies at night. Their particular purpose in doing so was to do battle with the spirit-forms of witches to defend the fertility of the local farmlands. This belief disappeared during the seventeenth century, largely because of persecution by the local Inquisition, which stigmatized the *benandanti* as themselves inspired by demons. Ginzburg immediately commented upon the apparent connection between the belief and the shamanic tradition of spirit-flight.[26] A Hungarian colleague, Gabor Klaniczay, soon located the *benendanti* as lying at the western geographical extreme of a spectrum of beliefs found in more recent folklore across the Balkans as far as Bulgaria and Hungary. They concerned human beings who possessed the gift of sending their spirits forth at night to protect their own communities from spectral attacks by witches or by members of rival villagers. Some were marked off by special features at birth such as the caul of the *benandanti*. At the Hungarian end of its range, this figure was represented by the *taltos*.

Carlo Ginzburg subsequently linked this material to records from Romania, Serbia and Macedonia, of magicians who communed with spirits while in trance, as clear evidence of 'typically shamanic rituals in a European setting'. He then proposed a much larger and more important conclusion: that the early modern European tradition of the witches' sabbath had drawn upon a pan-Eurasian one of the spirit-flight of shamans, which had inspired folk-beliefs as disparate as Scottish reports of a Queen of Elfane and her fairy followers, the Germanic tradition of the Wild Hunt, and the Italian one of the hosts of women who rode at night with the goddess Diana.[27] In this manner he explicitly rejected the diffusionist thesis of

Dioszegi, and added instead a further component to the universalist vision of Eliade. His interpretation depended on the characterization of shamanism as the ancient ecstatic technique of Eurasia, and greatly enriched it by proposing that the same technique lay behind much European folklore and a distinctive feature of early modern demonology.

Both approaches have their problems. The composite portrait of the Magyar *taltos* does indeed look strikingly similar to a shaman, but its elements tend not to appear together in the same tales; rather, they have been collected from different pieces of folklore in which they feature as individual details. None of them, even fitted together, suffice to turn the *taltos* into a figure who helps others by working with spirits in a dramatic public performance; the three most obvious attributes of the Siberian practitioner are missing. Mihaly Hoppál, Dioszegi's successor as the leading Hungarian expert in the field, concluded that there 'is no unambiguous indication of the place of shamanism in the ideology of the Hungarian settlers'.[28] Moreover, the geography of folk custom also counts against the diffusionist hypothesis. If Magyar shamanism had been the root of all the Balkan traditions of nocturnal spirit-battles, then the latter should radiate out from an epicentre in the main area of Magyar settlement. Instead, the cases in which the *taltos* is credited with waging spiritual combat to defend communities are all comparatively late in the recorded history of that figure – from the end of the eighteenth century – and concentrated on the southern fringe of Hungary.[29] The epicentre of these traditions of night-battles by the spirits of sleeping humans to protect themselves and their neighbours from harm is firmly in the South Slav lands – in Slovenia, Croatia, Bulgaria and Macedonia. To place these traditions under the heading of shamanism is to conceal how distinctive a regional belief it is. When Carlo Ginzburg found parallels for them, they were not from the Magyars or northern Slav regions but from the opposite coast of the Black Sea, in the western Caucasus.[30] Klaniczay pointed out from the beginning, and Ginzburg accepted, the crucial difference between them and Siberian shamanism: that the South Slav spirit-flights were experienced by private individuals during sleep, while those of Siberia were induced in the process of a public performance. To Klaniczay, this was enough to mean that the former were 'not shamanism proper'.[31]

Patterns of belief and custom, however, are rarely that neat and convenient, and the Balkan region does preserve one record of shamanism of the Siberian sort. In 1648 the Italian churchman Marco Bandini made a journey through Moldavia, now the eastern province of Romania. He found there 'sorcerers' whom the local population held in high esteem. They had the ability to see the future, cure illnesses and find stolen objects. Their technique was to chose a special place in which to work, and then to begin to whimper, twist their heads, roll their eyes, contort their mouths, grimace and shake all over. They then fell to the ground with hands and feet spreadeagled and lay motionless for up to four hours. When they recovered, they told their clients what they had seen.[32] Bandini did not make it clear whether these magicians worked with spirits, but the similarity of their mode of operation to that of shamans is obvious enough, and demands explanation. Bandini encountered no other practitioners like them during his travels, and they are not recorded anywhere else in the Balkans. Dioszegi suggested that they were associated with the Tchango, a Magyar tribe which had migrated into Moldavia and which might have taken a Siberian style of shamanism with them.[33] This is possible, but not susceptible of proof, and (as seen) the existence of Magyar shamanism is itself controversial. Another possibility is that the Moldavian practice was inspired by the trances of Islamic mystics (dervishes) in the neighbouring Ottoman Empire, and had developed independently into a technique resembling Siberian shamanism. When all is said and done, however, it remains true that popular customs can disperse and develop in apparently capricious ways. Another one recorded in what is now Romania is that of young men who supplied public parades and entertainments under the patronage of a mythical empress 'Irodeasa'. This is clearly a garbled version of Herodias, the supernatural female who led people in nocturnal processions and revels in stories recorded in Western Europe, and especially in Italy, from the middle ages onwards.[34] How she got to the far end of the Balkans is anybody's guess. Likewise, folk drama found in Greek communities in Macedonia and Asia Minor by the early twentieth century displayed a striking resemblance to the English Mummers' Play, but nobody has yet provided a convincing explanation for the similarity.[35] The magicians of Moldavia are in a rich tradition of cultural anomaly.

That tradition serves, however, to reinforce a situation in which scholars are able to construct hypotheses more or less according to their personal or ideological predispositions, whether these be to think in terms of ethnic, national or supranational identity, pan-human experience or local particularism, archaic survival or historical evolution. In this situation the terms 'shaman', 'shaman-ism', and 'shamanic' correspond neither to agreed conceptual categories nor to precise intellectual tools so much as to materials upon an artist's palette, with which academics create compositions of emotive and polemical power. This may indeed be a proper reflection of the status of expert knowledge in a post-modern world, and in those disciplines which have traditionally claimed to be arts rather than sciences – such as history – it is not an unfamiliar state of affairs. There may, however, be a deeper reason for the existence of it in the particular case of shamanism.

In the year 1720 a Swedish servant girl called Catharina Fagerberg, who wove linen in a baronial household, became afflicted with severe depression and anxiety, and blasphemous and murderous thoughts. After seven years, these were joined by pains, convulsions and semi-paralysis. Her sufferings ended when a 'good spirit' informed her that she was possessed by demons, and she expelled the latter by prayer. Her spirit-friend then told her that she had thereby acquired the power to perform the same service for others, and she proceeded to build up a considerable reputation as a healer of mysterious mental and physical afflictions. Treating these as the product of possession by evil entities, she cast out the latter by laying her hands on the sufferers and telling them to trust in God. In 1732 she was put on trial for these activities, but was acquitted when a clergyman testified to her piety and good character. Her belief-system shows a classic early-modern European mixture of 'learned' and 'popular' cultures, resting at one end on Scripture and a specifi-cally Lutheran theology of angels and demons, and at the other on

older and more localized traditions such as elf-shot and the tendency
of spirits to take animal forms.[36]

Had Fagerberg grown up in a native Siberian society, she would
certainly have become a shaman, and the Swedish academic who
has studied her, Carl-Martin Edsman, has pointed out the clear
parallels to shamanism in her story. Whether she herself should be
termed a shaman is a matter for individual scholarly judgement;
Edsman himself preferred to call her a 'folk-healer', and labels such
as 'faith-healer' or 'exorcist' seem just as culturally and technically
apposite. What must be significant is that a common point of
departure with that of shamans led to a different expression of the
same abilities, involving a much greater degree of tension with
the parent culture, and a proportionately greater difficulty in
assimilating her skills to dominant frameworks of belief.

I myself have a woman friend who is now in middle life and has
settled in the suburbs of an English city. In her youth she was
contacted by disembodied voices whom she identified as spirits and
whose promptings she ignored and resisted for years. One day, weary
of the struggle, she acknowledged their presence and asked them
what they wanted, whereupon 'they all cheered'. She then began to
work with them, and their advice and companionship helped to
steer her into a successful career as a therapist and healer, specializing in mysterious illnesses and emotional problems, and as an
adviser to individuals who experienced parapsychological phenomena similar to her own. She is not the only person of this kind
whom I have met personally; she is simply the one whom I know
best. On hearing her story, I was immediately struck by its resemblance to the formative experiences of a Siberian shaman, but when
undergoing her own development she had never heard of shamanism. If she located herself in any tradition, it was the
nineteenth-century western one of Spiritualism, and there was a
history of mediumship in her family; the hereditary element in her
situation is, of course, another parallel with Siberia. Later she found
others points of reference in native American culture, as filtered
through modern American authors and teachers. There is little
doubt that, in the context of aboriginal Siberia, she would have
become a shaman. In modern Britain, however, she has never found

any public role in which her experiences and qualities could be given expression, or even discussed. Far from being socially valued, they were not even socially respectable. In general, they were not recognised at all.

Piers Vitebsky seems to be correct, therefore, in suggesting that the traits which underpin Siberian shamanism occur naturally in individuals throughout humanity, although they are given different cultural expression at particular times and places. In Siberia, during recorded history, they were expressed in an unusually spectacular and socially esteemed manner. In early modern Europe they could be given a public role only with some difficulty and danger, and in the modern world they can hardly be expressed at all. The fact that western scholars have had to go to the far end of Eurasia to find a term for something apparently inherent in humanity may be directly related to this lack of recognition, as is the confusing breadth of phenomena to which it is now applied. At the heart of the modern scholarly fascination with what is called shamanism, and confusion over it, lies an unease caused by a wilful failure of comprehension.

12

The Discovery of a Shamanic Future

The time has come to return to Siberia, for some final reflections. Back in 1957, when Vilmos Dioszegi first proposed to visit the region to collect material for a study of shamanism, he received nothing but discouragement from his Soviet colleagues. They told him that the time when such an expedition would yield anything of value was long past, that shamanism had died out, and that his visit would amount to nothing but 'tourism'.[1] In a sense their attitude can be understood and forgiven, for they were recalling their own work in the 1920s and 1930s, when shamanism was still a living force in native society, and it was perfectly true that their own regime had stamped it out in the intervening decades. None the less, Dioszegi recovered a large trove of valuable data by talking to elderly people about their memories, and he remained heartily grateful that he had ignored the attempts to dissuade him from what proved to be such an important mission.

I should have borne his experiences in mind during my own travels in the Soviet Union in the mid 1980s, when experts informed me confidently that shamanism was completely extinct, and that all the former practitioners of it had died before 1970. I repeated that claim in a minor publication of my own,[2] and my shame in having done so is eased only slightly by the fact that scholars of more celebrity in the subject than myself, and with more freedom of movement, were fed the same sort of information.[3] The latter was itself part of the campaign of annihilation. At that period a relatively large number of people still survived who had been children at the time when shamans were active in native societies, and many more who had been told of that time by their parents. Even these, however, were not always willing to talk about such matters. Caroline Humphrey, who lived in a Buryat community in the 1960s and 1970s, later recalled how 'a grimly familiar cloud would descend if I brought up the subject',[4] and just the same could be said of my own experience. On the whole, people were willing to speak more freely if their comments were mocking or dismissive, although these too could sometimes have some real historical value; my favourite recollection of this sort was from a man who had worked in his youth on the Trans-Siberian railway. He remembered resentfully how a shaman in full ceremonial gear had come up to him and demanded money with the threat of using his powers to disrupt the signalling system if none was paid over.

It is quite certain that a number of former shamans survived into the 1980s. The question of whether any remained active is more difficult to resolve. Vladimir Basilov seemed genuinely undecided on the matter. Writing in 1984, he was unaware of any working in Siberia proper, but thought that they possibly still operated in the Islamic territories of Soviet Central Asia, where they had been absorbed into mainstream religious culture. Furthermore he had seen a photograph allegedly taken in Tuva in 1983, showing a female Soyot apparently performing as a shaman. He followed these observations, however, with a restatement of the party line, declaring that, if any did still exist, then 'the general tendency of the development of society inevitably dooms them to gradual extinction'.[5] An American anthroplogist working amongst the Sakha in the same period did not hear of any, but noted that people in private still told stories celebrating the prowess of the great shamans of old.[6] By apparent sharp contrast, the Buryat academic Taras Mikhailov could complain in 1987 that shamanism was still 'vigorous and persistent' among his people.[7] It is possible that he was literally correct, and that the Buryats were a striking exception to the rule; but once again the definitional problem may be at stake. Mikhailov never explained what he meant here by shamanism; if he was using it to cover old magico-religious customs in general, such as spells, charms and offerings, or else faith-healing and divination of all kinds, then the apparent anomaly is explained.

Attitudes to the subject were to change dramatically, like so much else, towards the end of the decade. An anticipation of this may be found in the work of the first native Siberian to emerge as a

world-class creative writer, the Chukchi Yuri Rytkheu. At the opening of the 1980s he was still subscribing to the official historical
orthodoxy that the Soviet state had been the saviour of aboriginal
peoples, emancipating them from servitude and demoralization. He
followed it likewise in contrasting this supposed benevolence and
wisdom with the destructive exploitation of traditional peoples by
capitalist states. What set his work off from the norm is that he was
already prepared to suggest that there had been some merits in the
traditional Chukchi way of life, and that his people should be
allowed to decide for themselves how much of it should be retained
or abandoned. By 1986 he was prepared to extend this argument to
shamanism, holding up its former practitioners for respect as individuals gifted in healing, wisdom and poetry. Two years later he
began to launch an all-out attack on what he now regarded as the
myths propagated to justify and extenuate Soviet Russian rule over
native Siberians, and to declare that the latter had in fact been
exploited and misled.[8]

By this time the Soviet system itself was beginning to disintegrate,
and the 1990s brought in a period in which Siberian natives were
able to campaign openly for greater local autonomy and a better
share of the profits of their former territories, and were relatively
free to revive selected features of their traditional cultures. To some
extent they have succeeded in all three. The place of shamanism in
this process is a complex one, and can be illustrated here by some
case-studies. One is from the Buryat village of Oost Oordat, where
some British musicians travelling the region in 1997 were introduced
to an inhabitant who was described to them as a hereditary shaman.
He claimed to have inherited the power on the death of his grandfather, a blacksmith, and now employed it as a healer. His sole
method was to move his hands over a person's body from head to
foot, cleansing it of evil spirits. One of the musicians later found an
identical exercise described in a book on Chinese medicine. Whether
the Buryat had been taught it by his forebear, or discovered it himself,
was never made clear, but he also gave a classic display of apparent
superhuman abilities of the sort long recorded of shamans, and one
which he specifically claimed to have been shown by his grandfather;
he passed a red-hot knife between his lips.[9] What at first sight seems

to be a straightforward case of the revival of tradition, therefore, becomes more problematic on closer inspection. The hereditary claim is unproven, the special costume, equipment, ceremonial, initiatory ritual and range of expertise of the older shamanism are all missing, and the provenance of the actual healing method used is uncertain. Siberian shamanism had always employed a wide range of practices, but this one does not seem to feature among them, and it is not one of those which have been used to distinguish shamanism from other kinds of magico-religious phenomena.

In Tuva, matters are yet more complicated. By the time that the musicians visited it, on the same journey, a number of different sorts of local personalities had assumed the name of shaman. One was a musician, who claimed to call up spirits during his stage show, and by this means automatically to cleanse the whole audience of evil forces. Another was the curator of the state museum in the capital, Kyzyl, who was using his academic expertise to encourage a revival of both the native religion and shamanism. A third was a Buddhist monk, who had also begun to claim to heal by shamanic means.[10] By 1998 a guild of shamans, the Association of the Tambour (drum), had been established in Kyzyl, apparently under the auspices of the museum curator. It had premises in a building divided into various offices, with a waiting room for clients and a number of practitioners in residence wearing traditional shamanic costumes and working for fees. The customers were called in by them for one-to-one consultations, as at a medical centre. A British journalist who visited the building in that year formed the impression that these treatments lasted an average ten minutes, and thought them a travesty of the old shamanism. He was, however, impressed by the Buddhist, who proved to be self-educated, both in his religion and in shamanism. He operated mainly as a herbalist, but also sometimes drove away evil spirits by drumming, chanting, and dancing in full costume, after the classic manner. He condemned the Association of the Tambour as novices.[11] That association has continued to flourish, and has developed into a tourist attraction.[12]

Similar complexities exist in attempting to unravel attitudes to shamanism since the end of the Soviet Union among the peoples of eastern central Siberia, the territory of the newly-established

Sakha Republic. Here information is available from studies made by western academics. In the early 1990s Piers Vitebsky found that the former shamans who survived among the Evens either accepted the abandonment of their vocation and were prepared to talk about it, or seemed still to believe in it but were very reticent. Shamanism had died out completely as an organized public practice, and various other forms of divination had expanded to fill the gap; Vitebsky felt that the Evens had become a 'post-shamanistic' society.[13]

The same label could well be applied to his portrait of the Sakha themselves during that period, although with differences occasioned by a much larger and more elaborate social group. He found only eight shamans identifiable at that period among a total Sakhan population of over 350,000. There was, however, a growing use of the term 'shamanism' to characterize the traditional, pre-Christian, religion. A revival of the latter was being sponsored by societies in the capital, Yakutsk, which consisted mostly of professional people like the museum director at Kyzyl. These regarded the old religion as being associated with ancient healing wisdom, and with the epic traditions of the Sakha, and used it as a metaphor for a caring relationship with the land. The latter was given a political edge by a concern to prevent the continued exploitation of Sakhan natural resources by Russians and other outsiders. The Minister for Culture then in office commented that 'shamanism is a void at the heart of things; everyone circles it and no one knows how to get in'.[14]

The few who thought that they had 'got in' were made the subject of a study by an American anthropologist, Marjorie Mandelstam Balzer, who also worked in the Sakha Republic in the early 1990s.[15] One was Vladimir Kondakov, the president of a newly-established Association of Folk Medicine and a healer who travelled widely to cure people in public performances. In 1991 he had assumed the label of *oyun*, but his right to it was denied by other Sakha, especially in Yakutsk, and he himself denounced as charlatans rival individuals who had recently started to portray themselves as shamans. He had acquired a costume and a drum, but it was not clear that he believed in spirit-helpers or entered trance; his only verifiable technique was to wave away 'bad energy' from clients with his hands. He claimed to have been trained by a famous old *oyun*, but his knowledge of Sakhan shamanism seemed to derive mainly from the old ethnographic studies.

The most respected of the newly-appeared Sakhan shamans at the time of Balzer's study was a young man who had acquired a formidable reputation as a magical healer. Like Kondakov he claimed to have been trained by an experienced *oyun* left over from the old days, and thus to stand in an unbroken tradition, but he provided more details of what this training had involved, which allow insights into the ways in which shamanism had survived or mutated during the decades of Soviet persecution. One such practitioner was a herbalist who also 'said incantations' and gave 'ritual massages', another a healer who cured people by calling his spirits as of old, but was very careful to work without drum or costume, and to avoid using the name of *oyun*. The former seems hard to distinguish from Western European practitioners of traditional cunning craft or modern 'alternative' medicine, while the latter was clearly a shaman in disguise.

The status of shamanism in post-Soviet Siberia is therefore both significant and problematic. Public attitudes to it are reversing rapidly, but it remains a contested area in which conflicts of both individual and national identity are subsumed. Elements of survival, revival, re-creation and re-imagining are all present and productive of controversy. In the process the lack of definition attached to the label of 'shaman' is assuming a new significance. All this makes for a situation quite complicated enough, but it is beginning to acquire a further dimension of complexity in its emerging relationship with a parallel movement in the West.

This appeared in the 1980s, and has been most commonly characterized as 'neoshamanism' or 'urban shamanism'. It represents an application to modern needs of techniques derived to some extent from traditional peoples, of the sort which scholars have dubbed shamanic. In the context of the present work, four aspects of it in particular deserve emphasis. The first is that, although it has spread throughout the western world, it is based in the United States and on the writings of two American anthropologists, Carlos Castaneda and Michael Harner. Both used studies of magical practices in tribal societies in Central and South America to provide examples of healing and personal transformation for people in industrialized nations. Both subsequently left the academy in order to write and teach for lay audiences, and indeed the authenticity of Castaneda's original fieldwork has been called into question; which has done little to diminish the popularity of his books. Overwhelmingly, the traditions on which the literature of this movement draws have been native American; when another of its most prominent authors, Nevill Drury, provided a series of cameos of tribal shamanism for his readers, every one of them came from the North American continent. None the less, Siberia still features in such works as the traditional source of information on the subject, and its shamanism is treated as the same phenomenon.

This is of some importance, because the relationships between native American cultures, native Siberian cultures and the scholarly construct of shamanism are by no means straightforward. Most of the characteristics of Siberian shamanism suggested above are also found in North America: the existence of specialists working with spirits to heal, divine, blight or defend; the use of entranced states and special equipment by these people; and the provision of performances by them before audiences. They are, however, not a consistent feature of native American society, but found singly or in various different combinations among particular peoples scattered across the continent. The role of the native American 'medicine men' is much slighter than that of the Siberian shamans, and they would probably not have received much special attention from scholars had it not been for the interest generated by the Siberian figures. This is largely because most young native men east of the Rocky Mountains passed through an initiation rite characterized by withdrawal, isolation and contact with guardian spirits; in other words, many of the formative experiences of Siberian shamans were undergone, in diluted form, by virtually all the male population. The medicine men only differed from the latter in degree, not in kind. Furthermore, these specialists rarely made spirit-flights or were in contact with dead ancestors who advised and empowered them. The peoples on the continent who had produced a shamanism most similar to that of Siberia were those who were geographically closest to the latter, especially the Inuit

of the Arctic regions. Some American natives have reacted vehemently against attempts by scholars to incorporate their culture
into the contruct of shamanism. Inez M. Talamantez, an Apache
who is Professor of Religious Studies at the University of California
at Santa Barbara, has declared of such attempts: 'they are stealing
our religion by calling our medicine men shamans ... Our language does not know shamans, and that name is used only by
neo-shamans; not our chanters'.

Such complex and difficult issues need to be borne in mind when
contemplating the 'core shamanism' which Harner developed from
his American materials to market to the developed world, as the
basic set of practices common to shamans the world over. It was
important to his interpretation that they were regarded as both
ancient and once universal; in other words they were ultimately part
of everybody's inheritance instead of being part of the culture of
certain peoples. Indeed, his distillation of them could be presented
as in some respects superior to their application in a tribal setting,
because they could achieve much faster results. Modern westerners
who learned them were 'returned to the eternal community of the
shaman, unlimited by the boundaries of space and time'.

Readers of Harner's textbook and customers at his workshops
learned techniques designed to lead them into an altered state of
consciousness in which they could perceive entrances to otherworlds
and go through them to explore spiritual landscapes. These techniques included steady repetitive rhythms on drum or rattle. Forms
of meditative dance allowed people to discover the form of animal
to whom they naturally corresponded and which could then function as their guardian spirit. They could then learn how to make
visionary journeys to restore power to themselves or to others, and
to heal, and to extract spiritual substances from the bodies of
patients which had been impairing their physical or mental health.
There are undoubtedly Siberian parallels for each component of
this assemblage; whether they represent the essence of Siberian
shamanism (which is after all Harner's claim), or a reworking of a
few features of it which are more important in the Americas, is not
a question which can be so easily resolved.[16]

The second aspect of neoshamanism which needs consideration

here is the relationship of the movement with Mircea Eliade. In essence, it was created by the combination of the creative writing of Castaneda and the practical manuals and workshops of Harner, and relies more on operative techniques and concepts than on ethnographic examples. None the less, its self-justifying concept of shamanism as a worldwide and ancient phenomenon is very much the vision provided by Eliade, and his book features as a respected text in its literature. It is hard to imagine that neoshamanism would have developed, at least in the form which it has taken, without the excitement with which that work infused the subject. In many ways, it represents a democratization and liberalization of Eliade's concept. In place of his secretly trained and initiated elite of spiritual warriors, pitted against essential evil for the common good, shamans can be anybody willing to learn the core set of practices. Futhermore, they are presumed to operate within a cosmos which is at worst morally neutral and more often essentially benevolent.

A third aspect of the relationship is that the new western shamanism represents a self-conscious, counter-cultural, reversal of attitudes dominant in western societies since those societies first encountered Siberian shamans. Instead of seeking to remove tribal magicians from the world as devil-worshippers, charlatans, maniacs or fanatics, it seeks to imitate some of their methods in order to serve the needs of a society which is increasingly seeking direct and personal experience of spirit-worlds and of divinity outside of institutional and dogmatic frameworks. In this sense it is practising what Eliade and Lewis preached. More than a reversal of sympathies has occurred, however; there has also been a shift of geographical emphasis, reflecting one of political, economic and military power. In the eighteenth century it was native Siberia – Europe's vast and mysterious hinterland – which supplied the main examples of the shaman as Other. Now it is native America, the emotional hinterland of the United States. I have myself, however, regularly seen photographs of Siberians, taken ultimately from the old ethnographic studies, used to advertise 'shamanic workshops' in Britain during the 1990s. The content is based on Harner, but the Siberian label is still potent.

The fourth consideration is that neoshamanism has swiftly

become a conceptual battleground in its own right. One controversy concerns the propriety of its appropriation and marketing of tribal beliefs and customs by members of the developed world; to some the process honours traditional societies, while to others it is a new form of exploitation and theft.[17] Another, less bitter, debate is over the extent to which it can be regarded and studied as the same phenomenon as the traditional techniques on which it is ostensibly based. Some writers have suggested that the word 'shamanism' be confined to societies in which those techniques were customary, and some looser term such as 'shamanic behaviour' used of their application in urbanized and industrialized nations.[18] A number of individuals operating in the latter have preferred to call themselves 'shamanic practitioners' rather than shamans. The absence of agreed definitions inside the academy makes any scholarly resolution of this debate most unlikely. At first sight none of these problems seem to be relevant to the reappearance of people openly identifying themselves as shamans in post-Soviet Siberia. They are, after all, members of societies with an immemorial tradition of such practices, kept up to within living memory and perhaps maintained since then in secret. None the less, the concentration of the new shamans among educated and professional city-dwellers, and the questions which some of them have raised over the authenticity of others, does produce some significant comparisons.

These comparisons, and the more controversial aspects of both the American and the Siberian movements, are likely to increase as they mesh, which is starting to happen at a number of points. In 1996 a book by a Russian author was published in San Francisco, describing a jouney across the Altai in quest of native mysticism and crafted to the tastes of American counter-cultural spirituality. As it made a point of failing to identify places and people with precision, ostensibly to protect the individuals concerned, it is hard to tell how literally the text should be read.[19] A different sort of link was established when the co-owner of a Seattle bookshop devoted to ancient and Eastern religions invited an elder of the Ulchi, one of the small peoples along the Amur, to give a talk in her city. The bookshop-owner concerned had grown up in Hawaii and subsequently become attracted to Taoism, but when she heard the Ulchi speak, she felt that 'This was it. I had found my people'. She has now founded a school in Seattle for the study of Ulchi culture.[20]

These are examples of the appropriation, or honouring, of native Siberian material to enrich contemporary American counter-culture. There is also an opposite form of interaction, whereby counter-cultural ideas from America penetrate Siberia, and the main vehicle for this to date has been Michael Harner's Foundation for Shamanic Studies, the organization set up to teach his 'core shamanism'. One of the devices adopted by the Foundation to meet complaints of exploitation has been to make grants of money to traditional peoples to assist them in preserving or reviving their own shamanic heritage. Inevitably (and reasonably) the practices selected for such reward represent those which conform to the Foundation's notion of what shamanism should be. At the time of writing it seems to have made one grant to native Siberians; this has been to the Association of the Tambour at Kyzyl. The Foundation has, however, gone further, by sending teachers to Tuva and Buryatia to instruct local people in its own 'core shamanism', apparently believing that by doing so it is helping to revive the aboriginal shamanic traditions of those regions. Some indication of the difference between the two is provided by a comment gathered from Buryats who had attended the Americans' workshops; that the latter seemed intent on teaching in two days abilities which in former times had needed years of training.[21]

Negotiating their way through all these changes and paradoxes are the group of scholars most concerned with Siberian shamanism, the academics of the former Soviet Union and its satellite states. For three centuries, until the late 1980s, the dominant tradition within which scholars of their nations had worked had been an imperialist and reformist one, designed to further the abolition of the phenomenon which they were studying, in the name of the improvement of human life. Now the regimes which governed them lost an ideology of hostility towards religiosity and spirituality of virtually any kind, while academic opinion and popular culture in the West tended towards a more sympathetic view of shamanism, as did the nationalist movements of native Siberians. Not enough time has passed for the impact of all these developments to become fully apparent, but a few tendencies are already visible. In 1992 the Hungarian Mihaly Hoppal could already publish his sense of a 'growing recent conviction' among professional scholars that shamanism had possessed 'some therapeutic value'. In that year he attended the first academic conference on the subject ever permitted upon Siberian soil. It was at Yakutsk, 'in a region where not long ago even the mere positive or neutral mention of shamanism was unthinkable'. Now he observed it to have become 'an integral part of identity-building self-awareness' there, and the conference closed with an appearance by a practising shaman, who called on spirits to assist the scholars present; in effect, giving them his blessing.[22] Three years later the American anthropologist Marjorie Balzer published the comment of 'one young ethnographer' among the Sakha:

> I'm more spiritual than I was when you met me in 1985. I've changed a lot. It is partly because I now see the ancient power of shamanism, and believe in some shamans' ability to cure, but it is also because I myself saw a spirit last year at a sacred lake.[23]

Notes

Notes to Introduction

1. On which see I. M. Lewis, 'What is a Shaman?', in Mihaly Hoppál (ed.), *Shamanism in Eurasia* (Göttingen: Herodot, 1984), pp. 3–12.
2. V. Voigt, 'Shaman: Person or Word', in Hoppál (ed.), *Shamanism in Eurasia*, p. 14; Gloria Flaherty, *Shamanism and the Eighteenth Century* (Princeton New Jersey: Princeton University Press, 1992), passim.
3. Lewis, 'What is a Shaman?', pp. 3–12; Voigt, 'Shaman-Person or Word?', pp. 13–20; R. Gilberg, 'How to Recognise a Shaman among Other Religious Specialists', in Hoppál (ed.), *Shamanism in Eurasia*, pp. 21–27; Gustav Rank, 'Shamanism as a Research Subject', in Carl-Martin Edsman (ed.), *Studies in Shamanism* (Stockholm: Almqvist and Wiksell, 1967), pp. 15–22; Johann Reinhard, 'Shamanism and Spirit-Possession: The Definitional Problem', in John T. Hitchcock and Rex T. Jones (ed.), *Spirit Possession in the Nepal Himalayas* (Warminster: Aries and Phillips, 1976), pp. 12–22; Åke Hultkranz, 'Ecological and Phenomenological Aspects of Shamanism', in Vilmos Dioszegi and Mihaly Hoppál (ed.), *Shamanism in Siberia* (Budapest: Akademiai Kiado, 1978), pp. 27–58, and 'The Place of Shamanism in the History of Religion', in Mihaly Hoppál and Otto von Sadovszky (ed.), *Shamanism Past and Present* (Budapest and Los Angeles: Hungarian Academy of Sciences and International Society for Trans-Oceanic Research, 1989), pp. 43–46; Caroline Humphrey, 'Theories of North Asian Shamanism', in Ernest Gellner (ed.), *Soviet and Western Anthropology* (London: Duckworth, 1980), pp. 242–44, and 'Shamanic Practices and the State in Northern Asia', in Nicholas Thomas and Caroline Humphrey (ed.), *Shamanism, History and the State* (Ann Arbor: University of Michigan Press, 1994), p. 192; Anna-Leena Siikala, *The Rite Technique of the Siberian Shaman* (Helsinki: FF Communications, Academia Scientarum Fennica, 1987), pp. 311, 319; Nevill Drury, *The Elements of Shamanism* (Shaftesbury: Element, 1989), pp. 1, 11; Roger Walsh, *The Spirit of Shamanism* (Los Angeles: Tarcher, 1990),

pp. 1–35; Mihaly Hoppál, 'Shamanism: An Archaic and/or Recent System of Beliefs', in Anna-Leena Siikala and Mihaly Hoppál, *Studies on Shamanism* (Helsinki and Budapest: Finnish Anthropological Society and Akademiai Kiado, 1992), pp. 117–31; Holger Kalweit, *Shamans, Healers and Medicine Men* (Boston, Massachusetts: Shambhala, 1992), p. 1; Piers Vitebsky, *The Shaman* (London: Macmillan, 1995), pp. 6–11; Roberte Hamayon, 'Are "Trance", "Ecstasy" and Similar Concepts Appropriate in the Study of Shamanism?', in Tae-Gon Kim and Mihaly Hoppál (ed.), *Shamanism in Performing Arts* (Budapest: Akademiai Kiado, 1995), pp. 17–34; Graham Harvey, 'Shamanism in Britain Today', *Performance Research*, 3 (1998), p. 16; Merete Demant Jakobsen, *Shamanism* (New York: Berghahn, 1999), pp. 1–12.

Notes to Chapter 1: The Creation of Siberia

1. Philip Johann Tabbert von Strahlenberg, *An Histori-Geographical Description of the North and Eastern Part of Europe and Asia* (1736).
2. F. A. Golder (ed.), *Bering's Voyages* (New York: American Geographical Society, 1922), i, p. 27; Yuri Semyonov, *Siberia: Its Conquest and Development* (London: Hollis and Carter, 1963), p. 153.
3. Ibid., p. 82.
4. Most of what follows is based on a mixture of personal experience and conversation. It is underpinned, however, by comments in most of the ethnographic literature cited below. For travel accounts spanning the twentieth century, see Bassett Digby, *Tigers, Gold and Witch-Doctors* (London: Bodley Head, 1928); Hugo Portisch, *I Saw Siberia* (London: Harrap, 1972); and Colin Thubron, *In Siberia* (London: Chatto and Windus, 1999).

Notes to Chapter 2: The Creation of Siberians

1. For what follows I have relied particularly on James Forsyth, *A History of the Peoples of Siberia* (Cambridge: Cambridge University Press, 1992), with additional material from Waldemar Bogoras, *The Chukchi* (Leiden: Brill, 1908), pp. 1–15; Waldemar Jochelson, *The Koryak* (Leiden: Brill, 1908), 406–7, and *The Yukaghir and the Yukagirized Tungus* (Leiden: Brill, 1926), pp. 2–16; A. Wood and R. A. French (ed.), *The Development of Siberia* (London: Macmillan, 1989), passim; Victor L. Mote, *Siberia: Worlds Apart* (Boulder, Colorado: Westview, 1998),

passim; S. A. Artiunov, 'Koryak and Itelmen', and 'Chukchi', in William W. Fitzhugh and Aron Crowell (ed.), *Crossroads of Continents* (Washington DC: Smithsonian Institution, 1988), pp. 31–35, 39–42.

2. It appears as accepted fact in Yuri Semyonov, *Siberia: Its Conquest and Development* (London: Hollis and Carter, 1963), p. 241. More ingeniously, Terence Armstrong, *Russian Settlement in the North* (Cambridge: Cambridge University Press, 1965), p. 119, argues that some native groups did disappear, but by absorption into others; which means that they survived under a different name. That such arguments were found in the Soviet Union is suggested by the declaration of the Association of the Peoples of the North, cited below.

3. Mote, *Siberia*, pp. 176–77.

4. This is once again based mainly on Forsyth. The information concerning the Enets is from Yekaterina D. Prokofyeva, 'The Costume of an Enets Shaman', in Henry N. Michael (ed.), *Studies in Siberian Shamanism* (Toronto: University of Toronto Press, 1963), p. 124.

5. Forsyth, *History*, pp. 74–81; Bogoras, *The Chukchee*, pp. 15–18; Jochelson, *The Koryak*, pp. 783–805; I. S. Gurvich, 'Ethnic Connections across the Bering Strait', in Fitzhugh and Crowell (ed.), *Crossroads of Continents*, pp. 20–21.

Notes to Chapter 3: The Transformation of Siberians

1. This summary, and much of what follows, is based on James Forsyth, *A History of the Peoples of Siberia* (Cambridge: Cambridge University Press, 1992), pp. 11–82; Terence Armstrong, *Russian Settlement in the North* (Cambridge: Cambridge University Press, 1965), pp. 14–113; Yuri Semyonov, *Siberia: Its Conquest and Development* (London: Hollis and Carter, 1963), pp. 1–241; David N. Collins, 'Russia's Conquest of Siberia', *European Studies Review*, 12 (1982), pp. 17–44.

2. Forsyth, *History*, p. 160.

3. Ibid., pp. 1–53, 122; Semyonov, *Siberia*, pp. 1–61; Vilmos Dioszegi, 'Pre-Islamic Shamanism of the Baraba Turks', in Dioszegi and Mihaly Hoppál (ed.), *Shamanism in Siberia* (Budapest: Akademiai Kiado, 1978), p. 83.

4. Victor Mote, *Siberia: Worlds Apart* (Boulder, Colorado: Westview, 1998), p. 71; Forsyth, *History*, pp. 170, 187, 225; S. M. Shirokogoroff, *Psychomental Complex of the Tungus* (London: Kegan Paul, 1935), p. 282; Caroline Humphrey and Urgunge Onon, *Shamans and Elders* (Oxford: Oxford University Press, 1996), pp. 141–42; Humphrey,

'Theories of North Asian Shamanism', in Gellner (ed.), *Soviet and Western Anthropology* (London: Duckworth, 1980), pp. 250–51.

5. N. Basilov, 'Chosen by the Spirits', in Marjorie Mandelstam Balzer (ed.), *Shamanism* (Armonk, New York: Sharpe, 1990), p. 39.

6. Vilmos Dioszegi, *Tracing Shamans in Siberia* (Oosterhout: Anthropological Publications, 1968), p. 207.

7. Forsyth, *History*, p. 188.

8. Ibid., pp. 147, 154–55, 178; E. L. Lvova, 'On the Shamanism of the Chulym Turks', in Dioszegi and Hoppál (ed.), *Shamanism in Siberia*, pp. 237–38; Z. P. Sokolova, 'A Survey of Ob-Ugrian Shamanism', in Hoppál and Sadovszky (ed.), *Shamanism Past and Present* (Budapest and Los Angeles: Hungarian Academy of Sciences and International Society for Trans-Oceanic Research, 1989), pp. 155, 158, 162–63.

9. Armstrong, *Russian Settlement*, p. 90; Forsyth, *History*, pp. 150, 178–85, 219; Dioszegi, *Tracing Shamans*, p. 125; Shirokogoroff, *Psychomental Complex*, pp. 396–97.

10. Forsyth, *History*, pp. 154–55, 178; Carla Corradi-Musi, 'Siberian Shamanism in the Eighteenth- to Nineteenth-Century Travellers Books', in Hoppál and Sadovszky (ed.), *Shamanism Past and Present*, pp. 71–73.

11. Georg Wilhelm Steller, *Beschriebung von dem Lande Kamschatka* (Leipzig, 1774), pp. 284–85; Mathieu de Lesseps, *Journal historique du voyage de M. de Lesseps, Consul de France* (Paris, 1790), i, pp. 128–29.

12. Caroline Humphrey, *Karl Marx Collective* (Cambridge: Cambridge University Press, 1983), pp. 373–74.

13. Jeremiah Curtin, *A Journey in Southern Siberia* (London, 1910), passim; *tailgan* described and photographed at pp. 44–52.

14. Shirokogoroff, *Psychomental Complex*, p. 397.

15. Dioszegi, *Tracing Shamans*, p. 125.

16. Forsyth, *History*, p. 155.

17. Ibid., p. 155.

18. Waldemar Jochelson, *The Koryak* (Leiden: Brill, 1926), pp. 13–16, 47–52, 123–24, 805–08; Ildiko Lehtinen, 'Artturi Kannisto in Siberia, 1901–06', in Juha Pentikainen et al. (ed.), *Shamans* (Tampere: Tampere Museums, 1999), pp. 77–83; quotation on p. 78.

19. Nicholas Witsen, *Noord en Oost Tataryen* (1682: repr. Amsterdam, 1785), ii, p. 896; N. A. Alekseev, 'Shamanism among the Turkic Peoples of Siberia', in Marjorie Mandelstam Balzer (ed.), *Shamanism* (Armonk, NY: Sharpe, 1990), pp. 78–79.

20. Martin Sauer, *An Account of a Topographical and Astronomical*

Expedition to the Northern Part of Russia (London, 1802), p. 61; Johann Georg Gmelin, *Reise durch Sibirien, vom dem Jahr 1733 bis 1743* (Göttingen, 1751–52), ii, p. 288; Ivan Ivanovich Lepechin, *Tagebuch der Reise durch verschiedene Provinzen des russischen Reiches in den Jahren 1768 und 1769*, trans. Christian Heinrich Hase (Altenburg, 1774–83), ii, p. 45; Petrus Simon Pallas, *Reise durch verschiedene Provinzen des russischen Reiches* (St Petersburg, 1776), iii, pp. 60, 223; De Lesseps, *Journal historique*, i, pp. 128–29; Daniel Gottlieb Messerschmidt, *Forschungreise durch Sibirien*, ed. E. Winter and N. A. Figurovski (Berlin, 1962–77), i, pp. 66–68.

21. Waclaw Sieroszewski, *Yakuti* (St Petersburg, 1896), pp. 394–96.

22. Jochelson, *The Koryak*, pp. 49–51; and Waldemar Jochelson, *The Yukaghir and the Yukaghirized Tungus* (Leiden: Brill, 1926), pp. 162, 196–201.

23. Alekseev, Nikolai Alekseevich, 'Shamanism among the Turkic Peoples of Siberia', in Balzer (ed.), *Shamanism in Eurasia*, pp. 88–89.

24. A. J. Juki, 'Notes on Selkup Shamanism', in Dioszegi and Hoppál (ed.), *Shamanism in Siberia*, p. 379.

25. Forsyth, *History*, pp. 242–61; Armstong, *Russian Settlement*, pp. 166–67; Mote, *Siberia*, p. 99.

26. Kai Donner, 'Ethnological Notes about the Yenisey-Ostyak', *Mémoires de la Société Finno-Ougrienne*, 66 (1933), p. 75; Forsyth, *History*, p. 267; Humphrey, *Karl Marx Collective*, p. 415.

27. Forsyth, *History*, pp. 209–394 (quotation from p. 394); Mote, *Siberia*, pp. 99–125.

28. Arkadiy F. Anismov, 'The Shaman's Tent of the Evenks', in Henry N. Michael (ed.), *Studies in Siberian Shamanism* (Toronto: Toronto University Press, 1963), pp. 121–22; Forsyth, *History*, pp. 288, 306, 309. For a classic Stalinist denunciation of shamanism, see I. M. Suslov, 'Shamanstvo i Borba s nim', *Sovietsky Sever*, 3–4 (1931), pp. 89–152.

29. Vitebsky, *The Shaman*, p. 136; Juha Pentikainen, 'The Shamans and Shamanism', in Pentikainen et al. (ed.), *Shamans*, pp. 33, 41.

30. Ibid.; Forsyth, *History*, pp. 287–88, 306, 338–39.

31. Humphrey, *Karl Marx Collective*, p. 414.

Notes to Chapter 4: The Records of Shamanism

1. Gloria Flaherty, *Shamanism and the Eighteenth Century* (Princeton, New Jersey: Princeton University Press, 1992), passim.

2. Marco Polo, *The Travels*, ed. Ernest Rhys (London, 1908), pp. 251–52; Piers Vitebsky, 'Some Medieval European Views on Mongolian

Shamanism', *Journal of the Anglo-Mongolian Society*, 1, pt 1 (1974), pp. 24–42.

3. 'Certain Notes Unperfectly Written by Richard Johnson', in Richard Hakluyt, *The Principal Navigations, Voyages, Traffiques and Discoveries of the English Nation* (Glasgow, 1903), ii, pp. 347–49. I have modernized the spelling and a few words.

4. Nicholas Witsen, *Noord en Oost Tataryen* (Amsterdam, 1785), ii, pp. 634, 896; drawing at pp. 662–63.

5. Flaherty, *Shamanism and the Eighteenth Century*, pp. 46, 48, 55, 58, 70–74, 82, 90; with additional material from Johann Georg Gmelin, *Reise durch Sibirien, vom dem Jahr 1733 bis 1743* (2 vols, Göttingen, 1751–52), ii, p. 46; and Johann Gottlieb Georgi, *Beschreibung aller Nationen des russischen Reichs* (St Petersburg, 1776–80), ii, p. 392. The long quotation is from John Bell, *Travels from St Petersburg in Russia to Diverse Parts of Asia* (Glasgow, 1763), i, pp. 206–07, 253–55.

6. Stephan Krascheninnikow, *The History of Kamtschatka and the Kuriliski Islands*, trans. James Grieve (Gloucester, 1764), p. 206.

7. Ibid., p. 215.

8. Carla Corradi-Musi, 'Siberian Shamanism in the Eighteenth- and Nineteenth-Century Travellers Books', in Mihaly Hoppál and Otto von Sadovszky (ed.), *Shamanism Past and Present* (Budapest and Los Angeles: Hungarian Academy of Sciences and International Society for Trans-Oceanic Research, 1989), p. 70.

9. V. M. Mikhailowskii, 'Shamanism in Siberia and European Russia', *Journal of the Anthropological Institute of Great Britain and Ireland*, 24 (1895), pp. 68–69.

10. V. M. Mikhailowskii, *Shamanstvo* (Moscow, 1892). The long passage quoted below is taken from Waclaw Sieroszewski, *Yakuti* (St Petersburg, 1896), pp. 639–42, as translated in M. A. Czaplicka, *Aboriginal Siberia: A Study in Social Anthropology* (Oxford: Oxford University Press), pp. 233–36.

11. Waldemar Jochelson, *The Koryak* (Leiden: Brill, 1908), pp. 1–15.

12. E.g. Kai Donner, 'Ethnological Notes about the Yenisey-Ostyak', *Mémoires de la Société Finno-Ougrienne*, 66 (1933), p. 5.

13. S. M. Shirokogoroff, *Psychomental Complex of the Tungus*, which was published in London (Kegan Paul, 1935).

14. A. A. Popov, *Materialy dlya Bibliografii Russkoi Literatury po Izucenigu Shamanstva Severo-Aziatskikh Narodov* (Leningrad, 1932).

15. Anisimov's *magnum opus* was *Religiya Evenkov* (Moscow, 1958). The passage quoted is taken from his essay 'The Shaman's Tent of

the Evenks and the Origin of the Shamanistic Rite', printed in translation in Henry N. Michael (ed.), *Studies in Siberian Shamanism* (Toronto: Toronto University Press, 1963), pp. 100–03.

16. Michael (ed.), *Studies in Siberian Shamanism*; Vilmos Dioszegi (ed.), *Popular Beliefs and Folklore Tradition in Siberia* (Bloomington: University of Indiana Press, 1968); Vilmos Dioszegi and Mihaly Hoppál (ed.), *Shamanism in Siberia* (Budapest: Akademiai Kiado, 1978); Mihaly Hoppál (ed.), *Shamanism in Eurasia* (Göttingen: Herodot, 1984); and Hoppál and von Sadowszky (ed.), *Shamanism Past and Present*; Balzer (ed.), *Shamanism*; Mihaly Hoppál and Juha Petikainen (ed.), *Northern Religions and Shamanism* (Budapest and Helsinki: Akademiai Kiado and Finnish Literature Society, 1992); Siikala and Hoppal, *Studies on Shamanism*; Mihaly Hoppál and Keith D. Howard (ed.), *Shamans and Cultures* (Budapest and Los Angeles: Akademiai Kiado and International Society for Trans-Oceanic Research, 1993); Marjorie Mandelstam Balzer (ed.), *Shamanic Worlds* (Armonk, New York: North Castle, 1997).

17. Dioszegi, *Tracing Shamans*, p. 209.

18. Alekseev, 'Shamanism among the Turkic Peoples', and Taras M. Mikhailev, 'Buryat Shamanism', in Balzer (ed.), *Shamanism*, pp. 108 and 115.

Notes to Chapter 5: What Shamans Did

1. E. Ysbrants Ides, *Driejaarige Reize naar China* (Amsterdam, 1698).

2. On which see Gloria Flaherty, *Shamanism and the Eighteenth Century* (Princeton, New Jersey: Princeton University Press, 1992), p. 23.

3. Kai Donner, *La Siberie* (Paris, 1946), 222, p. 222; Wilhelm Radlov, *Aus Siberien* (Leipzig, 1884), ii, p. 55; Anatoly Alekseev, 'Healing Techniques among Even Shamans', in Marjorie Mandelstam Balzer (ed.), *Shamanic Worlds* (Armonk, New York: North Castle, 1997), p. 160; Caroline Humphrey and Urgunge Onon, *Shamans and Elders* (Oxford: Oxford University Press, 1996), pp. 35–37; Leo Sternberg, *Gilyaki* (Moscow, 1905), pp. 90–92.

4. Humphrey and Onon, *Shamans and Elders*, p. 51.

5. Waldemar Jochelson, *The Yakut* (New York: Anthropological Reports of the American Museum of Natural History, 33.2, 1933), p. 105; Piers Vitebsky, *The Shaman* (London: Macmillan, 1995), p. 25.

6. Waclaw Sieroszewski, *Yakuti* (St Petersburg, 1896), p. 632; Jochelson, *The Yakut*, p. 106.

7. Anatoly Alekseev, 'Healing Techniques among Even Shamans' in Balzer, ed., *Shamanic Worlds*, p. 154; Waldemar Jochelson, *The Koryak* (Leiden: Brill, 1926), pp. 59–60.
8. Humphrey and Onon, *Shamans and Elders*, pp. 30–31.
9. Caroline Humphrey, 'Shamanic Practices and the State in Northern Asia', in Nicholas Thomas and Caroline Humphrey (ed.), *Shamanism, History and the State* (Ann Arbor: University of Michigan Press, 1994), p. 208.
10. Humphrey and Onon, *Shamans and Elders*, p. 183.
11. V. M. Mikhailowskii, 'Shamanism in Siberia and European Russia', *Journal of the Anthropological Institute of Great Britain and Ireland*, 24 (1895), p. 63; Yakut was, as said earlier, the name which Russians used for the Sakha.
12. Jochelson, *The Yakut*, p. 107; Sieroszewski, *Yakuti*, p. 628.
13. Jochelson, *The Yakut*, p. 122.
14. On this see Mircea Eliade, *Shamanism* (English edn, London: Routledge, 1964), p. 189.
15. E. A. Alekseenko, 'Categories of the Ket Shamans', in Vilmos Dioszegi and Mihaly Hoppál (ed.), *Shamanism in Siberia* (Budapest: Akademiai Kiado, 1978), pp. 255–64.
16. Leo Sternberg, *Gilyaki* (Moscow, 1905), pp. 72–74; Ivan A. Lopatin, *Goldi Amurskiye, Ussuriskiye i Sungariiskiye* (Vladivostok, 1922), pp. 50–60.
17. L. V. Khomich, 'A Classification of Nenets Shamans', in Dioszegi and Hoppál (ed.), *Shamanism in Siberia*, pp. 245–53.
18. Z. P. Sokolova, 'A Survey of the Ob-Ugrian Shamanism', in Mihaly Hoppál and Otto von Sadovsky (ed.), *Shamanism Past and Present* (Budapest and Los Angeles: Hungarian Academy of Sciences and International Society for Trans-Oceanic Research, 1989), p. 155.
19. This analysis is based upon that of Anna-Leena Siikala, *The Rite Technique of the Siberian Shaman* (Helsinki: FF Communications, Academia Scientarum Fennica, 1987), pp. 303–11. I am very grateful for Caitlin Matthews for lending me a copy of this work.
20. S. M. Shirokogoroff, *Psychomental Complex of the Tungus* (London: Kegan Paul, 1935), p. 315; Siikala, *Rite Technique*, p. 15; Eliade, *Shamanism*, pp. 182, 509; Humphrey, 'Shamanic Practices', pp. 198–200.
21. Petrus Simon Pallas, *Reise durch verschiedene Provinzen des russischen Reiches* (3 vols, St Petersburg, 1776), iii, pp. 62–64.
22. E.g. Waldemar Jochelson, *The Yukaghir and the Yukaghirized Tungus* (Leiden: Brill, 1926), pp. 196–205; Mikhailowskii, 'Shamanism in

Siberia and European Russia', pp. 97–126, and sources cited there; L. V. Khomich, 'Classification of Nenets Shamans', in Dioszegi and Hoppál, ed., *Shamanism in Siberia*, pp. 246–50; Waldemar Bogoras, *The Chukchee* (Leiden: Brill, 1908), p. 256; Eliade, *Shamanism*, pp. 215–29, and sources cited there; Carla Corradi-Musi, 'Siberian Shamanism in the Eighteenth- to Nineteenth-Century Travellers Books', in Hoppál and von Sadovszky (ed.), *Shamanism in Siberia* pp. 72–73.

23. Jochelson, *The Koryak*, p. 50.
24. Ivan Ivanovich Lepechin, *Tagebuch der Reise durch verschiedene Provinzen des russischen Reiches in Jahren 1768 und 1769*, trans. Christian Heinrich Hase (2 vols, Altenberg, 1774–83), ii, pp. 45–46.
25. Jochelson, *The Yukaghir*, pp. 102–03.
26. Eliade, *Shamanism*, pp. 183–84.
27. Bogoras, *The Chukchee*, pp. 430–31; Jochelson, *The Yukaghir*, pp. 208–09; P. I. Treyakov, *Turukhanskiye Kraya* (St Petersburg, 1871), pp. 220–22; Johann Georg Gmelin, *Reise durch Sibirien, vom dem Jahr 1733 bis 1743* (2 vols, Göttingen, 1751–52), ii, pp. 364–65; Dorji Banzarov, *Chernaya Vera ili Shamanstvu u Mongolov* (St Petersburg, 1891), pp. 107–15; V. F. Troschanski, *Evoludiya 'Chernaya Vera' (Shamanstva) u Yakutoi* (Kazan, 1901), p. 151; P. Hajdu, 'Classification of Samoyed Shamans', in Dioszegi (ed.), *Popular Beliefs*, pp. 147–73; Corradi-Musi, 'Siberian Shamanism in the Eighteenth- to Nineteenth-Century Travellers Books', pp. 70–73; Z. P. Sokolova, 'A Survey of the Ob-Ugrian Shamanism', in Hoppál and von Sadoszky (ed.), *Shamanism Past and Present*, pp. 156, 159; Khomich, 'Classification of Nenets Shamans', pp. 247–51.
28. Evdokiya Gaer, 'The Way of the Soul to the Otherworld and the Nanai Shaman', in Hoppál and von Sadovszky (ed.), *Shamanism Past and Present*, pp. 233–39.
29. Uno Harva, *Die religiosen Vorstellungen der Altaischen Volker* (Helsinki: Folklore Fellows Communications, 52.125, 1938), p. 547; Sieroszewski, *Yakuti*, pp. 642–44.
30. Khomich, 'Classification of Nenets Shamans', pp. 247–48; T. Lehtisalo, 'Entwurf einer Mythologie der Jurak-Samojeden', *Memoires de la Société Finno-Ougrienne*, 53 (1924), pp. 133–37.
31. Eliade, *Shamanism*, pp. 182, 208.
32. Arkadiy F. Anisimov, 'The Shaman's Tent of the Evenks', in Henry N. Michael (ed.), *Studies in Siberian Shamanism* (Toronto: Toronto University Press, 1963), pp. 84–123.
33. Lydia T. Black, 'Peoples of the Amur and Maritime Regions', in

William W. Fitzhugh and Aron Crowell (ed.), *Crossroads of Continents* (Washington DC: Smithsonian Institution, 1988), p. 29.

34. Pallas, *Reise*, iii, pp. 62–64; Corradi-Musi, 'Siberian Shamanism in the Eighteenth- and Nineteenth-Century Travellers Books', p. 70; Sokolova, 'Survey of the Ob-Ugrian Shamanism', p. 159.

35. A. F. Anisimov, 'Cosmological Concepts of the Peoples of the North', in Michael (ed.), *Studies in Siberian Shamanism*, pp. 157–229.

36. Mikhailowskii, 'Shamanism', p. 96; Troschanski, *Evoludiya 'Chernaya Vera' (Shamanstva) u Yakutoi* (Kazan, 1901), p. 110; Jochelson, *The Yukaghir*, pp. 208–12; Roberte Hamayon, 'Game and Games, Fortune and Dualism in Siberian Shamanism', in Hoppál and Pentikainen (ed.), *Northern Religions and Shamanism*, pp. 134–37.

37. Sokolova, 'Survey of the Ob-Ugrian Shamanism', p. 157; L. Krader, 'Shamanism: Theory and History in Buryat Society', in Dioszegi and Hoppál (ed.), *Shamanism in Siberia*, p. 229.

38. Jochelson, *The Yukaghir*, pp 162–64.

39. Roberte Hamayon, *La chasse à l'âme: esquisse d'une théorie du Chamanisme Siberien* (Nanterre: Société d'Ethnologie, 1990); 'Game and Games'; 'Shamanism in Siberia: From Partnership in Supernature to Counter-Power in Society', in Nicholas Thomas and Caroline Humphrey (ed.), *Shamanism, History and the State* (Ann Arbor: University of Michigan Press), pp. 76–89.

40. Jochelson, *The Yukaghir*, pp. 211–12.

Notes to Chapter 6: Shamanic Cosmologies

1. S. M. Shirokogoroff, *Psychomental Complex of the Tungus* (London: Kegan Paul, 1935), p. 294.

2. Waldemar Bogoras, *The Chukchee* (Leiden: Brill, 1908), pp. 281, 294.

3. This cosmology is recorded in most of the ethnographic literature used for this essay. For a convenient summary, see Uno Holmberg, *Finno-Ugric and Siberian Mythology* (New York; Cooper Square, 1964), pp. 175–238, 449–71.

4. Mircea Eliade, *Shamanism* (English edn, London, Routledge, 1964), pp. 259–73; quotation on p. 259.

5. Holmberg, *Finno-Ugric and Siberian Mythology*, pp. 307–40; Waldemar Jochelson, *The Koryak* (Leiden: Brill, 1908), p. 121; Bogoras, *The Chukchee*, pp. 303–33; Caroline Humphrey and Urgunge Onon, *Shamans and Elders* (Oxford: Oxford University Press, 1996), pp. 119–24; Jeremiah Curtin, *A Journey in Souther Siberia* (London, 1910), p. 173.

6. Holmberg, *Finno-Ugric and Siberian Mythology*, pp. 3–14, 463–82; V. N. Chernetsov, 'Concepts of the Soul among the Ob-Ugrians', in Henry N. Michael (ed.), *Studies in Siberian Shamanism* (Toronto: Toronto University Press, 1963), pp. 3–45.

7. Jochelson, *The Koryak*, pp. 341–60; and Waldemar Jochelson, *The Yukaghir and the Yukaghirized Tungus* (Leiden: Brill, 1926), pp. 298–309.

8. Holmberg, *Finno-Ugric and Siberian Mythology*, pp. 381–85.

9. See ibid., pp. 313–71, for other examples.

10. Ibid., pp. 371–80; Jochelson, *The Koryak*, p. 23; Humphrey and Onon, *Shamans and Elders*, p. 133.

11. F. Kon, quoted in Shirokogoroff, *Psychomental Complex*, p. 282; Nikolai Alekseevich Alekseev, 'Shamanism among the Turkic Peoples', in Marjorie Mandelstam Balzer (ed.), *Shamanism* (Armonk, New York: Sharpe, 1990), p. 93.

12. Philip C. Almond, *The British Discovery of Buddhism* (Cambridge: Cambridge University Press, 1988), passim.

13. A point made by Caroline Humphrey, 'Theories of North Asian Shamanism', in Ernest Gellner (ed.), *Soviet and Western Anthropology* (London: Duckworth, 1980), p. 249.

14. Bogoras, *The Chukchee*, p. 436; Shatlov, quoted in Vladimir N. Basilov, *Izbranniki Dukhov* (Moscow: Politizdat, 1984), pp. 123–24; Jochelson, *The Yukaghir*, pp. 201–05.

15. Vilmos Dioszegi, 'Pre-Islamic Shamanism of the Baraba Turks', in Vilmos Dioszegi and Mihaly Hoppál, *Shamanism in Siberia* (Budapest: Akademiai Kiado, 1978), p. 164.

16. E. L. Lvova, 'On the Shamanism of the Chulym Turks', in Dioszegi and Hoppál, *Shamanism in Siberia*, p. 239; Jochelson, *The Koryak*, p. 47.

17. Jochelson, *The Yakut*, pp. 107, 113–14; Sieroszewski, *Yakuti*, pp. 626–28; Nikolai A. Alekseev, 'Helping Spirits of the Siberian Turks', in Hoppál (ed.), *Shamanism in Eurasia*, p. 269.

18. Waclaw Sieroszewski, *Yakuti* (St Petersburg, 1896), pp. 626–28.

19. Leo Sternberg, *Gilyaki* (Moscow, 1905), pp. 42–74.

20. Leo Sternberg, 'Divine Election in Primitive Religion', in Congrès International des Americanistes, *Compte-rendu de la XXIe Session* (Goteborg, 1925), ii, pp. 475–87.

21. Arkadiy F. Anisimov, 'The Shaman's Tent of the Evenks', in Henry N. Michael (ed.), *Studies in Siberian Shamanism* (Toronto: Toronto University Press, 1963), pp. 84–97, 100–04; P. I. Tretyakov, *Turukhanskiye Kraya* (St Petersburg, 1891), p. 212.

22. Alekseev, 'Helping Spirits', pp. 269–71; Dioszegi, 'Tracing Shamans', pp. 53–67.
23. Jochelson, *The Yukaghir*, pp. 199–202; Shirokogoroff, *Psychomental Complex*, p. 272.
24. Ibid., 271.
25. Eliade, *Shamanism*, p. 6. For a counter-argument, see Johann Reinhard, 'Shamanism and Spirit Possession: The Definitional Problem', in John T. Hitchcock and Rex T. Jones (ed.), *Spirit Possession in the Nepal Himalayas* (Warminster: Aries and Phillips, 1976), passim.
26. Ivan A. Lopatin, 'A Shamanistic Performance to Regain the Favour of the Spirit', *Anthropos*, 35–36 (1940–41), pp. 352–55; and 'A Shamanistic Performance for a Sick Boy', ibid., 41–44 (1946–49), pp. 365–68.
27. Bogoras, *The Chukchee*, pp. 417, 438.
28. Sieroszewski, *Yakuti*, p. 634.
29. Tretyakov, *Turukhanskiye Kraya*, pp. 223–24.
30. Tatyana Bulgakaya, 'Why Does Nanai Shaman Chant?', in Tae-Gon Kim and Mihaly Hoppál (ed.), *Shamanism in Performing Arts* (Budapest: Akademiai Kiado, 1995), pp. 135–44; Shirokogoroff, *Psychomental Complex*, p. 369.
31. Tretyakov, *Turukhanskiye Kraya*, p. 212; Sieroszewski, *Yakuti*, pp. 223–24.
32. Shirokogoroff, *Psychomental Complex*, p. 366; Piers Vitebsky, *The Shaman* (London: Macmillan, 1995), pp. 92–93.

Notes to Chapter 7: Shamanic Apprenticeship and Equipment

1. Mircea Eliade, *Shamanism* (English edn, London: Routledge, 1964), pp. 13–21; Anna-Leena Siikala, 'Siberian and Inner Asian Shamanism', in Siikala and Mihaly Hoppál, *Studies on Shamanism* (Budapest and Helsinki: Finnish Anthropological Society and Akademiai Kiado, 1992), pp. 5–7.
2. Jeremiah Curtin, *A Journey in Southern Siberia* (London 1910), p. 105; N. N. Agapitov and M. N. Khangalov, *Materialy dlya Izuchenia Shamanstva i Sibiri*, Izvestia Vostochno-Sibiriskovo Otdzla Russkovo Geograficheskovo Obshchestva, 14.1–2 (1883), pp. 44–52; S. M. Shirokogoroff, *Psychomental Complex of the Tungus* (London: Kegan Paul, 1935), p. 345; G. N. Potanin, *Ocherki Severo-Zapadnoi Mongolii* (St Petersburg, 1881–83), iv, pp. 56–57; Vilmos Dioszegi, *Tracing Shamans in Siberia* (Oosterhout: Anthropological Publications, 1968), pp. 53–60, 136; Ulla Johansen, 'The Transmission of the Shaman's Position in

South Siberia', in Mihaly Hoppál and Keith D. Howard (ed.), *Shamans and Cultures* (Budapest and Los Angeles: Akademiai Kiado and International Society for Trans-Oceanic Research, 1993), pp. 193–94; Waldemar Jochelson, *The Yukaghir and the Yukaghirized Tungus* (Leiden: Brill, 1926), p. 163.

3. P. I. Tretyakov, *Turukhanskiye Kraya* (St Petersburg, 1891), pp. 210–11; R. Bielayewski, *Psezdka ki Lyedavitamu Maru* (Moscow, 1883), pp. 113–14; Alexander M. Castren, *Nordische Reisen und Forschungen* (St Petersburg, 1856–57), ii, p. 191; A. A. Popov, 'How Seraptie Djarvoskin of the Nganasans (Tavgi Samoyeds) Became a Shaman', in Vilmos Dioszegi (ed.), *Popular Beliefs and Folklore Tradition in Siberia* (Bloomington: Indiana University Press), pp. 137–38; Waldemar Bogoras, *The Chukchee* (Leiden: Brill, 1908), pp. 374, 413.

4. Kai Donner, 'Ethnological Notes about the Yenisey-Ostyak', *Memoires de la Société Finno-Ougrienne*, 66 (1933), p. 76; Tretyakov, *Turukhanskiye Kraya*, pp. 210–11; Castrén, *Nordische Reisen*, ii, p. 191; Hajdu, 'Classification of Samoyed Shamans', pp. 147–73.

5. Bogoras, *The Chukchee*, pp. 423, 450; Dioszegi, *Tracing Shamans*, p. 243.

6. Vladimir Basilov, 'Chosen by the Spirits', in Marjorie Mandelstam Balzer (ed.), *Shamanism* (Armonk, New York: Sharpe, 1990), pp. 9–10; Anna-Leena Siikala, 'The Interpretation of Siberian and Inner Asian Shamanism', in Siikala and Mihaly Hoppál, *Studies on Shamanism* (Budapest and Helsinki: Finnish Anthropological Society and Akademiai Kiado, 1992), pp. 5–6.

7. Dioszegi, *Tracing Shamans*, 243; G. N. Potanin, *Ocherki Severo-Zapadnoi Mongolii* (4 vols, St Petersburg, 1881–83), iv, pp. 56–57; Waldemar Jochelson, *The Koryak* (Leiden: Brill, 1926), pp. 47–52.

8. Curtin, *Journey in Southern Siberia*, p. 106; N. N. Agapitov and M. N. Khangalov, *Materialy dlya Izuchenia Shamanstva I Sibiri*, Izvestia Vostochno-Sibiriskovo Otdzla Russkovo Geograficheskovo Obshchestva, 14.1–2 (1883), pp. 44–52; Bogoras, *The Chukchee*, pp. 415–16, 421; V. M. Mikhailowskii, 'Shamanism in Siberia and European Russia', *Journal of the Anthropological Intitute of Great Britain and Ireland*, 24 (1895), pp. 85–86.

9. As in the case of the Nganasan shaman studied by A. A. Popov, in *Tavgytsy* (Moscow, 1936), pp. 84–90.

10. Bogoras, *The Chukchee*, pp. 421–28.

11. See for example Dioszegi, *Tracing Shamans*, pp. 141, 244, 279–80.

12. Ibid., p. 279.

13. Yekaterina De Provofyeva, 'The Costume of an Enets Shaman', in

Henry N. Michael (ed.), *Studies in Siberian Shamanism* (Toronto: Toronto University Press, 1963), p. 125.

14. Shirokogoroff, *Psychomental Complex*, pp. 271–72; Mikhailowskii, 'Shamanism', pp. 85–86; Castrén, *Nordische Reisen*, i, p. 191; Dioszegi, *Tracing Shamans*, pp. 238, 243, 288- 89.

15. Curtin, *Journey in Southern Siberia*, p. 106; Agapitov and Khangalov, *Materialy*, 44–52; Bogoras, *The Chukchee*, pp. 420–22; Jochelson, *The Koryak*, pp. 47–52.

16. G. M. Vasilevich, 'The Acquisition of Shamanistic Ability among the Evenki', in Vilmos Dioszegi (ed.), *Popular Beliefs and Folklore Tradition* (Bloomington: Indiana University Press, 1968), pp. 339–49.

17. Curtin, *Journey in Southern Siberia*, p. 106; Agapitov and Khangalov, *Materialy*, pp. 44–52; Dioszegi, *Tracing Shamans*, pp. 58–68.

18. G. V. Ksenofontov, *Legendy i Rasskazy u Yakutov, Buryat i Tungusov* (2nd edn, Moscow, 1930), pp. 44, 65, 102–03; Popov, *Tavgytsy*, pp. 84–90; Dioszegi, *Tracing Shamans*, pp. 58–68; Popov, 'Sereptie Djaruoskin', pp. 137–45.

19. Eliade, *Shamanism*, pp. 33–62.

20. Curtin, *Journey in Southern Siberia*, pp. 106–08; Agapitov and Khangalov, *Materialy*, pp. 44–52; Jorma Partanen, 'A Description of Buryat Shamanism', *Journal de la Société Finno-Ougrienne*, 51 (1941–42), pp. 10–15.

21. Mikhailowskii, 'Shamanism', pp. 85–86; Tretyakov, *Turukhanskiye Kraya*, pp. 210–11.

22. Dioszegi, *Tracing Shamans*, pp. 65–74.

23. Shirokogoroff, *Psychomental Complex*, p. 273; P. Hajdu, 'Classification of Samoyed Shamans', in Dioszegi (ed.), *Popular Beliefs*, pp. 147–73; G. M. Vasilevich, 'The Acquisition of Shamanistic Ability among the Evenki', ibid., pp. 339–49.

24. Shirokogoroff, *Psychomental Complex*, pp. 273, 383–85; Vasilevich, 'Acquisition of Shamanistic Ability', pp. 339–49.

25. Jochelson, *The Yukaghir*, pp. 196–201; Waclaw Sieroszewski, *Yakuti* (St Petersburg, 1896), pp, 626–31; Bogoras, *The Chukchee*, p. 415.

26. Petrus Simon Pallas, *Reise durch verschiedene Provinzen des russischen Reiches* (3 vols, St Petersburg, 1776), iii, p. 62.

27. Its career as an idea is charted by Vladimir Nikolaevich Basilov, 'Chosen by the Spirits', pp. 1–9; and Piers Vitebsky, *The Shaman* (London: Macmillan, 1995), pp. 139–40; and comprehensively rejected by Eliade, *Shamanism*, pp. 1–20. See also Roger Walsh, *The Spirit of Shamanism* (Los Angeles: Tarcher, 1990), chapter 7. Dioszegi's statements are in *Tracing Shamans*, pp. 314–15.

28. Arkadiy F. Anisimov, 'The Shaman's Tent', in Michael (ed.), *Studies in Siberian Shamanism*, pp. 121–23; Shirokogoroff, *Psychomental Complex*, p. 371.
29. Dioszegi, *Tracing Shamans*, pp. 244–45; Sieroszewski, *Yakuti*, p. 626.
30. Shaskov and Khangalov, both quoted in Mikhailowskii, 'Shamanism', pp. 130–132; Agapitov and Khangalov, *Materialy*, p. 46.
31. Shirokogoroff, *Psychomental Complex*, p. 287; Mihaly Hoppál, 'Shamanism: Universal Structures and Regional Symbols', in Hoppál and Howard (ed.), *Shamans and Cultures*, p. 191.
32. Wilhelm Radlov, *Aus Sibirien* (Leipzig, 1884), ii, p. 17; John Bell, *Travels from St Petersburg in Russia* (Glasgow, 1763), i, pp. 206–07.
33. Lvova, 'On the Shamanism of the Chulym Turks', in Dioszegi and Hoppál (ed.), *Shamanism in Siberia*, pp. 237–44.
34. Z. P. Sokolova, 'A Survey of the Ob-Ugrian Shamanism', in Hoppál and von Sadovszky (ed.), *Shamanism Past and Present*, p. 160; Richard Johnson 'Certain Notes, Unperfectly Written by Richard Johnson', in Richard Hakluyt, *The Principal Navigations, Voyages, Traffiques and Discoveries of the English Nation* (Glasgow edn, in 6 vols, 1903); Eliade, *Shamanism*, pp. 154–55.
35. Shirokogoroff, *Psychomental Complex*, p. 272; A. V. Smoljak, 'Some Elements of the Ritual Attire of Nanai Shamans', in Hoppál (ed.), *Shamanism in Eurasia* (Göttingen: Herodot, 1984), pp. 244–52.
36. Jochelson, *The Koryak*, p. 52; Bogoras, *The Chukchee*, pp. 457–60.
37. Shirokogoroff, *Psychomental Complex*, p. 289.
38. Nikolai Alekseevich Alekseev, 'Shamanism among the Turkic Peoples of Siberia', in Balzer (ed.), *Shamanism*, pp. 105–06.
39. Pallas, *Reise*, iii, pp. 181–82; Johann Georg Gmelin, *Reise durch Sibirien, von dem Jahr 1733 bis 1743* (2 vols, Göttingen, 1751–52), ii, pp. 11–13, 44–46, 345, 351–56; Mihaly Hoppál, 'The Changing Image of Siberian Shamans', in Siikala and Hoppál, *Studies on Shamanism*, pp. 176–81, Johann Gottlieb Georgi, *Beschreibung aller Nationen des russischen Reichs* (4 vols, St Petersburg, 1776–80), supplement, figs 44–86.
40. E.g. Shirokogoroff, *Psychomental Complex*, p. 287; Dioszegi, *Tracing Shamans*, pp. 65–76; Hajdu, 'Classification of Samoyed Shamans', pp. 147–73.
41. G. N. Potanin, *Ocherki Severo-Zapadnoi Mongolii* (4 vols, St Petersburg, 1881–83), iv, pp. 49–54.
42. Jochelson, *The Yukaghir*, pp. 169–71; Shirokogoroff, *Psychomental Complex*, p. 288.

43. Vilmos Dioszegi, 'The Problem of the Ethnic Homogeneity of Tofa (Karagas) Shamanism', in Dioszegi (ed.), *Popular Beliefs*, pp. 239–339.

44. Eliade, *Shamanism*, pp. 158–59; Dioszegi, *Tracing Shamans*, p. 317.

45. Dioszegi, 'The Problem of the Ethnic Homogeneity', in Dioszegi (ed.), *Popular* Beliefs, pp. 320–29.

46. Jochelson, *The Yukaghir*, pp. 169–91; and *The Yakut*, pp. 109–14.

47. Sources at n. 30, plus 'Certain Notes Unperfectly Written by Richard Johnson'; Witsen, *Noord en Oost Tataryen* (1682: repr. 2 vols, Amsterdam, 1785), ii, pp. 662–63; Vilmos Dioszegi, 'Pre-Islamic Shamanism of the Baraba Turks', in Dioszegi and Hoppál (ed.), pp. 83–167.

48. Jochelson, *The Yakut*, p. 118.

49. Mikhailowskii, 'Shamanism', pp. 80–83; Eliade, 'Shamanism', p. 175; Sokolova, 'Survey of the Ob-Ugrian Shamanism', p. 56; Lvova, 'On the Shamanism of the Chulym Turks', pp. 237–44; E. A. Alekseenko, 'Categories of the Ket Shamans', in Dioszegi and Hoppál (ed.), *Shamanism in* Siberia, pp. 255–64.

50. Eliade, *Shamanism*, pp. 168–73.

51. Mikhailowskii, 'Shamanism', p. 80. See also Dioszegi, 'Pre-Islamic Shamanism of the Baraba Turks', pp. 83–167; J. P. Potapov, 'Shamans' Drums of Altaic Ethnic Groups', in Dioszegi (ed.), *Popular Beliefs*, pp. 205–34; M. Jankovics, 'Cosmic Models and Siberian Shamans' Drums', in Hoppál (ed.), *Shamanism in Eurasia*, pp. 149–73.

52. Eliade, *Shamanism*, p. 175.

53. Pallas, *Reise*, iii, pp. 181–82; Agapitov and Khangalov, *Materialy*, pp. 42–44 and plate 3; Partenen, 'A Description of Buryat Shamanism', *Journal de la Société Finno-Ougrienne*, 51 (1941–42), pp. 10–15.

54. Dioszegi, *Tracing Shamans*, pp. 238–40; S. I. Vajnstejn, 'Shamanism in Tuva at the Turn of the Twentieth Century', in Hoppál (ed.), *Shamanism in Eurasia*, pp. 353–73.

55. Lvoba, 'On the Shamanism of the Chulym Turks', pp. 237–44; Sokolova, 'Survey of the Ob-Ugrian Shamanism', pp. 155–64.

56. Jochelson, *The Koryak*, pp. 5–53; Mikhailowskii, 'Shamanism', pp. 141–52; Yekaterina D. Prokofyeva, 'The Costume of an Enets Shaman', in Michael (ed.), *Studies in Siberian Shamanism*, pp. 125–52.

57. Dioszegi, *Tracing Shamans*, pp. 106–07; Vasilevich, 'Acquisition of Shamanistic Ability', pp. 341–47.

58. Dioszegi, *Tracing Shamans*, p. 309.

Notes to Chapter 8: Shamanic Performance

1. Vilmos Dioszegi, *Tracing Shamans in Siberia* (Oosterhout: Anthropological Publications, 1968), pp. 314–15.
2. Johann Gottlieb Georgi, *Beschreibung aller Nationen des russischen Reichs* (4 vols, St Petersburg, 1776–80), i, p. 14; Waclaw Sieroszewski, *Yakuti* (St Petersburg, 1896), p. 637.
3. Arkadiy F. Anisimov, 'The Shaman's Tent in the Evenks', in Henry N. Michael (ed.), *Studies in Siberian Shamanism* (Toronto: Toronto University Press), p. 102.
4. Dioszegi, *Tracing Shamans*, pp. 278, 310–11.
5. Waldemar Jochelson, *The Yukaghir and the Yakaghirized Tungus* (Leiden: Brill, 1926), pp. 196–201.
6. Mircea Eliade, *Shamanism* (English edn, London: Routledge, 1964), p. 257; Piers Vitebsky, *The Shaman* (London: Macmillan, 1995), pp. 6–11; Caroline Humphrey and Urgunge Onon, *Shamans and Elders* (Oxford: Oxford University Press, 1996), p. 31.
7. Ann-Leena Siikala, *The Rite Technique of the Siberian Shaman* (Helsinki: FF Communications, Academia Scientarum Fennica, 1987), p. 321; and 'The Interpretation of Siberian and Central Asia Shamanism', in Siikala and Mihaly Hoppál, *Studies on Shamanism* (Budapest and Helsinki: Finnish Anthropological Society and Akademiai Kiado, 1992), pp. 11, 21; Johann Reinhard, 'Shamanism and Spirit Possession: The Definitional Problem', in John T. Hitchcock and Rex T. Jones (ed.), *Spirit Possession* (Warminster: Aries and Phillips, 1976), passim.
8. Sieroszewski, *Yakuti*, p. 637; S. M. Shirokogoroff, *Psychomental Complex of the Tungus* (London: Kegan Paul, 1935), pp. 304–06, 324–25; G. N. Potanin, *Ocherki Severo-zapadnoi Mongolii* (4 vols, St Petersburg, 1881–83), iv, pp. 80–87; Wilhelm Radlov, *Aus Sibirien* (2 vols, Leipzig, 1884), ii, pp. 20–50; V. M. Mikhailowskii, 'Shamanism in Siberia and European Russia', *Journal of the Anthropological Institute of Great Bitain and Ireland*, 24 (1895), pp. 97–98; Waldemar Jochelson, *The Yakut* (New York: Anthropological Reports of the American Museum of Natural History, 33.2, 1933), p. 109; V. I. Anuchin, *Ocherk Shamanstva u Yeniseiskikh Ostyakov* (St Petersburg, 1914), pp. 28–31; Shatlov, quoted in Vladimir Nikolaevich Basilov, *Izbranniki Dukhov* (Moscow: Politizdat, 1984), pp. 123–24; T. Lehtisalo, 'Entwurf einer Mythologie der Jurak-Samojeden', *Mémoirés de la Société Finno-Ougrienne*, 53 (1924), pp. 133–37, 145–70; Waldemar Bogoras, *The Chukchee* (Leiden: Brill, 1908), pp. 426, 438, 441; Anna-Leena Siikala, 'Two Types of Shamanizing and

Categories of Shamanic Songs', in Siikala and Hoppál, *Studies on Shamanism*, pp. 41–55; Anisimov, 'The Shaman's Tent', pp. 104–5; Dioszegi, *Tracing Shamans*, pp. 238–40; E. L. Lvova, 'On the Shamanism of the Chulym Turks', in Dioszegi and Hoppál, *Shamanism in Siberia*, pp. 237–44; E. A. Alekseenko, 'Categories of the Ket Shamans', in Dioszegi and Hoppál, *Shamans in Siberia*, pp. 255–64. The two full narratives given below are those in P. I. Tretyakov, *Turukhanskiye Kraya* (St Petersburg, 1891), pp. 217–18, and Potanin, *Ocherki*, iv, pp. 64–68.

9. Ivan A. Lopatin, 'A Shamanistic Performance to Regain the Favour of the Spirit', *Anthropos*, 35–36 (1940–41), pp. 365–68; Tatyana Bulgakova, 'Why Does Nanai Shaman Chant?', in Tae-Gon Kim and Mihaly Hoppál (ed.), *Shamanism in Performing Arts* (Budapest: Akademiai Kiado, 1995), p. 139; John Bell, *Travels from St Petersburg in Russia* (2 vols, Glasgow, 1763), i, pp. 253–55; Waldemar Jochelson, *The Koryak* (Leiden: Brill, 1908), pp. 49, 51; Jochelson, *The Yukaghir*, pp. 201–05; V. M. Mikhailowskii, 'Shamanism in Siberia and European Russia', *Journal of the Anthropological Institute of Great Britain and Ireland*, 24 (1895), pp. 66, 96; Bogoras, *The Chukchee*, pp. 435–36; Anisimov, 'The Shaman's Tent', pp. 100–03.

10. Jochelson, *The Yukaghir*, pp. 205–08; Alexander M. Castrén, *Nordische Reisen und Forschungen* (2 vols, St Petersburg, 1856–57), i, pp. 172–74; Grigory Novitskii, *Kratkoe Opisanie o Narodye Ostyatskom*, ed. L. Maikov (St Petersburg, 1884), pp. 48–49; Potanin, *Ocherki*, iv, pp. 60–62; Carla Corradi-Musi, 'Siberian Shamanism in the Eighteenth- and Nineteenth-Century Travellers Books', in Mihaly Hoppál and Otto von Sadovszky (ed.), *Shamanism Past and Present* (Budapest and Los Angeles; Hungarian Academy of Sciences and International Society for Trans-Oceanic Research, 1989), pp. 72–73; Bogoras, *The Chukchee*, pp. 433–40; Anna-Leena Siikala, 'Two Types of Shamanizing', in Siikala and Hoppál (ed.), *Studies on Shamanism*, pp. 41–55.

11. E.g. K. F. Karjalienen, *Die Religion der Jugra-Volker* (2 vols, Helsinki, 1921–27), ii, pp. 308–10.

12. Anisimov, 'The Shaman's Tent', pp. 100–05.

13. Richard Johnson, 'Certain Notes Unperfectly Written by Richard Johnson', in Richard Hakluyt, *The Principal Navigations, Voyages, Traffiques and Discoveries of the English Nation* (Glasgow edn, in 6 vols, 1903); John Bell, *Travels from St Petersburg in Russia* (2 vols, Glasgow, 1763), i, pp. 253–55; Grigory Novitskii, *Kratkoe Opisanie o Narodye Ostyakom*, ed. L. Maikov (St Petersburg, 1884), pp. 48–49.

14. Shirkogoroff, *Psychomental Complex*, pp. 328, 365, 379.

15. Potanin, *Ocherki*, iv, pp. 60–62.
16. Vitebsky, *The Shaman*, pp. 80–81.
17. M. J. Zornickaja, 'Dances of Yakut Shamans', in Dioszegi and Hoppál (ed.), *Shamanism in Siberia*, pp. 299–307.
18. Dioszegi, *Tracing Shamans*, pp. 283–90.
19. Z. P. Sokolova, 'Survey of the Ob-Ugrian Shamanism', in Hoppál and von Sadovszky (ed.), *Shamanism Past and Present*, pp. 161–62.
20. Vladimir Nikolaevich Basilov, 'Chosen by the Spirits', in Marjorie Mandelstam Balzer (ed.), *Shamanism* (Armonk, New York: Sharpe, 1990), pp. 28–29.
21. Shirokogoroff, *Psychomental Complex*, p. 311.
22. Bogoras, *The Chukchee*, pp. 424, 441; Eliade, *Shamanism*, p. 219; Sieroszewski, *Yakuti*, p. 635.
23. Sieroszewski, *Yakuti*, p. 636; Shirokogoroff, *Psychomental Complex*, pp. 304–06; Anisimov, 'The Shaman's Tent', pp. 84–97.
24. Wilhelm Radlov, *Aus Sibirien* (2 vols, Leipzig), ii, pp. 20–50.
25. Bastian, quoted in Mikhailowskii, 'Shamanism', p. 70.
26. Shirokogoroff, *Psychomental Complex*, p. 330.
27. Caroline Humphrey and Urgunge Onon, *Shamans and Elders* (Oxford: Oxford University Press, 1996), p. 261.
28. 'Certain Notes Unperfectly Written by Richard Johnson'; Bell, *Travels from St Petersburg*, i, pp. 253–55; Johann Georg Gmelin, *Reise durch Sibirien, vom dem Jahr 1733 bis 1743* (2 vols, Göttingen, 1751–52), ii, pp. 44–46.
29. Shirokogoroff, *Psychomental Complex*, pp. 325–33; Anisimov, 'The Shaman's Tent', 100–02.
30. Basilov, 'Chosen by the Spirits', p. 13.
31. Bogoras, *The Chukchee*, p. 433.
32. 'Certain Notes Unperfectly Written by Richard Johnson'.
33. Gmelin, *Reise durch Sibirien*, ii, pp. 44–46. See also Bell, *Travels from St Petersburg*, i, pp. 253–55; Stephan Krascheninnikow, *The History of Kamschatka and the Kurilski Islands*, trans. James Grieve (Gloucester, 1764), p. 230.
34. Jochelson, *The Koryak*, pp. 50–52.
35. Bogoras, *The Chukchee*, p. 442.
36. Ibid., pp. 426, 429, 436–37.
37. Ibid., pp. 421, 438–40.
38. Sieroszewski, *Yakuti*, p. 628; Vitebsky, *The Shaman*, p. 120; Shirokogoroff, *Psychomental Complex*, p. 332.
39. Basilov, 'Chosen by the Spirits', pp. 16–21.

Notes to Chapter 9: Knots and Loose Ends

1. S. M. Shirokogoroff, *Psychomental Complex of the Tungus* (London, Kegan Paul, 1935), p. 379; G. M. Vasilevich, 'The Acquisition of Shamanistic Ability among the Evenki', in Vilmos Dioszegi (ed.), *Popular Beliefs and Folklore Tradition* (Bloomington: Indiana University Press, 1968), pp. 346–49; Arkadiy F. Anismov, 'The Shaman's Tent of the Evenks', in Henry N. Michael (ed.), *Studies in Siberian Shamanism* (Toronto: Toronto University Press), pp. 121–22.

2. Waclaw Sieroszewski, *Yakuti* (St Petersburg, 1896), p. 627; Waldemar Bogoras, *The Chukchee* (Leiden: Brill, 1908), pp. 425, 432, 441; Z. P. Sokolova, 'Survey of the Ob-Ugrian Shamanism', in Mihaly Hoppál and Otto von Sadovszky (ed.), *Shamanism Past and Present* (Göttingen: Herodot, 1984), p. 161; Anatoly Alekseev, 'Shamanism among the Turkic Peoples', in Marjorie Mandelstam Balzer (ed.), *Shamanic Worlds* (Armonk, New York: Sharpe, 1990), pp. 88–89.

3. Åke Olmmarks, *Studium zum Problem des Schamanismus* (Lund, 1939), pp. 101–13; J. Balazs, 'The Hungarian Shaman's Technique of Trance Induction', in Dioszegi (ed.), *Popular Beliefs*, pp. 53–75; Mircea Eliade, *Shamanism* (English edn, London: Routledge, 1964), p. 221; Anna-Leena Siikala, 'The Interpretation of Siberian and Inner Asian Shamanism', in Siikala and Mihaly Hoppál, *Studies in Shamanism* (Budapest and Helsinki: Finnish Anthropological Society and Akademiai Kiado, 1992), p. 11.

4. K. F. Karjalainen, *Religion der Jugra-Volker* (2 vols, Helsinki, 1921–27), iii, pp. 306–08, 315–17.

5. Kai Donner, 'Ethnological Notes about the Yenisey-Ostyak', *Memoires de la Société Finno-Ougrinne*, 66 (1933), pp. 81–82.

6. T. Lehtisalo, 'Entwurf einer Mythologie der Jurak-Samojeden', *Memoires de la Société Finno-Ougrinne*, 53 (1924), p. 150.

7. Waldemar Bogoras, *The Chukchee* (Leiden: Brill, 1908), p. 425; Waldemar Jochelson, *The Koryak* (Leiden: Brill, 1908), p. 120.

8. For notable examples, see P. I. Tretyakov, *Turukhanskiye Kraya* (St Petersburg, 1891), pp. 217–18; G. N. Potanin, *Ocherki Severo-Zapadnoi Mongolii* (4 vols, St Petersburg, 1881–83), iv, pp. 64–68, 86–87; Wilhelm Radlov, *Aus Sibirien* (2 vols, Leipzig, 1884), ii, pp. 40–50; A. A. Popov, *Tavgytsy* (Moscow, 1936), pp. 84–90; Ksenofontov, *Legendy i Rasskazy u Yakutov, Buryat i Tungusov* (2nd edn, Moscow, 1930), pp. 44–65, 102–03; Lehtisalo, 'Entwurf einer Mythologie', pp. 133–37; Dioszegi, Vilmos *Tracing Shamans in Siberia* (Oosterhout: Anthropological

Publications, 1968), pp. 56–67; Evdokiya Gaer, 'The Way of the Soul to the Otherworld and the Nanai Shaman', in Hoppál and von Sadovszky (ed.), *Shamanism Past and Present* , pp. 233–39; Uno Harva, *Die religiosen Vorstellungen der altaischen Volker* (Helsinki: Folklore Fellows Communications, 52.125, 1938), pp. 558–59; Waldemar Jochelson, *The Koryak* (Leiden: Brill, 108), p. 93.

9. Paul Devereux, *Shamanism and the Mystery Lines* (London: Quantum, 1992).

10. Alby Stone, *Straight Track, Crooked Road: Leys, Spirit-Paths and Shamanism* (Wymeswold: Heart of Albion Press, 1998), pp. 13–27.

11. Shirokogoroff, *Psychomental Complex*, p. 336; Harva, *Die religiosen Vorstellungen*, pp. 268–72, 547; Sieroszewski, *Yakuti*, pp. 639–44.

12. Sources at p. 238.

13. Anisimov, 'The Shaman's Tent', p. 102.

14. Johann Georg Gmelin, *Reise durch Sibirien, vom dem Jahr 1733 bis 1743* (2 vols, Göttingen, 1751–52), ii, p. 288.

15. Bogoras, *The Chukchee*, p. 413; Caroline Humphrey, *Karl Marx Collective* (Cambridge: Cambridge University Press, 1983), p. 404; Alekseev, 'Shamanism among the Turkic Peoples', pp. 78, 85; Shirokogoroff, *Psychomental Complex*, p. 386; S. I. Vajnstein, 'Shamanism in Tuva at the Turn of the Twentieth Century', in Hoppál (ed.), *Shamanism in Europe*, p. 353; Dioszegi, *Tracing Shamans*, p. 209.

16. Shirokogoroff, *Psychomental Complex*, p. 386; Waldemar Jochelson, *The Yukaghir and the Yugkaghirized Tungus* (Leiden: Brill, 1926), pp. 193–94.

17. Bogoras, *The Chukchee*, 413–15; Jochelson, *The Koryak*, pp. 49–60; Jochelson, *The Yukaghir*, pp. 193–94; P. Hajdu, 'Classification of Samoyed Shamans', in Dioszegi (ed.), *Popular Beliefs*, pp. 147–73.

18. Yekaterina D. Prokofyeva, 'Costume of an Enets Shaman', in Michael (ed.), *Studies in Siberian Shamanism*, pp. 124–26; Gmelin, *Reise durch Siberien*, ii, pp. 82–84.

19. V. M. Mikhailowskii, 'Shamanism in Siberia and European Russia', *Journal of the Anthropological Institute of Great Britain and Ireland*, 24 (1895), p. 129; Sieroszewski, *Yakuti*, p. 631; Nikolai Alekseevich Alekseev, 'Shamanism among the Turkic Peoples of Siberia ', in Balzer (ed.), *Shamanism*, p. 78.

20. Jochelson, *The Yukaghir*, pp. 193–94.

21. Troschanski, *Evoludiya 'Chernaya Vera' (Shamanstva) u Yakutoi* (Kazan, 1901), pp. 120–25.

22. M. A. Czaplicka, *Aboriginal Siberia* (Oxford: Oxford University Press, 1914), p. 200.
23. Humphrey, *Karl Marx Collective*, p. 404; Roberte Hamayon, 'Is There a Typically Female Exercise of Shamanism in Patrilinear Societies such as the Buryat?', in Hoppál (ed.), *Shamanism in Eurasia*, pp. 307–18.
24. A point made by Hamayon, 'Is There a Typically Female Exercise of Shamanism?', pp. 307–08.
25. Sieroszewski, *Yakuti*, pp. 78–94; Hamayon, 'Is There a Typically Female Exercise of Shamanism?', pp. 307–18; Jochelson, *The Koryak*, pp. 744–45.
26. Leopold von Schrenk, *Amurkago Kraya* (St Petersburg, 1903), ii, pp. 11–13; E. I. Rombandeeva, 'Some Observances and Customs of the Mansi (Voguls) in Connection with Childbirth', in Dioszegi (ed.) *Popular Beliefs*, pp. 77–83.
27. James Forsyth, *A History of the Peoples of Siberia* (Cambridge: Cambridge University Press, 1992), pp. 286–87.
28. Bogoras, *The Chukchee*, p. 132.
29. Jochelson, *The Koryak*, pp. 52–53; Jochelson, *The Yukaghir*, pp. 193–95; Sieroszewski, *Yakuti*, p. 631.

Notes to Chapter 10: The Discovery of a Shamanic World

1. Johann Gottlieb Georgi, *Beschreibung aller Nationen des russichen Reiches* (4 vols, St Petersburg), iii, p. 375; S. M. Shirokogoroff, *Psychomental Complex of the Tungus* (London, Kegan Paul, 1935), pp. 282–86.
2. V. Voigt, 'Shaman: Person or Word?', in Mihaly Hoppál (ed.), *Shamanism in Eurasia* (Göttingen: Herodot, 1984), p. 16.
3. The debate is summarized in Mihaly Hoppál, 'The Origin of Shamanism and the Siberian Rock Art', in Anna-Leena Siikala and Mihaly Hoppál, *Studies on Shamanism* (Budapest and Helsinki: Finnish Anthropological Society and Akademiai Kiado, 1992), pp. 132–49.
4. The sources are cited and discussed in Berthold Laufer, 'Origin of the Word Shaman', *American Anthropologist*, new series, 19 (1917), pp. 361–71.
5. Ibid.; Shirokogoroff, *Psychomental Complex*, p. 269; Voigt, 'Shaman: Person or Word?', pp. 13–15.
6. Cf. Shirokogoroff, *Psychomental Complex*, pp. 281–86.
7. See the survey provided by V. N. Basilov, 'The Study of Shamanism in Russian Ethnography', in Hoppál (ed.), *Shamanism in Eurasia*,

pp. 46–63; and Gustav Rank, 'Shamanism as a Research Subject', in Carl-Martin Edsman (ed.), *Studies in Shamanism* (Stockholm: Almqvist and Wiksell, 1967), pp. 15–22.

8. Arkadiy F. Anisimov, 'The Shaman's Tent of the Evenks', in Michael (ed.), *Studies in Siberian Shamanism*, pp. 84–123; and Cosmological Concepts of the Peoples of the North', ibid., pp. 157–229; I. S. Vdovin, 'Social Foundations of Ancestor Cult among the Yukaghirs, Koryaks and Chukchis', in Vilmos Dioszegi and Mihaly Hoppál (ed.), *Shamanism in Siberia* (Budapest: Adamediai Kiado, 1978), pp. 405–18; Taras M. Mikhailov, 'Buryat Shamanism', in Marjorie Mandelstam Balzer (ed.), *Shamanism*, pp. 110–20 (Armonk, New York: Sharpe, 1990).

9. All discussed in Caroline Humphrey, 'Theories of North Asian Shamanism', in Ernest Gellner, *Soviet and Western Anthropology* (London, Duckworth), pp. 246–50.

10. Ibid., pp. 246, 249–50.

11. Ibid., pp. 250–52; and Caroline Humphrey, 'Shamanic Practices and the State', in Nicholas Thomas and Caroline Humphrey (ed.), *Shamanism, History and the State* (Ann Arbor: University of Michigan Press, 1994), pp. 198–208.

12. Discussed by Mirceade Eliade, *Shamanism* (English edn, London: Routledge, 1964), pp. 495–502; and Humphrey, 'Theories of North Asian Shamanism', pp. 244–45.

13. Waldemar Jochelson, *The Koryak* (Leiden: Brill, 1908), pp. 47–52; Eliade, *Shamanism*, p. 253.

14. Z. P. Sokolova, 'A Survey of the Ob-Ugrian Shamanism', in Mihaly Hoppál and Otto von Sadovszky (ed.), *Shamanism Past and Present* (Budapest and Los Angeles: Hungarian Academy of Sciences and International Society for Trans-Oceanic Research, 1989), pp. 155–56; E. L. Lvova, 'On the Shamanism of the Chulym Turks', in Dioszegi and Hoppál (ed.), *Shamanism in Siberia*, pp. 237–44.

15. Humphrey, 'Theories of North Asian Shamanism', pp. 248–49.

16. On which see Mihaly Hoppál, 'Studies on Eurasian Shamanism', in Mihaly Hoppál and Keith D. Howard (ed.), *Shamans and Cultures* (Budapest and Los Angeles: Akademiai Kiado and International Society for Trans-Oceanic Research, 1993), pp. 259–60.

17. Eliade, *Shamanism*, passim: quotations on pp. 4, 8, 33, 508, 509.

18. Ibid., p. 247.

19. Ibid., pp. 183–84, 221, 256. For an example of the splicing effect, see p. 218.

20. Ibid., pp. 45–62, 122–44, 288–366.
21. Ibid., pp. 361–66.
22. I. M. Lewis, *Ecstatic Religion* (Harmondsworth: Penguin, 1971), passim; quotations on pp. 15, 49, 178, 189, 205.
23. Cf. Mihaly Hoppál, 'Shamanism: An Archaic and/or Recent System of Beliefs', in Siikala and Hoppal (ed.), *Studies on Shamanism*, p. 117; Rank, 'Shamanism as a Research Subject', pp. 15–22; Åke Hultkranz, 'The Place of Shamanism in the History of Religion', in Hoppál and von Sadowszky (ed.), *Shamanism Past and Present*, pp. 43–46.
24. Eliade, *Shamanism*, pp. 45–50, 122–44; Piers Vitebsky, *The Shaman* (London: Macmillan, 1995), p. 50; Hultkranz, 'The Place of Shamanism', Lewis, *Ecstatic Religion*, passim.
25. The impression is stated as orthodoxy in Roger Walsh, *The Spirit of Shamanism* (Los Angeles: Tarcher, 1990), chapter 2; and challenged in Vitebsky, *The Shaman*, pp. 29, 32. Åke Hultkranz, 'The Shaman in Myths and Tales', in Tae-Gon Kim and Mihaly Hoppál (ed.), *Shamanism in Performing Arts* (Budapest; Akademiai Kiado), p. 147.
26. Hultkranz, 'The Place of Shamanism', pp. 47–88.
27. Vitebsky, *The Shaman*, pp. 8–11, 30.

Notes to Chapter 11: The Discovery of a Shamanic Past

1. Vladimir Nikolaevich Basilov, 'Chosen by the Spirits', in Marjorie Mandelstam Balzer (ed.), *Shamanism* (Armonk, New York: Sharpe, 1990), pp. 39–40.
2. S. H. Nyberg, *Die Religionen des Alten Iran* (1937: repr. Osnabrück: Zeller, 1966); W. B. Henning, *Zoroaster: Politician or Witch-Doctor?* (Oxford: Oxford University Press, 1951). For latest thoughts see Touraj Daryaee, 'Shamanistic Elements in Zoroastrianism', *The Pomegranate*, 13 (2000), pp. 31–37.
3. F. M. Cornford, *Principium Sapientiae* (Cambridge: Cambridge University Press, 1952), pp. 88–106; E. R. Dodds, *The Greeks and the Irrational* (Berkeley: University of California Press, 1951), pp. 135–78; Walter Burkert, *Structure and History in Greek Mythology and Ritual* (Berkeley: University of California Press, 1979), pp. 78–96; quotation on p. 96; Jan Bremmer, *The Early Greek Concept of the Soul* (Princeton: Princeton University Press, 1983), p. 47.
4. Horst Kirchner, 'Ein archäologischer Beitrag zur Urgeschichte des Schamanismus', *Anthropos*, 47 (1952), pp. 244–86; Karl J. Narr, 'Baren-zeremoniell und Schamanismus in der Alteren Steinzeit Europas',

Saeculum, 10, pt 3 (1959), pp. 233–72; Mirceade Eliade, *Shamanism* (English edn, London: Routledge, 1964), pp. 503–04.

5. Andreas Lommel, *Shamanism: The Beginnings of Art* (New York: McGraw-Hill, 1967). The reactions were collected in *Current Anthropology,* 11 (1970), pp. 39–48.

6. David Lewis-Williams and Thomas Dowson, 'The Signs of All Times', *Current Anthropology,* 29 (1988), pp. 201–45; Jean Clottes and David Lewis-Williams, *The Shamans of Prehistory* (New York: Abrams, 1998).

7. For the classic hostile outburst, see Paul Bahn, 'Stumbling in the Footsteps of St Thomas', *British Archaeology,* 31 (1998), p. 18. The debates are overviewed by Robert Layton, 'Shamanism, Totemism and Rock Art', *Cambridge Archaeological Journal,* 10 (2000), pp. 169–86.

8. Clottes and Lewis-Williams, *Shamans of Prehistory,* p. 59.

9. Jeremy Dronfield, 'Subjective Vision and the Source of Irish Megalithic Art', *Antiquity,* 69 (1995), pp. 539–49; and 'Entering Alternative Realities: Cognition, Art and Architecture in Irish Passage Tombs', *Cambridge Archaeological Journal,* 6 (1996), pp. 37–52; and ensuing discussion in ibid., pp. 55–72. Robert J. Wallis makes a good speculative interpretation of the great Neolithic ceremonial complex at Avebury in terms of shamanism, appended as a booklet to his important thesis 'Autoarchaeology and Neoshamanism: The Sociopolitics of Ecstasy' (unpublished Ph.D. thesis, Southampton University, 2000).

10. Cf. Aubrey Burl, *Prehistoric Avebury* (New Haven: Yale University Press, 1979), and *Rites of the Gods* (London: Dent, 1981), pp. 150–54.

11. N. K. Chadwick, 'Shamanism among the Tatars of Central Asia', *Journal of the Royal Anthropological Institute,* 66 (1936), pp. 75–112.

12. *Poetry and Prophecy* (Cambridge: Cambridge University Press, 1942).

13. Ibid., p. 58.

14. Alwyn Rees and Brinley Rees, *Celtic Heritage: Ancient Tradition in Ireland and Wales* (London: Thames and Hudson, 1961), pp. 17, 236, 256, 305, 310.

15. Daniel F. Melia, 'The Irish Saint as Shaman', *Pacific Coast Philology,* 18 (1983), pp. 37–42.

16. Joseph Nagy, 'Shamanic Aspects of the Bruidhean Tale', *History of Religions,* 20 (1981), pp. 302–22 (the definition is on p. 303); Leslie Ellen Jones, *Druid, Shaman, Priest: Metaphors of Celtic Paganism* (Enfield: Hisarlik, 1998), pp. 97–126.

17. Translated by Jeffrey Gantz, *Early Irish Myths and Sagas* (Harmondsworth: Penguin, 1981), p. 65.

18. V. M. Mikhailowskii, 'Shamanism in Siberia and European Russia', *Journal of the Anthropological Institute of Great Britain and Ireland,* 24 (1895), pp. 151–55.

19. Ibid., pp. 155–57.

20. J. Pentikainen, 'The Saami Shaman', in Mihaly Hoppál (ed.), *Shamanism in Eurasia* (Göttingen: Herodot, 1984), pp. 125–48; Tore Åhlback and Jan Bergman (ed.), *The Saami Shaman Drum* (Abo: Scripta Instituti Donneriani Aboensis, 12, 1987). The information on Finnish folk magic is based on a personal communication from Laura Stark-Arola of Helsinki University, 9 December 2000. Dr Stark-Arola works with the great Finnish expert on Siberian shamanism, Anna-Leena Siikala, who is preparing a book on that of the Finns.

21. Cited in Inger Zachrisson, 'The Saami Shaman Drums', in Ahlback and Bergmann (ed.), *The Saami Shaman Drum,* chapter 4; R. Grambo, 'Shamanism in Norwegian Popular Legends', in Hoppál (ed.), *Shamanism in Eurasia,* pp. 391–92.

22. The most convenient overview is in H. R. Ellis Davidson, 'Hostile Magic in the Icelandic Sagas', in Venetia Newall (ed.), *The Witch Figure* (London: Routledge, 1973), pp. 20–42.

23. This figure is identified from a worldwide sample of material in Ronald Hutton, 'The Global Context of the Scottish Witch-Hunts', in Julian Goodare (ed.), *The Scottish Witch-Hunt in Context* (Edinburgh: Edinburgh University Press, forthcoming). The succeeding paragraphs of the present work are also drawn from that essay, where full references are given.

24. Cf. Vilmos Dioszegi, *Tracing Shamans in Siberia* (Oosteehout: Anthropological Publications, 1968), pp. 23–24, 204–05.

25. Ibid., pp. 61–65; Mihaly Hoppál, 'Traces of Shamanism in Hungarian Folk Beliefs'; and 'The Role of Shamanism in Hungarian Ethnic Identity', in Anna-Leena Siikala and Mihaly Hoppál, *Studies on Shamanism* (Budapest and Helsinki: Finnish Anthropological Society and Akademiai Kiado, 1992), pp. 156–68, 169–75; Jeno Fazekas, 'Hungarian Shamanism: Material and History of Research', in Henry N. Michael (ed.), *Studies in Siberian Shamanism* (Toronto: Toronto University Press, 1963), pp. 97–119.

26. Carlo Ginzburg, *The Night Battles: Witchcraft and Agrarian Cults in the Sixteenth and Seventeenth Centuries,* trans. J. and Tedeschi (London: Routledge, 1983); Cf. Carlo Ginzburg, *I Benandanti* (Turin, 1966).

27. Gabor Klaniczay, 'Shamanistic Elements in Central European

Witchcraft', in Hoppál (ed.), *Shamanism in Eurasia*, pp. 404–22; Carlo Ginzburg, *Ecstasies: Deciphering the Witches' Sabbath*, trans. R. Rosenthal (Harmondsworth: Penguin, 1992), passim; quotation on p. 194. Cf. Carlo Ginzburg, *Storia notturna* (Turin, 1989).

28. Sources as at n. 25; quotation from Hoppál, 'The Role of Shamanism in Hungarian Ethnic Identity', p. 173.

29. Eva Pocs, *Between the Living and the Dead: A Perspective on Witches and Seers in the Early Modern Age* (Budapest: Central European University Press, 1999), pp. 73–105, 121–64; Gabor Klaniczay, 'Shamanistic Elements in Central European Witchcraft', in Hoppál (ed.), *Shamanism in Eurasia*, pp. 416–20.

30. Ginzburg, *Ecstasies*, pp. 162–65.

31. Ibid., p. 171; Klaniczay, 'Shamanistic Elements', pp. 420–22; quotation on p. 421.

32. Quoted in Ginzburg, *Ecstasies*, p. 188; and Hoppál, 'The Role of Shamanism in Hungarian Ethnic Identity', in Siikala and Hoppál (ed.), *Studies on Shamanism*, pp. 170–71.

33. Ginzburg, *Ecstasies*, p. 194 and n. 64.

34. Ibid., pp. 90–105, 189.

35. Ronald Hutton, *The Stations of the Sun: A History of the Ritual Year in Britain* (Oxford: Oxford University Press, 1996), pp. 77–78.

36. Carl-Martin Edsman, 'A Swedish Female Folk Healer', in Carl-Martin Edsman (ed.), *Studies in Shamanism* (Stockholm: Almqvist and Wiksell, 1967), pp. 120–65.

Notes to Chapter 12: The Discovery of a Shamanic Future

1. Vilmos Dioszegi, *Tracing Shamans in Siberia* (Oosterhout: Anthropological Publications, 1968), p. 38.

2. Ronald Hutton, *The Shamans of Siberia* (Glastonbury: Isle of Avalon Press, 1993), p. 18.

3. Such as Mihaly Hoppál: Hoppál, 'Shamanism: An Archaic and/or Recent System of Beliefs', in Anna-Leena Siikala and Mihaly Hoppál (ed.), *Studies on Shamanism* (Budapest and Helsinki: Finnish Anthropological Society and Akademiai Kiado, 1992), pp. 118–19.

4. Caroline Humphrey and Urgunge Onon, *Shamans and Elders* (Oxford: Oxford University Press, 1996), p. 1.

5. Vladimir Nikolaevich Basilov, 'Chosen by the Spirits', in Marjorie Mandelstam Balzer (ed.), *Shamanism* (Armonk, New York: Sharpe, 1990), pp. 31, 43–46.

6. Marjorie Mandelstam Balzer, 'Introduction', in Balzer (ed.), *Shamanism*, p. vii.
7. Taras M. Mikhailov, 'Buryat Shamanism', in Balzer (ed.), *Shamanism*, p. 115.
8. His pronouncements are chronicled in James Forsyth, *A History of the Peoples of Siberia* (Cambridge: Cambridge University Press, 1992), pp. 366, 369, 397–408.
9. Ken Hyder, 'Global Ear: Siberia', *The Wire* (April 1998), p. 22. I am grateful to 'Bendle' for supplying me with this article.
10. Ibid., p. 23.
11. Colin Thubron, *In Siberia* (London: Chatto and Windus, 1999), pp. 99–107.
12. A colleague from my own university department found it treated as such on a recent visit to Kyzyl.
13. Piers Vitebsky, 'Landscape and Self-Determination among the Eveny', in Elisabeth and Croll and David Parkin (ed.), *Bush Base: Forest Farm* (London: Routledge, 1992), pp. 223–46.
14. Piers Vitebsky, 'From Cosmology to Environmentalism: Shamanism as Local Knowledge in a Global Setting', in Richard Fardon (ed.), *Counterworks: Managing the Diversity of Knowledge* (London: Routledge, 1995), pp. 182–203.
15. Marjorie Mandelstam Balzer, 'Two Urban Shamanisms: Unmasking Leadership in Fin-de-Soviet Siberia', in George E. Marcus (ed.), *Perilous States* (Chicago: University of Chicago Press, 1993), pp. 131–64.
16. Classic texts of the movement are Carlos Castaneda, *The Teachings of Don Juan: A Yaqui Way of Knowledge* (Berkeley: University of California Press, 1968); Michael Harner, *The Way of the Shaman* (San Francisco: Harper and Row, 1980); Nevill Drury, *The Elements of Shamanism* (Shaftesbury: Element Books, 1989). For a critical overview see Daniel C. Noel, *The Soul of Shamanism: Western Fantasies, Imaginal Realities* (New York: Continuum, 1997). For comparisons between North American and Siberian shamanism, see Mirceade Eliade, *Shamanism* (English edn, London: Routledge, 1964), pp. 288–335; Juha Pentikainen, 'The Shamans and Shamanism', in Hoppál (ed.), *Shamanism in Eurasia* (Göttingen: Herodot, 1984), pp. 43–44 (quotation from Talamantez on p. 44); Åke Hultkrantz, 'On the History of Research in Shamanism', in Pentikainen et al. (ed.), *Shamans* (Tampere: Tampere Museums, 1999), pp. 59–61. My summary of 'core shamanism' is derived from Michael Harner, *The Way of the Shaman* (San Francisco: Harper and Row, 1980; third edn, 1990); quotation on p. xv.

17. The best recent discussion of these issues by a British author is in Robert Wallis's unpublished Southampton University Ph.D. thesis, 'Autoarchaeology and Neoshamanism'.

18. Merete Demant Jakobsen, *Shamanism* (New York: Berghahn, 1999), pp. 157–222, debates these matters at length.

19. Olga Kharitidi, *Entering the Circle: Ancient Secrets of Wisdom Discovered by a Russian Psychiatrist* (San Francisco: Harper San Francisco, 1996).

20. *Seattle Times*, 2 April 2000, p. M2. I am grateful to Gordon Cooper for supplying me with this article.

21. Wallis, 'Autoarchaeology and Neoshamanism', pp. 190–91.

22. Hoppál, 'Shamanism: An Archaic and/or Recent System of Beliefs', in Siikala and Hoppál, *Studies on Shamanism*, p. 121; and 'Studies on Eurasian Shamanism', pp. 266, 280.

23. Marjorie Mandelstam Balzer, 'The Poetry of Shamanism', in Tae-Gon Kim and Mihaly Hoppál (ed.), *Shamanism in Performing Arts* (Budapest: Akademiai Kiado, 1995), p. 174.

Bibliography

Agapitov, N. N., and Khangalov, M. N., *Materialy dlya Izuchenia Sha-manstva i Sibiri* (Izvestia Vostochno-Sibiriskovo Otdzla Russkovo Geograficheskovo Obshchestva, 14.1–2, 1883).

Åhlback, Tore, and Bergman, Jan (ed.), *The Saami Shaman Drum* (Abo: Scripta Instituti Donneriani Aboensis, 12, 1987).

Alekseenko, E. A., 'Categories of the Ket Shamans', in Dioszegi and Hoppál (ed.), *Shamanism in Siberia*, pp. 255–64.

Alekseev, Anatoly, 'Healing Techniques among Even Shamans', in Balzer (ed.), *Shamanic Worlds*, pp. 153–61.

Alekseev, Nikolai Alekseevich, 'Helping Spirits of the Siberian Turks', in Hoppál (ed.), *Shamanism in Eurasia*, pp. 268–79.

—, 'Shamanism among the Turkic Peoples of Siberia', in Balzer (ed.), *Shamanism*, pp. 78–108.

Almond, Philip C., *The British Discovery of Buddhism* (Cambridge: Cambridge University Press, 1988).

Anisimov, Arkadiy F., 'Cosmological Concepts of the Peoples of the North', in Michael (ed.), *Studies in Siberian Shamanism*, pp. 157–229.

—, *Religiya Evenkov* (Moscow, 1958).

—, 'The Shaman's Tent of the Evenks', in ibid., pp. 84–123.

Anuchin, V. I., *Ocherk Shamanstva u Yeniseikikh Ostayakov* (St Petersburg, 1914).

Armstrong, Terence, *Russian Settlement in the North* (Cambridge: Cambridge University Press, 1965).

Artiunov, S. A., 'Chukchi' in Fitzhugh and Crowell (ed.), *Crossroads of Continents*, pp. 39–42.

—, 'Koryak and Itelmen', in ibid., pp. 31–35.

Bahn, Paul, 'Stumbling in the Footsteps of St Thomas', *British Archaeology*, 31 (1998), p. 18.

Balzer, Marjorie Mandelstam (ed.), *Shamanic Worlds* (Armonk, New York: North Castle, 1997).

—, (ed.), *Shamanism* (Armonk, New York: Sharpe, 1990).

—, 'The Poetry of Shamanism', in Kim and Hoppál (ed.), *Shamanism in Performing Arts*, pp. 171–87.

—, 'Two Urban Shamanisms: Unmasking Leadership in Fin-de-Soviet Siberia', in Marcus (ed.), *Perilous States*, pp. 131–64.

Banzarov, Dorji, *Chernaya Vera ili Shamanstvu u Mongolov* (St Petersburg, 1891).

Basilov, Vladimir Nikolaevich., 'Chosen by the Spirits', in Balzer (ed.), *Shamanism*, pp. 1–46.

—, *Izbranniki Dukhov* (Moscow: Politizdat, 1984).

—, 'The Study of Shamanism in Russian Ethnography', in Hoppál (ed.), *Shamanism in Eurasia*, pp. 46–63.

Bell, John, *Travels from St Petersburg in Russia* (2 vols, Glasgow, 1763).

Bielayewski, R., *Psezdka ki Lyedavitamu Maru* (Moscow, 1883).

Black, Lydia T., 'Peoples of the Amur and Maritime Regions', in Fitzhugh and Crowell (ed.), *Crossroads of Continents*, pp. 24–30

Bogoras, Waldemar, *The Chukchee* (Leiden: Brill, 1908).

Bulgakaya, Tatyana, 'Why Does Nanai Shaman Chant?', in Kim and Hoppál (ed.), *Shamanism in Performing Arts*, pp. 135–44.

Burkert, Walter, *Structure and History in Greek Mythology and Ritual* (Berkeley: University of California Press, 1983).

Burl, Aubrey, *Prehistoric Avebury* (New Haven: Yale University Press, 1979).

—, *Rites of the Gods* (London: Dent, 1981).

Castaneda, Carlos, *The Teachings of Don Juan: A Yaqui Way of Knowledge* (Berkeley: University of California Press, 1968).

Castrén, Alexander M., *Nordische Reisen und Forschungen* (2 vols, St Petersburg, 1856–57).

Chadwick, N. K., *Poetry and Prophecy* (Cambridge: Cambridge University Press, 1942).

—, 'Shamanism among the Tatars of Central Asia', *Journal of the Royal Anthropological Institute*, 66 (1936), pp. 75–112.

Chernetsov, V. N., 'Concepts of the Soul among the Ob-Ugrians', in Michael (ed.), *Studies in Siberian Shamanism*, pp. 3–45.

Clottes, Jean, and Lewis-Williams, David, *The Shamans of Prehistory* (New York: Abrams, 1998).

Collins, David N, 'Russia's Conquest of Siberia', *European Studies Review*, 12 (1982), pp. 17–44.

Corradi-Musi, Carla, 'Siberian Shamanism in the Eighteenth- to Nineteenth- Century Travellers Books, in Hoppál and von Sadovszky (ed.), *Shamanism Past and Present*, pp. 69–73.

Cornford, F. M., *Principium Sapientiae* (Cambridge: Cambridge University Press, 1952).

Croll, Elisabeth, and Parkin, David (ed.), *Bush Base: Forest Farm* (London: Routledge, 1995).

Curtin, Jeremiah, *A Journey in Southern Siberia* (London, 1910).

Czaplicka, M. A., *Aboriginal Siberia* (Oxford: Oxford University Press, 1914).

Daryaee, Touray, 'Shamanistic Elements in Zoroastrianism', *The Pomegranate*, 13 (2000), pp. 31–37.

Davidson, H. R. Ellis, 'Hostile Magic in the Icelandic Sagas', in Venetia Newall (ed.), *The Witch Figure* (London: Routledge, 1973), pp. 20–42.

Devereux, Paul, *Shamanism and the Mystery Lines* (London: Quantum, 1992).

Digby, Bassett, *Tigers, Gold and Witch-Doctors* (London: Bodley Head, 1928).

Dioszegi, Vilmos, (ed.), *Popular Beliefs and Folklore Tradition in Siberia* (Bloomington: Indiana University Press, 1968).

—, 'The Problem of the Ethnic Homogeneity of Tofa (Karagas) Shamanism', in ibid., pp. 239–339.

—, *Tracing Shamans in Siberia* (Oosterhout: Anthropological Publications, 1968).

—, and Hoppál, Mihaly (ed.), *Shamanism in Siberia* (Budapest: Akademiai Kiado, 1978), 'Pre-Islamic Shamanism of the Baraba Turks', in Dioszegi and Hoppál (ed.), *Shamanism in Siberia*, pp. 83–167.

Dodds, E. R., *The Greeks and the Irrational* (Berkeley: University of California Press, 1951).

Donner, Kai, 'Ethnological Notes about the Yenisey-Ostyak', *Mémoires de la Société Finno-Ougrienne*, 66 (1933), pp. 75–95.

—, *La Siberie* (Paris, 1946).

Dronfield, Jeremy, 'Entering Alternative Realities: Cognition, Art and Architecture in Irish Passage Tombs', *Cambridge Archeological Journal*, 6 (1996), pp. 37–52.

—, 'Subjective Vision and the Source of Irish Megalithic Art', *Antiquity*, 69 (1995), pp. 539–49.

Drury, Nevill, *The Elements of Shamanism* (Shaftesbury: Element, 1989).

Edsman, Carl-Martin (ed.), 'A Swedish Female Folk Healer', in ibid., pp. 120–65.

—, *Studies in Shamanism* (Stockholm: Almqvist and Wiksell, 1967).

Eliade, Mircea, *Shamanism* (English edn, London: Routledge, 1964).

Farndon, Richard (ed.), *Counterworks: Managing the Diversity of Knowledge* (London: Routledge, 1995).

Fazekas, Jeno, 'Hungarian Shamanism: Material and History of Research', in Michael (ed.), *Studies in Siberian Shamanism*, pp. 97–119.

Fitzhugh, William W., and Crowell, Aron (ed.), *Crossroads of Continents* (Washington, DC: Smithsonian Institution, 1988).

Flaherty, Gloria, *Shamanism and the Eighteenth Century* (Princeton, New Jersey: Princeton University Press, 1992).

Forsyth, James, *A History of the Peoples of Siberia* (Cambridge: Cambridge University Press, 1992).

Gaer, Evdokiya, 'The Way of the Soul to the Otherworld and the Nanai Shaman', in Hoppál and von Sadovszky (ed.), *Shamanism Past and Present*, pp. 233–39.

Gantz, Jeffrey, *Early Irish Myths and Sagas* (Harmondsworth: Penguin, 1981).

Gellner, Ernest (ed.), *Soviet and Western Anthropology* (London: Duckworth, 1980).

Georgi, Johann Gottlieb, *Beschreibung aller Nationen des russischen Reichs* (4 vols, St Petersburg, 1776–80).

Gilberg, R., 'How to Recognise a Shaman among Other Religious Specialists?', in Hoppál (ed.), *Shamanism in Eurasia*, pp. 21–27.

Ginzburg, Carlo, *Ecstasies: Deciphering the Witches' Sabbath*, trans. R. Rosenthal (Harmondsworth: Penguin, 1992).

—, *The Night Battles: Witchcraft and Agrarian Cults in the Sixteenth and Seventeenth Centuries*, trans. J. and A. Tedeschi (London: Routledge, 1983).

Gmelin, Johann Georg, *Reise durch Sibirien, vom dem Jahr 1733 bis 1743)* (2 vols, Göttingen, 1751–52).

Golder, F. A. (ed.), *Bering's Voyages* (New York: American Geographical Society, 2 vols 1922).

Goodare, Julian (ed.), *The Scottish Witch-Hunt in Context* (Edinburgh: Edinburgh University Press, forthcoming).

Grambo, 'Shamanism in Norwegian Popular Legends', in Hoppál (ed.), *Shamanism in Eurasia*, pp. 391–403.

Gurvich, 'Ethnic Connections Across Bering Strait', in Fitzhugh and Crowell (ed.), *Crossroads of Continents*, pp. 18–21.

Hajdu, P., 'Classification of Samoyed Shamans' in Dioszegi (ed.), *Popular Beliefs*, pp. 147–73.

Hamayon, Roberte, 'Are "Trance", "Ecstasy" and Similar Concepts Appropriate in the Study of Shamanism?', in Kim and Hoppál (ed.), *Shamanism in Performing Arts*, pp. 17–34.

—, 'Game and Games, Fortune and Dualism in Siberian Shamanism', in Hoppál and Pentikainen (ed.), *Northern Religions and Shamanism*, pp. 134–37.

—, 'Is There a Typically Female Exercise of Shamanism in Patrilinear Societies such as the Buryat?', in Hoppál (ed.), *Shamanism in Eurasia*, pp. 307–18.

—, *La chasse a l'âme: esquisse d'une théorie du Chamanisme Siberien* (Nanterre: Société d'Ethnologie, 1990).

—, 'Shamanism in Siberia: From Partnership in Supernature to Counter-Power in Society', in Thomas and Humphrey (ed.), *Shamanism, History and the State*, pp. 76–89.

Harner, Michael, *The Way of the Shaman* (San Francisco: Harper and Row, 1980).

Harva, Uno, *Die religiosen Vorstellungen der altaischen Volker* (Helsinki: Folklore Fellows Communications, 52.125, 1938).

Harvey, Graham, 'Shamanism in Britain Today', *Performance Research*, 3 (1998), pp. 10–30.

Henning, W. B., *Zoroaster: Politician or Witch-Doctor?* (Oxford: Oxford University Press, 1951).

Hitchcock, John T., and Jones, Rex T. (ed.), *Spirit Possession in the Nepal Himalayas* (Warminster: Aries and Phillips, 1976).

Holmberg, Uno (alias Uno Harva), *Finno-Ugric and Siberian Mythology* (New York: Cooper Square, 1964).

Hoppál, Mihaly (ed.), *Shamanism in Eurasia* (Göttingen: Herodot, 1984).

—, and von Sadovszky, Otto (ed.), *Shamanism Past and Present* (Budapest and Los Angeles: Hungarian Academy of Sciences and International Society for Transoceanic Research, 1989).

—, 'Shamanism: An Archaic and/or Recent System of Beliefs', in Siikala and Hoppál, *Studies on Shamanism*, pp. 117–13.

—, 'Shamanism: Universal Structures and Regional Symbols', in ibid., pp. 181–92.

—, 'The Changing Image of Siberian Shamanism', in ibid., pp. 176–81.

—, 'The Origin of Shamanism and the Siberian Rock Art', in ibid., pp. 132–49.

—, 'The Role of Shamanism in Hungarian Ethnic Identity', in ibid., pp. 169–75.

—, 'Traces of Shamanism in Hungarian Folk Beliefs', in ibid., pp. 156–68.

—, and Howard, Keith D. (ed.), *Shamans and Cultures* (Budapest and Los Angeles: Akademiai Kiado and International Society for Trans-Oceanic Research, 1993).

—, and Pentikainen, Juha (ed.), *Northern Religions and Shamanism* (Budapest and Helsinki: Akademiai Kiado and Finnish Literature Society, 1992).

Hultkranz, Åke, 'Ecological and Phenomenological Aspects of Shamanism', in Dioszegi and Hoppál (ed.), *Shamanism in Siberia*, pp. 27–58.

—, 'On the History of Research in Shamanism', in Pentikainen et al. (ed.), *Shamans*, pp. 51–70.

—, 'The Place of Shamanism in the History of Religion', in Hoppál and von Sadovszky (ed.), *Shamanism Past and Present*, pp. 43–46.

—, 'The Shaman in Myths and Tales', in Kim and Hoppál (ed.), *Shamanism in Performing Arts*, pp. 145–55.

Humphrey, Caroline, *Karl Marx Collective* (Cambridge: Cambridge University Press, 1983).

—, 'Shamanic Practices and the State in North Asia', in Thomas and Humphrey (ed.), *Shamanism, History and the State*, pp. 191–228.

—, 'Theories of North Asian Shamanism', in Gellner (ed.), *Soviet and Western Anthropology*, pp. 242–51.

—, and Onon, Urgunge, *Shamans and Elders* (Oxford: Oxford University Press, 1996).

Hutton, Ronald, 'The Global Context of the Scottish Witch-Hunt', forthcoming in Goodare (ed.), *The Scottish Witch-Hunt in Context.*

—, *The Shamans of Siberia* (Glastonbury: Isle of Avalon Press, 1993).

—, *The Stations of the Sun: A History of the Ritual Year in Britain* (Oxford: Oxford University Press, 1996).

Hyder, Ken, 'Global Ear: Siberia', *The Wire* (April 1998), pp. 21–24.

Ides, E. Ysbrants, *Drejaarige Reize naar China* (Amsterdam, 1698).

Jakobsen, Merete Demant, *Shamanism* (New York: Berghahn, 1999)

Jankovics, M., 'Cosmic Models and Siberian Shamans' Drums', in Hoppál (ed.), *Shamanism in Eurasia*, pp. 149–73.

Jochelson, Waldemar, *The Koryak* (Leiden: Brill, 1908).

—, *The Yukagir and the Yukaghirized Tungus* (Leiden: Brill, 1926).

—, *The Yakut* (New York: Anthropological Reports of the American Museum of Natural History, 33.2, 1933).

Johansen, Ulla, 'The Transmission of the Shaman's Position in South Siberia', in Hoppál and Howard (ed.), *Shamans and Cultures*, pp. 193–99.

Johnson, Richard, 'Certain Notes Unperfectly Written by Richard Johnson', in Richard Hakluyt, *The Principal Navigations, Voyages, Traffiques and Discoveries of the English Nation* (Glasgow edn, in 6 vols, 1903).

Jones, Leslie Ellen, *Druid, Shaman, Priest: Metaphors of Celtic Paganism* (Enfield: Hisarlik, 1998).

Juki, A. J., 'Notes on Selkup Shamanism', in Dioszegi and Hoppál (ed.), *Shamanism in Siberia*, pp. 375–80.

Kalweit, Howard, *Shamans, Healers and Medicine Men* (Boston, Massachusetts: Shambhala, 1992).

Karjalienen, K. F., *Die Religion der Jugra-Volker* (2 vols, Helsinki, 1921–27).

Kharitidi, Olga, *Entering the Circle: Ancient Secrets of Wisdom Discovered by a Russian Psychiatrist* (San Franscisco: Harper SanFrancisco, 1996).

Khomic, L. V., 'A Classification of Nenets Shamans', in Dioszegi and Hoppál (ed.), *Shamanism in Siberia*, pp. 245–53.

Kim, Tae-Gon, and Hoppál, Mihaly (ed.), *Shamanism in Performing Arts* (Budapest: Akademiai Kiado, 1995).

Kirchner, Horst, 'Ein archäologischer Beitrag zur Urgeschichte des des Schamanismus', *Anthropos*, 47 (1952), pp. 244–86.

Klaniczay, Gabor, 'Shamanistic Elements in Central European Witchcraft', in Hoppál (ed.), *Shamanism in Eurasia*, pp. 404–22.

Krader, L., 'Shamanism: Theory and History in Buryat Society', in Dioszegi and Hoppál (ed.), *Shamanism in Siberia*, pp. 228–41

Krascheninnikow, Stephan, *The History of Kamtschatka and the Kuriliski Islands*, trans. James Grieve (Gloucester, 1764).

Ksenofontov, *Legendy i Rasskazy u Yakutov, Buryat i Tungusov* (second edn, Moscow, 1930).

Laufer, Berthold, 'Origin of the Word Shaman', *American Anthropologist*, new series 19 (1917), pp. 361–71.

Layton, Robert, 'Shamanism, Totemism and Rock Art', *Cambridge Archaeological Journal*, 10 (2000), pp. 169–86.

Lehtinen, Ildiko, 'Artturi Kannisto in Siberia', in Pentikainen et al. (ed.), *Shamans*, pp. 71–89.

200   SHAMANS

Lehtisalo, T., 'Entwurf einer Mythologie der Jurak-Samojeden', *Mémoires de la Société Finno-Ougrienne*, 53 (1924), pp. 128–39.

Lepechin, Ivan Ivanovich, *Tagebuch der Reise durch verschiedene Provinzen des russischen Reiches in den Jahren 1768 und 1769*, trans. Christian Heinrich Hase (2 vols, Altenburg, 1774–83).

Lesseps, Mathieu de, *Journal historique du voyage de M. de Lesseps, Consul de France* (2 vols, Paris, 1790).

Lewis, Ioan M., *Ecstatic Religion* (Harmondsworth: Penguin, 1971)

—, 'What is a Shaman?', in Hoppál (ed.), *Shamanism in Eurasia*, pp. 3–12.

Lewis-Williams, David, and Dowson, Thomas, 'The Signs of All Times', *Current Anthropology*, 11 (1970), pp. 201–45.

Lommel, Andreas, *Shamanism: The Beginnings of Art* (New York: McGraw-Hill, 1967).

Lopatin, Ivan A., 'A Shamanistic Performance for a Sick Boy', *Anthropos*, 41–44 (1946–49), pp. 365–68.

—, *Goldi Amurskiye, Ussuriskye i Sungariiskiye* (Vladivostok, 1922), 'A Shamanistic Performance to Regain the Favour of the Spirit', *Anthropos*, 35–36 (1940–41), pp. 352–55.

Lvova, E. L., 'On the Shamanism of the Chulym Turks', in Dioszegi and Hoppál (ed.), *Shamanism in Siberia*, pp. 237–44.

Marcus, George E. (ed.), *Perilous States* (Chicago: University of Chicago Press, 1993).

Melia, Daniel F., 'The Irish Saint as Shaman', *Pacific Coast Philology*, 18 (1983), pp. 37–42.

Messerschmidt, Daniel Gottlieb, *Forschungreise durch Sibirien*, ed. E. Winter and N. A. Figurovski (2 vols, Berlin, 1962–77).

Michael, Henry N. (ed.), *Studies in Siberian Shamanism* (Toronto: Toronto University Press, 1963).

Mikhailev, Taras M., 'Buryat Shamanism', in Balzer (ed.), *Shamanism*, pp. 110–20.

Mikhailowskii, V. M., 'Shamanism in Siberia and European Russia', *Journal of the Anthropological Institute of Great Britain and Ireland*, 24 (1895), pp. 62–100, 126–58.

—, *Shamanstvo* (Moscow, 1892).

Mote, Victor, *Siberia: Worlds Apart* (Boulder, Colorado: Westview, 1998).

Nagy, Joseph, 'Shamanic Aspects of the Bruidhean Tale', *History of Religions*, 20 (1981), pp. 302–22.

Narr, Karl J., 'Barenzeremoniell und Schamanismus in der alteren Steinzeit Europas', *Saeculum*, 10, pt 3 (1959), pp. 233–72.

Noel, Daniel, *The Soul of Shamanism: Western Fantasies, Imaginal Realities* (New York: Continuum, 1997).

Novitskii, Grigory, *Kratkoe Opisanie o Narodye Ostyakom*, ed. L. Maikov (St Petersburg, 1884).

Nyberg, S. H., *Die Religionen des Alten Iran* (1937: repr. Osnabrück: Zeller, 1966).

Ohlmarks, Åke, *Studium zum Problem des Schamanismus* (Lund, 1939).

Pallas, Petrus Simon, *Reise durch verschiedene Provinzen des russischen Reiches* (3 vols, St Petersburg, 1776).

Partenen, Jorma, 'A Description of Buryat Shamanism', *Journal de la Société Finno-Ougrienne*, 51 (1941–42), pp. 10–15.

Pentikainen, Juha, 'The Saami Shaman', in Hoppál (ed.), *Shamanism in Eurasia*, pp. 125–48.

—, 'The Shamans and Shamanism', in ibid., pp. 29–50.

—, et al. (ed.), *Shamans* (Tampere: Tampere Museums, 1999).

Pocs, Eva, *Between the Living and the Dead: A Perspective on Witches and Seers in the Early Modern Age* (Budapest: Central European University Press, 1999).

Polo, Marco, *The Travels*, ed. Ernest Rhys (London, 1908).

Popov, A. A., 'How Seraptie Djarvoskin of the Nganasans (Tavgi Samoyeds) Became a Shaman', in Dioszegi (ed.), *Popular Beliefs and Folklore Tradition*, pp. 137–45.

—, *Materialy dlya Bibliografii Russkoi Literatury po Izucenigu Shamanstva Severo-Azaitskikh Narodov* (Leningrad, 1932).

—, *Tavgytsy* (Moscow, 1936).

Portisch, Hugo, *I Saw Siberia* (London: Harrap, 1972).

Potanin, G. N., *Ocherki Severo-Zapadnoi Mongolii* (4 vols, St Petersburg, 1881–83).

Potapov, 'Shamans' Drums of Altaic Ethnic Groups', in Dioszegi (ed.), *Popular Beliefs and Folklore Tradition*, pp. 205–34.

Prokofyeva, Yekaterina D., 'The Costume of an Enets Shaman', in Michael (ed.), *Studies in Siberian Shamanism*, pp. 124–56.

Radlov, Wilhelm, *Aus Siberien* (2 vols, Leipzig, 1884).

Rank, Gustav, 'Shamanism as a Research Subject', in Edsman (ed.), *Studies in Shamanism*, pp. 15–22.

Rees, Alwyn, and Rees, Brinley, *Celtic Heritage: Ancient Tradition in Ireland and Wales* (London: Thames and Hudson, 1961).

Reinhard, Johan, 'Shamanism and Spirit-Possession: The Definitional Problem', in Hitchcock and Jones (ed.), *Spirit Possession*, pp. 12–22

Rombandeeva, E. I., 'Some Observances and Customs of the Mansi (Voguls) in Connection with Childbirth', in Dioszegi (ed.), *Popular Beliefs and Folklore Tradition*, pp. 77–83.

Sauer, Martin, *An Account of a Topographical and Astronomical Expedition to the Northern Part of Russia* (London, 1802).

Schrenk, Leopold von, *Amurskago Kraya* (St Petersburg, 1903).

Semyonov, Yuri, *Siberia: Its Conquest and Development* (London: Hollis and Carter, 1963).

Shirokogoroff, S. M., *Psychomental Complex of the Tungus* (London: Kegan Paul, 1935).

Sieroszewski, Waclaw, *Yakuti* (St Petersburg, 1896).

Siikala, Anna-Leena, 'The Interpretation of Siberian and Inner Asian Shamanism', in ibid., pp. 15–25.

—, *The Rite Technique of the Siberian Shaman* (Helsinki: FF Communications, Academia Scientarum Fennica, 1987).

—, 'Two Types of Shamanizing and Categories of Shamanic Songs', in ibid., pp. 41–55.

—, and Hoppál, Mihaly, *Studies on Shamanism* (Budapest and Helsinki: Finnish Anthropological Society and Akademiai Kiado, 1992).

Smoljak, A. V., 'Some Elements of the Ritual Attire of Nanai Shamans', in Hoppál (ed.), *Shamanism in Eurasia*, pp. 244–52.

Sokolova, Z. P., 'A Survey of Ob-Ugrian Shamanism', in Hoppál and von Sadovszky (ed.), *Shamanism Past and Present*, pp. 155–64.

Steller, Georg Wilhelm, *Beschriebung von dem Lande Kamschatka* (Leipzig, 1774).

Sternberg, Leo, 'Divine Election in Primitive Religion', in Congrès International des Americanistes, *Compte-Rendu de la XXIe Session* (Goteborg, 1925), ii, pp. 475–87.

—, *Gilyaki* (Moscow, 1905).

Stone, Alby, *Straight Track, Crooked Road: Leys, Spirit-Paths and Shamanism* (Wymeswold: Heart of Albion Press, 1998).

Strahlenburg, Philip John Tabbert von, *An Histori-Geographical Description of the North and Eastern Part of Europe and Asia* (1736).

Suslov, I. M., 'Shamanstvo i Borba s nim', *Sovietsky Sever*, 3–4 (1931), pp. 89–152.

Thomas, Nicholas, and Humphrey, Caroline (ed.), *Shamanism, History and the State* (Ann Arbor: University of Michigan Press, 1994).

Thubron, Colin, *In Siberia* (London: Chatto and Windus, 1999).

Tretyakov, P. I., *Turukhanskiye Kraya* (St Petersburg, 1891).

Troschanski, *Evoludiya 'Chernaya Vera' (Shamanstva) u Yakutoi* (Kazan, 1901).

Vajnstejn, S. I., 'Shamanism in Tuva at the Turn of the Twentieth Century', in Hoppál (ed.), *Shamanism in Eurasia*, pp. 353–73.

Vasilevich, G. M., 'The Acquisition of Shamanistic Ability among the Evenki', in Dioszegi (ed.), *Popular Beliefs and Folklore Tradition*, pp. 339–49.

Vdovin, I. S., 'Social Foundations of Ancestor Cult among the Yukaghirs, Koryaks and Chukchis', in Dioszegi and Hoppál (ed.), *Shamanism in Siberia*, pp. 405–18.

Vitebsky, Piers, 'From Cosmology to Environmentalism: Shamanism as Local Knowledge in a Global Setting', in Fardon (ed.), *Counterworks*, pp. 182–203.

—, 'Landscape and Self-Determination among the Eveny', in Croll and Parkin (ed.), *Bush Base: Forest Farm*, pp. 223–46.

—, 'Some Medieval European Views on Mongolian Shamanism', *Journal of the Anglo-Mongolian Society*, 1, pt 2, pp. 24–42.

—, *The Shaman* (London: Macmillan, 1995).

Voigt, V., 'Shamanism: Person or Word?', in Hoppál (ed.), *Shamanism in Eurasia*, pp. 13–20.

Wallis, Robert J., 'Autoarchaeology and Neoshamanism: The Sociopolitics of Ecstasy' (unpublished Ph.D. thesis, Southampton University, 2000).

Walsh, Roger, *The Spirit of Shamanism* (Los Angeles: Tarcher, 1990).

Witsen, Nicholas, *Noord en Oost Tataryen* (1682: repr. 2 vols, Amsterdam, 1785).

Wood, A., and French, R. A. (ed.) *The Development of Siberia* (London: Macmillan, 1989).

Zachrisson, Inger, 'The Saami Shaman Drums', in Åhlback and Bergmann (ed.), *The Saami Shaman Drum*, chapter 4.

Zornickaja, M. J., 'Dances of Yakut Shamans', in Dioszegi and Hoppál (ed.), *Shamanism in Siberia*, pp. 299–307.

Index

Adamnan, St 134
Africa, and shamanism 125, 126, 127
agrarian systems, and shamanism 133
Ainu people 12–13
Alekseev, Nikolai Alekseevich 43, 106
alhacci (conjuror) 48
Altaian peoples
  and ancestor-worship 116
  and Buddhism 17–18
  and cosmology 60, 62, 64
  and Oirot nation 10, 12
  and rites of passage 47
  and ritual drum 81, 82
  and sacrifice 92
  and shamans
    black and white 50
    clan 51
    costume 79
    performance 93
    vocation 71
  and spirit-journey 88–9
  and spirits 64, 89–90
amagyat (personal guardian) 64, 67, 75, 77
Amur peoples, and shamans 51
ancestor
  ancestor-spirits 40, 59, 117
  cult of 116–7
  and shamanic vocation 72–3

animals
  and animal-double 40–2, 64, 67, 103, 158
  imitation of 90–1
  and shape-changing 103
  and spirit-world 63–4, 91
Anisimov, Arkadiy F. 38–42, 60, 64, 77, 86, 93, 99, 104, 116
Anokhin, A. V. 50
anthropology
  early studies 35–8, 49–50, 85–6, 94–5
  modern studies 51, 54–8, 120–4, 129–35, 155–6, 161–2
  Soviet studies 38–44, 76–7, 86, 90–1, 99, 116–19
apprenticeship 69–76, 92
Armstrong, Terence 165 n. 2a
art, Palaeolithic 130–3
assistants 39, 41–2, 92
Association of Folk Medicine 155
Association of the Peoples of the North, declaration 11, 165 n. 2a
Association of the Tambour 154, 161
Athanasy, St 65
audience, and shamanic performance 92–3, 97, 136
Australia
  and rock art 132
  and shamanic practices 126, 127
Avvakum vii, 47

Bai-Yulgen (deity) 92
Balazs, J. 101–2
Balkans, and shamanism 145–6
Balzer, Marjorie Mandelstam 155–6, 162
Bandini, Marco 146
Baraba Turks 78–9
Bashkir people, and shamans 53
Basilov, Vladimir 70, 71, 97, 152
bear festival 47
bear-spirits 56, 64
Bell, John 32–3, 94
benandanti (Italian shaman-figure) 144
Bering Strait, as marking cultural division 142
Bering, Vitus Jonassen 4
bö (shaman) 47, 78, 92, 103–4, 107
Bogoras, Waldemar
    and Chukchi 59–60, 76, 93, 95–6, 100, 102, 105–6, 109
    as ethnographer 35, 77
Bremmer, Jan 130
Buddhism
    as academic construct 63
    conversions to 17–18
    influence of 62–3, 113–18, 120, 139
    and mysticism 118
    and shamans 18, 22, 24, 93, 154
budtode (high-ranking shaman) 106
bull-feast 135
Burkert, Walter 130
Buryat people 10, 12, 76
    and Buddhism 17–18
    and Christianity 19–20
    conquests by 13–14
    and cosmology 60–1

and healing 104, 153–4
and history of shamanism 116, 117
increase in numbers 16
and native scholarship 35
and neoshamanism 161
and ritual drum 81
and shamans 24, 26, 33, 51, 55–7, 69, 105, 152
    black 142
    equipment 82
    female 107
    initiation ceremonies 74–5
    training 72
    vocation 69, 71
and shape-changing 103
and Soviet modernization 26
and spirit-journey 88
and spirit-roads 104
and spirits 64, 71, 78, 89
and status of women 108
and tailgan ceremony 18, 19–20, 57–8, 92
and terminology 47

Castaneda, Carlos 156–9
Castren, Alexander 35
Catherine the Great
    and religious toleration 18, 22
    and shamanism 22, 29
Celtic studies, and shamanism 134–5, 140
Chadwick, Nora 134
chanting 36–7, 86, 91
Cherimise people 136–7
childbirth 53–4, 106, 108
Christianity
    compared with shamanism 125
    conversion to 16, 17, 18–19, 49, 66, 137–8

early contacts with 62
and shamans 22, 24, 29, 93, 116
and syncretism 19–22
Chukchi people
and cosmology 59–60, 62, 66
and culture 13, 24, 77, 153
and diet 102
and divination 55
and language 12
and Russian conquest 14, 16
and shamans 76–7, 105
costume 79
family 51, 70, 119
female 106
payment of 100
performance 91, 93, 95
training 72
vocation 70–1
and the 'soft man' 109–10
and Soviet modernization 25
and spirit-journey 88, 100
and spirit-possession 89–90
and spirits 63, 66, 70–1, 88
Chulym Turks 64, 79, 81, 82, 119
Chuvahe people 136–7
Chuwan clan 16
clairvoyance 54
clans
and clan identity 57, 116–17
clan shamans 51, 76, 77, 100,
117, 119, 141
and hereditary nature of
shamanism 69
inter-clan rivalries 77
and shamanic costumes 80
Clement of Alexandria 114
cold, immunity to 97
collectivization, in Siberia 24, 25
community
and inter-shaman rivalry 77–8

and recognition of shamans 69,
74–6, 148–9
and shamanic performance 91
consciousness, altered states vii,
29, 48, 67, 82, 97, 110, 127
and drugs 101
and neoshamanism 158
Cornford, Franic M. 130, 133–4
cosmology
shamanic 21, 56, 59–67
and spirit-roads 103–4
three-layer 60
see also spirits
costumes, ritual 32, 33, 36, 39,
50, 78–80, 83, 110, 119, 154,
155
in European shamanism 134,
140, 143
investiture with 75
and symbolic decoration 30,
79–81, 90, 99, 134
Cottes, Jean 132
Council of Assistance to the
Peoples of the North 24
cultures, Siberian 13, 17, 24–5,
34, 61, 153
early studies of 35–8
Soviet studies of 38–44, 76–7,
86, 90–1, 99, 116–19

dance, shamanic 33, 41–2, 65–6,
86, 89–91, 97, 158
Daur Mongols 49, 99
death
and functions of shamans 55
visionary experience of 74
deities
and cosmology 60
and external influence 116
images 19–20, 23, 56

diet 102
Dioszegi, Vilmos
  and European shamanism
    143–5, 146
  and shamanic equipment 80, 83
  and shamanic illness 71–2, 77
  and shamanic performance 85,
    86, 91
  and Soviet ethnography 42–3,
    151
disease
  effects of European disease 34
  see also healing
divination 51, 54–8, 90, 92, 110,
    155
  in Europe 136–7
  by women 106, 107
Djaruoskin, Sereptie 73–4
Dodds, Eric R. 130, 133–4
dogs, sacrifice of 21
Donner, Kai 102
Dowson, Thomas 131–2
dreams
  interpretation 34, 48
  and shamanic training 72–3
  and spirit-double 61, 64
dress see costumes
Dronfield, Jeremy 133
drugs 100–2, 132
druids, and shamanism 134–5, 140
drum, ritual 23, 25, 30, 32, 36–7,
    39–42, 79, 81, 86, 90, 143
  among Saami 137, 138
  and decoration 81–2
  and spirit-journey 89
Drury, Nevill 157

ecstasy, as shamanic technique
    40–2, 66, 121, 125, 145
Edsman, Carl-Martin 148

Eirik's Saga 139–40
Eliade, Mircea
  and comparative study of
    shamanism 120–7, 129–31, 145
  and cosmology 60, 103, 121–2
  and divination 54–5
  and drug use 101, 102
  and neoshamanism 159
  and ritual drum 81–2
  and shamans
    apprenticeship 69, 72, 74
    definition of 65, 80–2, 87–8,
      134
    family 119
    role 51, 54, 57, 65, 121–2
  and spirit-journey 87–8, 121–2
  and spirit-roads 103
Elizabeth Petrovna, Tsarina 14
Empedocles 130
enenalan (shaman) 47
Enet people 11, 14
  and animal-doubles 103
  and drug use 102
  and ritual drum 82
  and shamans
    costume 80
    female 72, 106
    and training 72
    and vocation 70–1, 72
  and spirit-journey 88
  and spirits 64, 66–7, 70–1
Engels, Friedrich 116
equipment, ritual 78, 81–3, 107,
    110, 143
  destruction of 23, 26
  see also costume; drum; spirit
Eskimo 12, 62, 95, 142, 157–8
ethnicity
  and geography 11–12
  and language 13

ethnography
  early studies 35–8, 49–50, 85–6, 94–5
  modern studies 51, 54–8, 76–7, 120–4, 129–35, 155–6, 161–2
  Soviet 38–44, 73–4, 76–7, 86, 90–1, 99, 116–19, 151
Europe
  shamanism in 133–49
  witches in 141–2
Even people 11–12, 14
  and cosmology 65
  and shamans 24, 47, 51
  and traditional culture 25, 48
Evenk people 11, 13
  and animal-doubles 103
  and Buddhism 17
  and cosmology 60, 62, 64–6
  and healing 38–40, 92
  and mythology 116
  and ritual drum 81
  and shamans 24, 25, 26, 33, 38–42, 51, 56, 58
    costume 79, 80
    equipment 78, 82, 83
    female 105–6, 116
    initiation 75
    performance 86, 91–4, 99
    survival 155
    training 72–3
  in Soviet scholarship 76–7
  and spirit-journey 88
  and spirit-roads 103–4
  and spirits 64–7, 71, 89–90
  studies of 38–42
  and syncretism 20
evil
  and shamanic fight against 121, 123
  and witches 141

exploitation
  economic 17, 25, 34, 116, 155
  by neoshamanism 160–1

Fagerberg, Catharina 147–8
families, family shamans 51, 70, 118–19
Felinska, Eva 34
Finland
  and folk magicians 138, 140
  and witches 142–3
Finns, and Siberian peoples 38
fishing 25, 56
  collectivization of 25
  and sacrifice 18
Flaherty, Gloria 29, 32
fly agaric mushrooms 100–2
folklore, studies 35, 62, 143–5
Forsyth, James 17
Fostbroeda Saga 139
Foundation for Shamanic Studies 161
Frazer, Sir James 121, 124
fur trade 15, 17, 23, 25

gas extraction 25
Gebler (Russian exile) 53–4
Georgi, Johann Gottlieb 33, 85, 113
Ginzburg, Carlo 144–5
Gmelin, Johann Georg 1, 22, 94, 104, 106
Greeks, ancient, and shamanism 130, 134
Gumilov, L. N. 116

Hamayon, Roberte 57, 107
Harner, Michael 156–7, 158–9, 161
Harvardar Saga 139

healing 25, 26, 35–7, 38–42, 58,
92, 110
  in European shamanism 138,
  147–8
  limitations of 53–4
  practitioners 48–9, 51, 138,
  153–4
  and spirit-roads 104
  and the spirit-world 52–3, 56,
  61, 66, 90
  by women 106
heaven, in traditional cosmologies
60
Henning, W. B. 129
heredity, and shamanism 69–70,
136, 148, 153–4
Herodias 146
hetolatirgin (diviners) 55
Hinduism, influence of 113, 120
Historia Norvegiae 138–9, 141
Hoppál, Mihaly 78, 145, 162
horses, sacrifice of 18, 19–20, 57–8
Hultkranz, Åke 126–7, 130
Humphrey, Caroline 48–9, 51, 87,
92, 107, 117, 119, 151–2
Hungary
  and shamanism 143–5
  and Siberian peoples 42, 119,
  143
hunter-gatherers, and shamanism
126–7, 131, 132–3
hunting
  exclusion of women from 108
  and role of shamans 48, 56–8
  and sacrifice 18
hypnosis, shamanism as 96–8

ican (sorcerer) 48
Iceland
  and Saami magicians 139–41

  and witches 142–3
Ides, E. Ysbrants 47
iemzya (Chuvashe functionary)
137
iicheen (wise person) 48
illness
  as caused by spirits 52–3, 56,
  61, 66, 129, 153
  and shamanic vocation 71–2,
  143
illusion, shamanism seen as 33,
94–5, 97
images, religious 19, 23, 39, 56,
79, 91
imperialism, and anthropology
34–5
improvisation, in shamanic
performance 91
initiation, shamanic 74–5, 121,
134, 143, 157
Inuit see Eskimo
Ireland, medieval, and shamanism
134–6, 140
Islam
  assimilation into 129, 138, 152
  conversions to 17
  early contacts with 62, 116, 146
Italy, and shamanism 144
Itelmen people 12
  and forced conversions 18, 19
  and shamans 34
  and transexuality 109
Ivanov (Russian merchant) 34

Jochelson, Waldemar 77
  as ethnographer 35, 122
  and family shamans 118–19
  and Koryaks 21, 23, 37, 61–2,
  65, 79, 94–5, 102, 106, 108,
  109, 118

and Sakhas 48, 49–50, 53–4, 81, 107
and shamanism as hypnosis 96
and transexuality 109–10
and Yukaghirs 57–8, 65, 76, 86–7, 90, 105
Johansen, Ulla 69–70
Johnson, Richard 30–2, 55, 79, 92, 94, 101, 117–18, 139
Jones, Leslie Ellen 135

kam (shaman) 47
and costumes 79–80, 82
history of term 115
and shamanic illness 71–2
and shamanic performance 89–93, 97
and spirit-helpers 77
Kannisto, Artturi 21–2
Karjalainen, K. F. 102
kart (diviner) 136
kasanti (shaman) 50, 55
Kazakhstan, and Islam and shamanism 129, 138
Ket language 13, 14
Ket people 9, 11, 13
and collectivization 25
and drug use 102
and family shamans 51, 70
and ritual drum 81
and shamanic vocation 72
and spirit-journey 88
studies of 50
Khakass nation 10, 12, 23, 91, 100
Khangalov, M. N. 35, 70
Khant people 11, 13, 76
and Christianity 18, 20
and cosmology 60, 61
and divination 55
and drug use 102

and Finns 38
and Magyars 143
and ritual equipment 81, 82
and shamans 51, 55–6, 70, 119, 133
costume 79
initiation 75
payment of 100
and spirit-journey 88–9
and spirits 63–4, 66–7, 89–90
and traditional religion 19, 25–6
Khodin clan 16
Khomoro clan 16
Kirgiz people 115
Klaniczay, Gabor 144, 145–6
Kondakov, Vladimir 155–6
körbüöccü (prophet) 48
Koryak people
and Christianity 21
and cosmology 64, 65, 66
and drug use 102
and language 12
and magic specialists 48
reduction in numbers 25
and ritual equipment 82
and Russian colonialism 16, 21, 25
and shamanism 23, 51, 53, 118–19
and shamans
costume 79
family 118–19
female 106
performance 94–5
training 72
vocation 71
and spirits 64, 65–6, 71, 89
and status of women 108
studies of 35
and terminology 47

and traditional religion 61–2
and transexuality 109
Krascheninnikow, Stephen 33, 34

language
    and ethnicity 13
    knowledge of 38
    and territory 13
    variety 9–10, 11–13
Lebed Turks 81, 82
Leningrad, Museum of the History
    of Religion and Atheism 26
Lepechin, Ivan Ivanovich 53
Lesseps, Mathieu de 33–4
Lewis, Ioan 124–6, 159
Lewis-Williams, David 131–2
lingustics, evidence from 114–15
logging 25
Lommel, Andreas 131
Lopatin, Ivan A. 65–6

magic
    and Christianity 22
    and divination 56–7
    early records of 30–3, 35–7
    in European literatures 138–41
    and healing 52
    and hunting 56–8, 132
    and old men 48
    and old women 34, 48
    practitioners 48–9
magicians, and shamans 29–30,
    48–9, 54–5, 87, 143
Magyars, and shamanism 143–4,
    145–6
Mampyi (shaman) 93
manaric (hysteric) 48
Manchu state 14, 99, 117
Mansi people 11
    and Finns 38

and forced conversions 18, 21
and Magyars 143
and payment of shamans 100
and shamans 55–6, 119, 133
and status of women 108
and traditional religion 19, 55
Marx, Karl 116
medicine
    alternative viii, 156
    natural 48, 52, 53
medicine men, and shamans 124,
    157–8
mediums, and shamans vii, 65,
    87, 96, 148
Megasthenes 114
Melanesia, and absence of
    Shamanism 123, 127
Melia, Daniel 134
menstruation, seen as dangerous
    106, 108
Messerschmidt, Daniel 33
Mikhailov, Taras Maksimovich
    43, 116, 152
Mikhailowskii, V. M. 35, 70
mining 25
modernization policies 23–7, 29
Moldavia, and sorcerers 146–7
Mongol court, magicians and
    shamans 29–30, 55, 115, 118
Mongols
    and shamans 49, 62, 99,
        117–18
    in Siberia 10, 14
monks, Buddhist 17, 114–15
    and shamans 18, 22, 24, 154
Mordvin people 137
mushrooms, fly agaric 100–2
music
    instruments 82
    see also drum; songs

muzhan (diviner) 136
mysticism
  Buddhist 118
  Islamic 129, 146
  and shamanism 121–2
mythology, origins of 62, 116

Nagy, Joseph 134–5
Nanai people 12, 13
  and Buddhism 17
  and Christianity 19
  and shamanic costume 79
  and shamans 25, 47–8, 50,
    55–7, 71
  and spirit-journey 88
  and spirits 64, 66, 70, 89
nationalism
  Finnish 38
  and imperialism 34–5
  and religion 19
  and study of folklore 35, 143
native Americans 11, 62, 109,
  148, 157–9
Nedigal people 12, 13
nemanti (shaman) 50
Nenet people 11, 14
  and conversions to Christianity
    18, 19
  and ritual drum 82
  and shamans 50–1, 55, 79, 139
    costume 50, 79, 80
  and Soviet modernization 24, 25
  and spirit-journey 88
  and spirit-possession 90
  and traditional religion 19, 24,
    30–2
neoshamanism 156–61
nga (shaman) 73–4
Nganasan people 11, 24
  and ritual drum 82

and shamans, family 51
  performance 93, 97
  training 73
and spirit-journey 88
and spirits 71
Nicholas, St, and shamanism 19, 20
Nivkh people 12–13
  and bear festival 47
  and shamans 34, 47, 79, 115
  and spirits 64, 71
  and status of women 108
North America, and shamanism
  124, 125, 142, 156–61
Nyberg, S. H. 129

Ohlmarks, Åke 100–2
oil industry 25
Oirot nation 10, 12
Orochi people 12
  and Buddhism 17
  and Christianity 19
  and cosmology 65
  and shamans 71, 79
  and spirit-possession 89
Orok people 12, 13
  and Christianity 19
Ostyak peoples 9
otohut (healer) 48
Owein ap Urien, as shamanic
  knight 135
oyun (shaman) 47, 48, 105, 156
  and divination 55, 56
  as hereditary role 70
  recognition of 76
  and ritual costume 80, 155
  and sacrifice 104
  and shamanic performance 91,
    96, 155
  and spirit-assistants 64, 66–7, 75
  'white' and 'black' 49–50

paganism, and shamanism viii
Palaeolithic era 127, 130–3
Pali language 114
Pallas, Petrus Simon 33, 52, 76
pastoralism, and shamanism 126,
    133
payment of shamans 99–100, 154
pellyaskis (Votyak functionary) 136
performance 35–7, 85–98, 110,
    122, 136, 140, 145–6
    and definition of shamanism vii
    seen as trickery 33–4, 94–7
petroglyphs 114
pipe, smoking 36, 42, 101
poets, as shamans 130, 134–5
Polo, Marco 29, 52
Popov, A. A. 73–4, 97–8
possession by spirits 40, 65, 87–8,
    89–90, 125
Potanin, G. N. 35, 90
Potapov, L. P. 116
priests, shamans as 58, 116, 124
prophecy 54
Pythagoras 130

Rashid-eddin 115
rattles, ritual 82
recitation 42, 86
Rees, Alwyn and Brinley 134
reindeer-herders 11–12, 105
Reinhard, Johann 87, 88
religion
    and contribution of shamanism
        120–4
    see also Buddhism; Christianity;
        Hinduism; Islam
religion, traditional
    revival of 155
    Soviet attacks on 24, 151–3
    and status of shamans 47–8

see also cosmology; deities;
    shamanism; shamans; spirits
rites of passage, and shamans 47,
    74
Russia
    activity of 47–58
    conquest of Siberia 3, 10–11,
        13, 15–17, 29, 49, 137
    and decline of indigenous
        peoples 10–11, 16–17
    and decline of traditional
        religion 19–23, 54
    and Siberian ethnic groups 9–14
    see also Soviet Russia
Rytkheu, Yuri 153

Saami people (Lapps) 137–41,
    142–4
sacrifice
    ban on 18
    continuance of 20, 21–2
    exclusion of women from 108
    of horses (*tailgan*) 18, 19–20,
        57–8, 92, 108
    and shamanic initiation 74, 75
    and shamanic performance 91–2
    and shamans 47, 55, 57
    and spirit-roads 104
Sagay people
    and shamans, equipment 82–3
        initiation 75
        training 72–3
St Olaf's Saga 139
Sakha people 10, 12
    and animal-doubles 103
    and Christianity 19, 49
    conquests by 13–14
    and cosmology 61, 62, 64–7
    and dance 90–1
    and divination 55

expansion in numbers 16
and inter-clan rivalries 77
and magic specialists 48, 51
and ritual drum 81
and shamanism 23, 35–7, 49, 51, 54–6, 70, 76, 105, 152
and shamans
costume 80–1
female 106–8, 110
initiation 75
payment of 100
performance 85, 91, 96
survival 155–6
training 72–3
vocation 70–1
and spirit-journey 88
and spirit-roads 104
and spirits 64, 65, 66, 67, 71, 89
and status of women 108
and terminology 47
and transexuality 109
Sakha Republic 155
samana/shamana (Buddhist monk) 114
sambana (shaman) 55
Samoyedic-speakers 11, 13, 14, 30, 32, 76
and cosmology 60
and shamans 47, 70, 75, 79–80
see also Enet people; Nenet people; Nganasan people; Selkup people
San people 127, 131–3
Savone (Enet shaman) 72, 106
Scandinavia
and shamanism 137–40, 147–8
and witches 141–2
schamanka (female shaman) 1–4
Scratching-Woman (shaman) 95–6
Selkup people 11, 14

and drug use 102
and female shamans 106
and ritual drums 81
and shamanic costume 80
and shamanism 23–4, 47, 56, 70
Semyonov, Yuri 165 n. 2a
sexuality, and spirits 109
sha-men (Buddhist monk) 114–15
shamanism
as academic construct vii, 3, 26–7, 48–9, 51–2, 55, 147, 157
comparative studies 118–27
definitions vii–viii, 54, 65, 87, 124–6, 131, 134–5, 152
in Europe 133–49
as hereditary 69–70, 136, 148, 153–4
history of vii, 29, 113–19, 123, 139
limitations of 53–4
as mental illness 67, 71, 77
opposition to 24–6, 43–4, 137, 156
'possession' 40, 65, 87–8, 89–90, 125
in prehistory 127, 131–3
preservation of 19–23, 151–6
records of 29–44
'soul-journey' 87–9
'urban' 156–61
world-wide diffusion of 124–7, 144–5, 158–9
see also cosmology
shamans
activity of 52–8
and age of vocation 71
and apprenticeship 69–76, 92
and assistants 92–3
and Buddhist monks 18, 22, 24, 154

and Christianity 22
clan 51, 76, 77, 100, 117, 119,
    141
family 51, 70, 118–19
'father-shaman' 74–5
female 32–3, 71, 72, 90, 104–9,
    110, 116, 152
and functional division 49–51
initiation 74–5, 121, 134, 143,
    157
and magicians 29–30, 48–9,
    54–5, 87, 143
and mediums vii, 65, 87, 96, 148
and Mongol magicians 29–30,
    55, 115, 118
and personality types 76
priestly role 58, 116, 124
recognition of 74–6
repression of 25–6, 43–4, 151–2
and rituals 35–7, 38–42
and rivalries 77–8
state opposition to 22–3, 52,
    116, 156
status in traditional religions
    47–8
and terminology vii, 32, 47–51,
    58
training 72–4, 76, 119, 136,
    155–6
as troubleshooters 51, 58
'white' and 'black' 49–50, 142
see also consciousness; costume;
    costumes; divination; drum;
    equipment; healing;
    performance; spirit-helper;
    spirit-world; vocation
shape-changing 103, 141, 143
shaytan 32
Shestakoff, Afanassy 16
shingkelevun rite 56, 58

Shirokogoroff, S. M. 38, 58, 59
and cosmology 61, 62, 64–5
and development of shamanism
    113, 115, 118
and divination 51
and Evenks 65–7, 76–80, 83, 91,
    92–3, 99, 103–4, 105
and healing 66
and payment of shamans 99,
    100
and shamanic costume 79, 80
and shamanic performance 90,
    91, 92
and shamanism as hypnosis
    96–7
Shonchur (shaman) 97
Shor people 12, 78
shrines
    burning of 18, 23
    domestic 118
    hidden 19–20
    women excluded from 108
Siberia
    and early use of 'shaman' vii, 32
    economic exploitation 17, 25,
        34, 116, 155
    effects of collectivization 24, 25
    and European settlement 14, 17,
        21, 24–5, 136
    exile to 35
    extent 3–4
    geography 4–5
    as homeland of shamanism viii,
        121, 126
    and Hungarians 42, 119, 143
    languages 9–10, 11–13
    peoples 6–7, 9–13, 15–17, 110
    reactions to 5–7
    Russian colonialism 3, 10–11,
        13, 15–19, 29, 34, 49, 137

Soviet modernization 23–7, 29, 153
and survival of shamanism 151–6
see also cultures
Sibir, khanate 3, 17
The Siege of Drum Damghaire 140
Sierszewski, Waclaw
and female shamans 106–8, 110
and functions of shamans 49–50, 77
and Sakhans 35–7, 66, 76, 85, 96, 100, 110
Siikala, Anna-Leena
and drug use 101, 102
and shamanic illness 71
and shamanic performance 87–8, 89
and shamans as troubleshooters 51, 58
and vocation 69
siurinka (shaman) 50
skeleton, shamanic costume as 80–1
smiths, and magic 48, 108, 153
'soft man' 109–10
Sokolova, Z. P. 102
Soloviev, 106
songs, shamanic 37, 39–42, 65–6, 86, 91
and audience refrains 33, 39, 92–3, 106
souls
'multiple' 61
stealing of 66
South America
and drug use 102
and shamanism 124, 125, 127
South Slavs, and spirit-flights 145

Soviet Russia
and ethnographic studies 38–44, 73–4, 76–7, 90–1, 116–19, 151
and Finns 38
and indigenous nations 9–10
and modernization 23–7, 29, 116, 153
and self-determination 23, 153
and status of women 109, 116
Soyot people 12, 105
and Buddhism 17, 62
and inter-clan rivalries 77
and shamans, costume 80
equipment 82, 83
female 152
performance 86, 97
training 72
vocation 71–2
and spirit-journey 88
space, sacred 74, 91
spirit-duels 77, 104, 139–40, 143, 145
spirit-flight 72–3, 91, 100, 110
of animal-double 40–2
and cosmology 60–1
and definition of shamanism viii, 53, 82, 87–9, 121, 134
in European traditions 140, 143–6
and healing 52, 92
and neoshamanism 158
in North American tradition 157
and shamanic costume 81
and shape-changing 10, 103
and spirit-roads 103–4
spirit-helpers 75, 91, 103, 136–7, 142
as animals 63–4
and definition of shaman 65–7, 87, 90

evil 78
  and healing 66
  inheriting 70
  modern shamanism 155
  and spirit-duels 77
  summoning 39–40, 65, 79, 86
spirit-journey see spirit-flight
spirit-roads 103–4
spirit-world 70–1, 76, 93–4, 121,
  124, 127
  and definition of shamanism
    vii, 61, 63–7
  and healing 52–3, 56, 61, 66, 90
spirits
  ancestor-spirit 40, 59, 117
  and animal-double 40–2, 64, 67,
    103
  as cause of illness 52–3, 56, 61,
    66, 129, 153
  and divination 55
  evil 33, 56, 78
  good and evil 78, 141, 153
  guardian 63, 64, 67, 75, 77, 103,
    158
  and 'multiple' souls 61
  possession by 40, 65, 87–8,
    89–90, 125
  and sexuality 109
  and shamans 63–7, 70–1, 76
  spirit-double 61
  spirit-images 39, 79, 91
  summoning of 36–7, 39–41, 48,
    86, 89, 138
  see also cosmology; spirit-flight
Stalinism
  effects on traditional cultures
    24–5, 77
  and ethnographic studies 38, 86,
    99
staves, ritual 82

Strabo 114
Strahlenberg, Philip Johann
  Tabbert von 3
syncretism 19–22, 116

tadibei (shamans) 47, 51
tailgan (horse sacrifice) 18, 19–20,
  57–8, 92
  exclusion of women from 108
Talamantez, Inez M. 158
Taliesin, as shamanic poet 135
taltos (Hungarian shaman-figure)
  143–5
Tatars 9, 11
  'Blacksmith' 12
Tchango (Magyar tribe) 146
Teleut people 10
  and shamans 51, 78, 105
  and spirits 64
tietaja (Finnish magician) 138
Tiuspiut (shaman) 23
tobacco, as drug 101
Tofa people 12
  and Christianity 19, 20
  and shamans 51, 80, 83
Togail bruidne Da Derga 135
totemism, and origins of
  shamanism 116
training, shamanic 72–3, 76, 119,
  136, 155–6
trance 86, 87, 91, 93, 131
  and communication with spirits
    55
  drug-induced 100–2, 132
  in Europe 137–9, 144
  and hypnosis 97
  in Islamic mysticism 129
  and modern shamanism 155
transexuality 109–10
travel see spirit-flight

tribute, payment of 15–16, 17, 21, 23
trickery, shamanism seen as 33–4, 94–7
Trinity, and traditional religion 20, 21–2
Troschanski, V. F. 107
Tungus language 114–15
Tungusic-speakers 9, 10, 11–12, 14, 16, 32
  and cosmology 59, 64–6
  and hereditary nature of shamanism 69
  and shamanic initiation 75
  see also Even people; Evenk people; Sakha people
tuno (shaman-figure) 136
Turkestan, and Islam and shamanism 129, 138
Turkic-speakers 5, 9, 10, 11, 12, 32, 76
  and ritual drums 81
  and shamans 47, 64, 69, 71, 119
    costume 78–9
    payment of 100
    perfomance 91
  and spirits 88
  see also Khakass nation; Oirot nation; Soyot people
tüülleekh kihi (dream interpreter) 48

udahan (female shaman) 48, 106–7
Udeghe people 12
udgan (female shaman) 107
Ulchi people 12, 13, 160–1
Unangan people 12
universalism, and shamanism 124–7, 131, 144–5, 149, 158–9

Vainstein, S. I. 116–17
Vasilevich, G. M. 99
Vatnsdaela Saga 139
Vdovin, I. S. 116
vedin (Votyak functionary) 136
Veniaminov, Ioann (archbishop of eastern Siberia) 19
ventriloquism 95–6
visions
  drug-induced 102, 132
  and shamanic training 72–4
Vitebsky, Piers 67, 70, 87, 96, 126, 127, 149, 155
vocation, shamanic 69–72, 75, 85, 92, 155
  and payment 99–100, 154
Voigt, V. 113
Votyak people 136, 137, 143

'White-Lord-Creator' 49
William of Rubruck 29–30, 55, 115, 139
wise-folk 137, 138, 142
witches 141–2, 144
Witsen, Nicholas vii, 32, 47, 52
women
  and magic 34, 48
  as shamans 32–3, 71, 72, 90, 104–9, 110, 116, 152
  as singers 93, 106
  status of 107–9, 116
  see also udahan
world tree 40, 60, 79

Yakut nation 10
Yandin clan 16
ye-keela (animal spirit) 64
yekyua (spirit-helpers) 64
Ynglinga Saga 139

Yukaghir people 12
  and cosmology 65
  and divination 55, 56
  and Russian conquest 11, 14, 16
  and shamanism 23, 51, 55,
    57–8, 69, 76
  and shamans
    female 105
    performance 86–7

  and spirit-flight 88
  and spirit-possession 89–90
  and traditional religion 62
  and transexuality 109
Yupik people 12, 14, 95

Zhukovskaya, N. L. 117
Zoroastrianism, and influence of
  shamanism 129–30